First World War
and Army of Occupation
War Diary
France, Belgium and Germany

25 DIVISION
Divisional Troops
Royal Army Medical Corps
77 Field Ambulance
1 September 1915 - 28 February 1919

WO95/2239/3

The Naval & Military Press Ltd
www.nmarchive.com
Published in association with The National Archives

Published by

The Naval & Military Press Ltd

Unit 10 Ridgewood Industrial Park,
Uckfield, East Sussex,
TN22 5QE England
Tel: +44 (0) 1825 749494

www.naval-military-press.com
www.nmarchive.com

This diary has been reprinted in facsimile from the original. Any imperfections are inevitably reproduced and the quality may fall short of modern type and cartographic standards.

© **Crown Copyright**
Images reproduced by permission of The National Archives, London, England, 2015.

Contents

Document type	Place/Title	Date From	Date To
Heading	WO95/2239/3 77 Field Ambulance		
Heading	77th Fld Ambulance Sep 1915 Feb 1919		
Heading	77th Field Ambulance Vol I Sept & Oct 15		
War Diary	Oultersteene	01/09/1915	04/09/1915
War Diary	Southampton	26/09/1915	26/09/1915
War Diary	Le Havre	27/09/1915	28/09/1915
War Diary	Steenbecque	29/09/1915	29/09/1915
War Diary	Oultersteene	30/09/1915	17/10/1915
War Diary	Bailleul	18/10/1915	01/11/1915
Miscellaneous	A Form. Messages And Signals.	25/10/1915	25/10/1915
Miscellaneous	C Form (Duplicate). Messages And Signals.	30/10/1915	30/10/1915
Heading	77th F.A. Vol 2 Nov 15		
War Diary	Bailleul	07/11/1915	30/11/1915
Heading	77th F.A. Vol. 3 Dec 1915		
War Diary	Bailleul	02/12/1915	30/12/1915
Heading	25th Div 77th Fa. Vol 4 Jan 1916		
War Diary	Bailleul	02/01/1916	26/01/1916
War Diary	Pradelles	29/01/1916	29/01/1916
Map	25th Divisional Area		
Miscellaneous	77th Field Ambulance Feb 1916		
War Diary	Pradelles	04/02/1916	29/02/1916
Heading	77 F Amb Vol 6 March 1916		
War Diary	Pradelles	09/03/1916	09/03/1916
War Diary	Outersteene	09/03/1916	09/03/1916
War Diary	P. 26 Reference 36. B.	10/03/1916	10/03/1916
War Diary	Valhuon	11/03/1916	15/03/1916
War Diary	Maisnil-St-Pol	16/03/1916	28/03/1916
Heading	25th Div. No 77 F Amb April 1916		
War Diary	Mesnil-St-Pol	01/04/1916	08/04/1916
War Diary	Mesnil	10/04/1916	18/04/1916
War Diary	Acq	19/04/1916	30/04/1916
Heading	25th Div 77 F. Amb May 1916		
War Diary	Acq	02/05/1916	30/05/1916
Heading	77 F.A. June 1916		
War Diary	Tinquette	02/06/1916	04/06/1916
War Diary	Canteleux	15/06/1916	15/06/1916
War Diary	Fienvillers	18/06/1916	18/06/1916
War Diary	Pernois	20/06/1916	20/06/1916
War Diary	Berneuil	25/06/1916	25/06/1916
War Diary	Toutencourt	28/06/1916	28/06/1916
War Diary	Harponville	30/06/1916	30/06/1916
War Diary	Contay	02/07/1916	02/07/1916
Heading	25th Division No 77 Field Ambulance July 1916		
War Diary	Contay	03/07/1916	03/07/1916
War Diary	Vadencourt	04/07/1916	17/07/1916
War Diary	Beauval	20/07/1916	20/07/1916
War Diary	Warnicourt Wood	22/07/1916	22/07/1916
War Diary	Acheux	23/07/1916	27/07/1916
War Diary	Bertrancourt	27/07/1916	30/07/1916
Heading	25th Div. 77th Field Ambulance August 1916		

War Diary	Bertrancourt	04/08/1916	09/08/1916
War Diary	Puchevillers	15/08/1916	25/08/1916
War Diary	Louven Court	27/08/1916	28/08/1916
War Diary	Clairfaye Farm	31/08/1916	31/08/1916
Heading	War Diary (Medical) 77th Field Ambulance Volume XII September 1916		
War Diary	Clairfaye Farm	02/09/1916	07/09/1916
War Diary	Louvencourt	09/09/1916	10/09/1916
War Diary	Lonquevellete	11/09/1916	11/09/1916
War Diary	Beaumetz	12/09/1916	12/09/1916
War Diary	Donquerelle Farm	18/09/1916	24/09/1916
War Diary	Longuevillete	25/09/1916	25/09/1916
War Diary	Arqueves	26/09/1916	28/09/1916
War Diary	Hedauville	29/09/1916	30/09/1916
War Diary	Bouzincourt	01/10/1916	10/10/1916
War Diary	North Chimney Albert	15/10/1916	22/10/1916
War Diary	Albert	20/10/1916	20/10/1916
War Diary	Val. De Maison	23/10/1916	26/10/1916
War Diary	Longuevillete	26/10/1916	29/10/1916
War Diary	Pont. De. Nieppe	30/10/1916	31/10/1916
Heading	25th Div. 77th Field Ambulance Nov. 1916		
War Diary	Pont. De. Nieppe.	01/11/1916	30/11/1916
Heading	25th Div 77th Field Ambulance Dec 1916		
War Diary	Pont-De-Nieppe	01/12/1916	29/12/1916
War Diary	In Field	30/12/1916	30/12/1916
Heading	25th Div 77th Field Ambulance Jan 1917		
War Diary	Pont de Nieppe	03/01/1917	31/01/1917
Heading	77th Field Ambulance Feb 1917		
War Diary	Pont-De-Nieppe	01/02/1917	20/02/1917
War Diary	Flettre	23/02/1917	28/02/1917
Heading	77th Field Ambulance March 1917		
War Diary	Flettre	01/03/1917	11/03/1917
War Diary	Lynde	13/03/1917	18/03/1917
War Diary	Borre	19/03/1917	20/03/1917
War Diary	Outersteene	21/03/1917	22/03/1917
War Diary	Steentje	28/03/1917	31/03/1917
Heading	77th F A. April 1917		
War Diary	Steen-Je	01/04/1917	02/04/1917
War Diary	Bailleul	03/04/1917	23/04/1917
War Diary	T. 19.b.4.5 Sheet 28.	24/04/1917	29/04/1917
War Diary	Outersteene	30/04/1917	30/04/1917
Heading	No. 77 F.a. May 1917		
War Diary	Outersteene	01/05/1917	11/05/1917
War Diary	T.19.b.4.5. Corps Major Chewing Station Westhof	13/05/1917	19/05/1917
War Diary	Westhof. Dressing Station.	20/05/1917	25/05/1917
War Diary	T. 19 by 4.8.	28/05/1917	31/05/1917
War Diary	T. 19. by 9.5. Sheet 28.	31/05/1917	31/05/1917
Heading	No. 77 F A. June 1917		
War Diary	T. 19. by.4.5 Sheet 28	01/06/1917	01/06/1917
War Diary	T. 19. b.4.5	03/06/1917	20/06/1917
War Diary	T. 19. b.4.5 Sheet 28	21/06/1917	22/06/1917
War Diary	Le.Tir. Anglais St. Hazebrouck	24/06/1917	24/06/1917
War Diary	Haverskerque	25/06/1917	25/06/1917
War Diary	Auchy-Au-Bois	26/06/1917	26/06/1917
War Diary	Coyecque	27/06/1917	27/06/1917
Heading	War Diary Medical 77th F. Ambulance		

War Diary	Coyecque	02/07/1917	05/07/1917
War Diary	Steenbecque	06/07/1917	06/07/1917
War Diary	C 21b. 25 Sheet 28	07/07/1917	09/07/1917
War Diary	Sheet 28 H. 29.a.5.9	09/07/1917	11/07/1917
War Diary	H.29.a.5.9	16/07/1917	24/07/1917
War Diary	H. 26.d.	24/07/1917	31/07/1917
Heading	War Diary Medical 77th F. Ambulance 25th Division August 1917		
War Diary	H. 26 d.	01/08/1917	01/08/1917
War Diary	H. 29.a 5.9	06/08/1917	06/08/1917
War Diary	H. 28.d.5.9. Sheet 28. N.W. 1/40,000	07/08/1917	10/08/1917
War Diary	Chateau Hendricques	11/08/1917	13/08/1917
War Diary	Lambouver Farm Sheet 28 E 21.	14/08/1917	17/08/1917
War Diary	Steenvorde	18/08/1917	30/08/1917
Heading	War Diary Medical 77th Field Ambulance		
War Diary	Steenvorde	01/09/1917	01/09/1917
War Diary	Waratah Farm	02/09/1917	02/09/1917
War Diary	Dickebush	04/09/1917	09/09/1917
War Diary	Vansohier Farm	09/09/1917	09/09/1917
War Diary	Caestre	10/09/1917	10/09/1917
War Diary	Thiennes	11/09/1917	11/09/1917
War Diary	Hurionville	12/09/1917	30/09/1917
Heading	War Diary Medical 77th F. Ambulance October 1917		
War Diary	Hurionville	01/10/1917	03/10/1917
War Diary	Bethune	04/10/1917	05/10/1917
War Diary	Mesplaux Farm	06/10/1917	31/10/1917
Heading	War Diary Medical 77th Field Ambulance November 1917		
War Diary	Mesplaux Farm	02/11/1917	17/11/1917
War Diary	Mesplaux Farm X 14 A.9.6. By Combined Bethune Map	25/11/1917	26/11/1917
War Diary	Mesplaux Farm Bethune Combined Sheet X 14.a 9.6	26/11/1917	26/11/1917
War Diary	Mesplaux Farm X 14. a 9.6 Bethune Combined Map	26/11/1917	27/11/1917
War Diary	Hurionville Rg 5 A Hazebrouck	26/11/1917	29/11/1917
War Diary	Capelle Sur La Lys.	30/11/1917	30/11/1917
Heading	77th Field Ambulance R A M C December 1917		
War Diary	Capelle Sur-La-Lys.	01/12/1917	01/12/1917
War Diary	Crepy	02/12/1917	03/12/1917
War Diary	Courcelles Les Comte	05/12/1917	05/12/1917
War Diary	Barastre	05/12/1917	08/12/1917
War Diary	Favreuil	09/12/1917	31/12/1917
Heading	No. 77 F.a. Jan 1918		
Heading	War Diary Medical 77th Field Ambulance. R.A.M.C. January 1918		
War Diary	57. C Favreuil	01/01/1918	14/01/1918
War Diary	Favreuil	28/01/1918	31/01/1918
Heading	War Diary Medical 77th Field Ambulance. 28th Feb'y 1918		
War Diary	Favreuil	04/02/1918	13/02/1918
War Diary	Courlelle Le Comte 57c A21.a.0.9	14/02/1918	21/02/1918
War Diary	Courlelle	22/02/1918	28/02/1918
Heading	77th Field Ambulance Mar 1918		
Heading	War Diary Medical 77th Field Ambulance March 1918		
War Diary	Courcelle Le-Compte	03/03/1918	10/03/1918
War Diary	Buchanan Camp Achiet-Le Grand.	12/03/1918	18/03/1918
War Diary	Om March	21/03/1918	21/03/1918

War Diary	Nr Lock Camp	21/03/1918	21/03/1918
War Diary	Buchanan Camp Achiet-Le-Grand	20/03/1918	21/03/1918
War Diary	Nr Loch Camp	21/03/1918	24/03/1918
War Diary	Brickfield	24/03/1918	24/03/1918
War Diary	Bucquoy	25/03/1918	25/03/1918
War Diary	Hebertune	25/03/1918	26/03/1918
War Diary	Bienvillers	26/03/1918	27/03/1918
War Diary	Coigneux	27/03/1918	27/03/1918
War Diary	Puchvillers Canaples	28/03/1918	31/03/1918
War Diary	Doullens	31/03/1918	31/03/1918
War Diary	Ref Map 5 A Hazebrouck	31/03/1918	31/03/1918
War Diary	Ravelsburg	31/03/1918	31/03/1918
Heading	War Diary Medical 77th Field Ambulance. April 1917		
War Diary	Ravelsburg Camp Sheet 28 S 15 Central	01/04/1918	01/04/1918
War Diary	Romilly. Camp Sheet 28 T27.C.5.D	05/04/1918	10/04/1918
War Diary	Pont d'Achelles Sheet 36 B.8.b.1.5	10/04/1918	10/04/1918
War Diary	Pont d'Achelles	10/04/1918	10/04/1918
War Diary	Westhof Camp Sheet 28 T19.b.4.4.	10/04/1918	10/04/1918
War Diary	Westhof	10/04/1918	11/04/1918
War Diary	Berthen Sheet 5 A Hazebrouck	11/04/1918	12/04/1918
War Diary	Berthen	12/04/1918	16/04/1918
War Diary	R 19 A. 33 Sheet 27	16/04/1918	16/04/1918
War Diary	Sheet 27 R 19.a.3.3	16/04/1918	16/04/1918
War Diary	Q 12. D.6.6.	16/04/1918	16/04/1918
War Diary	K 35.a.5.2	17/04/1918	19/04/1918
War Diary	Sheet 27 K 35 a.5.2.	21/04/1918	21/04/1918
War Diary	Sheet 27. Dozinghem	22/04/1918	22/04/1918
War Diary	F11.a.5.7	23/04/1918	25/04/1918
War Diary	Dozingham	25/04/1918	25/04/1918
War Diary	M.6.a.2.9 Sheet 28	26/04/1918	26/04/1918
War Diary	Vansohier Fm Sheet 28 G 21.c.5.7	25/04/1918	28/04/1918
War Diary	Vansohier Fm G 21. 6.5.7 Sheet 28	28/04/1918	28/04/1918
War Diary	Dozingham Sheet F 11 C 5.7 Sheet 27	29/04/1918	30/04/1918
Heading	War Diary Medical 77th F Ambulance May 1918		
War Diary	Dozingham F 11 a.5.7. Sheet	01/05/1918	01/05/1918
War Diary	Remy Siding 5A Hazebrouck Sheet	01/05/1918	02/05/1918
War Diary	Remy Siding	03/05/1918	04/05/1918
War Diary	K 32 Sheet 27	05/05/1918	05/05/1918
War Diary	Bissezeele	06/05/1918	08/05/1918
War Diary	Sheet 22 Soissons Archie-Le Pontaine	11/05/1918	16/05/1918
War Diary	Marteqny	24/05/1918	27/05/1918
War Diary	Bouvancourt	27/05/1918	27/05/1918
War Diary	Marteqny	28/05/1918	28/05/1918
War Diary	Arcis-Le-Ponsart		
War Diary	Vezilly	28/05/1918	28/05/1918
War Diary	Verneuil	29/05/1918	29/05/1918
War Diary	Damans	30/05/1918	30/05/1918
War Diary	La Chapelle	30/05/1918	30/05/1918
War Diary	La Chapelle	30/05/1918	31/05/1918
Heading	War Diary Medical 77th Field Ambulance R.A.M.C. June 1918		
War Diary	La Chapelle	30/05/1918	31/05/1918
War Diary	Maumit-en Brie	01/06/1918	01/06/1918
War Diary	Beaunay	01/06/1918	01/06/1918
War Diary	Chateau-de-la Gravelle	04/06/1918	07/06/1918
War Diary	Chateau De La Gravelle	10/06/1918	10/06/1918

War Diary	?	10/06/1918	16/06/1918
War Diary	Gourgancon	17/06/1918	22/06/1918
War Diary	Connantray	23/06/1918	24/06/1918
War Diary	Sommesous	25/06/1918	26/06/1918
War Diary	In The Train	27/06/1918	27/06/1918
War Diary	Prehedre	28/06/1918	30/06/1918
Heading	War Diary Medical July 1918		
War Diary	Prehedre	01/07/1918	03/07/1918
War Diary	Lebiez	04/07/1918	30/07/1918
War Diary	Enquin And Baillon	31/07/1918	31/07/1918
Heading	War Diary Medical 77th Field Ambulance Aug 1918		
War Diary	Enguin	01/08/1918	19/08/1918
War Diary	Barlin	20/08/1918	30/08/1918
War Diary	Ruitz	31/08/1918	31/08/1918
Miscellaneous	G.H.Q. 3rd Echelon	14/10/1918	14/10/1918
Heading	War Diary Medical 77th Field Ambulance September		
War Diary	Pernes	01/09/1918	01/09/1918
War Diary	Crepy	02/09/1918	02/09/1918
War Diary	Lebiez	03/09/1918	03/09/1918
War Diary	Leboisle	04/09/1918	04/09/1918
War Diary	Plessiel	05/09/1918	05/09/1918
War Diary	Foucacourt Les Nesle	06/09/1918	06/09/1918
War Diary	Villers	07/09/1918	24/09/1918
War Diary	Foucaucourt Les Nesle	25/09/1918	25/09/1918
War Diary	Molliens Vidame	20/09/1915	20/09/1915
War Diary	Ailly Somme	27/09/1918	27/09/1918
War Diary	Querrieu	28/09/1918	28/09/1918
War Diary	Franvillers	29/09/1918	29/09/1918
War Diary	Bernafay Wood	30/09/1918	30/09/1918
Heading	War Diary Of 77th Field Ambulance From 1st-31st October 1918		
War Diary	Bernafay Wood	01/10/1918	01/10/1918
War Diary	Bois De L'Eppinette	02/10/1918	02/10/1918
War Diary	St. Emilie	03/10/1918	03/10/1918
War Diary	Bellicourt Road	04/10/1918	04/10/1918
War Diary	Hargicourt	05/10/1918	07/10/1918
War Diary	Bellicourt Grandcourt Road	08/10/1918	08/10/1918
War Diary	Contained	08/10/1918	08/10/1918
War Diary	Estrees	09/10/1918	10/10/1918
War Diary	Busigny	11/10/1918	12/10/1918
War Diary	Elincourt.	13/10/1918	16/10/1918
War Diary	Honnechy	17/10/1918	18/10/1918
War Diary	St. Souplet	19/10/1918	21/10/1918
War Diary	Farm	22/10/1918	24/10/1918
War Diary	Cross Roads	25/10/1918	29/10/1918
War Diary	Honnechy	30/10/1918	31/10/1918
Heading	War Diary Medical Services 77th Field Ambulance		
War Diary	Honnechy	01/11/1918	06/11/1918
War Diary	Le Cateau	07/11/1918	09/11/1918
War Diary	Landrecies	10/11/1918	10/11/1918
War Diary	Bousies	11/11/1918	13/11/1918
War Diary	Pommereuil	14/11/1918	28/11/1918
War Diary	Quievy	29/11/1918	30/11/1918
Heading	War Diary Of O.B. 77 Field Ambulance for the month of December 1918		
War Diary	Quievy	01/12/1918	31/12/1918

Heading	War Diary & Infantry January of O.b 77 Field Ambulance to month of January 1919		
War Diary	Quievy	01/01/1919	03/01/1919
War Diary	Vendegies	04/01/1919	31/01/1919
Heading	War Diary Of The Officer 77th Field Ambulance for the Month of February 1919		
War Diary	Vendegies Au Bois	01/02/1919	07/02/1919
War Diary	Vendegies	08/02/1919	25/02/1919
War Diary	Iwuy	21/02/1919	28/02/1919

notes/2239

3) 27 Field Avenue

25TH DIVISION
MEDICAL

77TH FLD AMBULANCE
SEP 1915 - FEB 1919

121/7594

25th Division

77th Field Ambulance
Vol I

Sept & Oct 15

Army Form C. 2118.

WAR DIARY
or
~~INTELLIGENCE SUMMARY.~~
(Erase heading not required.)

Folio III.

Place	Date	Hour	Summary of Events and Information	Remarks and references to Appendices
OULTERSTEENE	1/9/15	9 p.m.	Sent B Section to open a rest station in a Chateau at BAILLEUL in the RUE DE MUSÉE. Took over a quantity of stores drugs & hospital clothing left behind by a previous Field Ambulance. A.D.C sections remain here. We are drawing sick from our Brigade area to casualty clearing station at BAILLEUL. One of our heavy draught horses sick with Pneumonia. Weather very fine.	
"	2/9/15	9 p.m.	Church Parade. Nothing to report	
"	3/9/15	9 p.m.	Church Parade. Visited B Section. Veterinary surgeon visited & shot the sick horse.	
"	4/9/15	9 p.m.	Nothing to report. Visited B Section at BAILLEUL. Informed that No 2 advanced depôt of Medical Stores is at BAILLEUL also No 2 Motor Ambulance Convoy. The two other Field Ambulances of the Division have fixed up dressing stations at ARMENTIÈRE & PONT DE NIEPPE. This Ambulance is being held in reserve in a rest camp	

Folio 1.
Army Form C. 2118

77th Field Ambulance

WAR DIARY
or
INTELLIGENCE SUMMARY.
(Erase heading not required.)

Place	Date	Hour	Summary of Events and Information	Remarks and references to Appendices
SOUTHAMPTON	26/9/15	7 p.m	The 77th Field Ambulance left Camp 38 Aldershot for Southampton. Entrained in two trains which departed at 12:30 & 1:30 p.m. respectively. On arrival at SOUTHAMPTON the F.A. were embarked on two ships 6 Officers & 3 Chaplains and 131 men F.A. were embarked on one ship the remainder of personnel & transport on another.	
LE HAVRE	27/9/15	2 p.m	Both Steamers arrived & the F.A. disembarked without accident & proceeded to rest camp No 5 arriving 2 p.m.	
LE HAVRE	28/9/15	2.30 p.m	Left rest camp & entrained at point 1 Gare de Marchandise	
STEENBECQUE	29/9/15 12 noon		Arrived & detrained. Received orders to proceed to MONT. DE MERRIS. On march received orders to proceed to billets at OULTERSTEENE. Arrived 7 p.m and billeted.	

Army Form C. 2118.

Folio 2.

WAR DIARY
or
INTELLIGENCE SUMMARY.
(Erase heading not required.)

Place	Date	Hour	Summary of Events and Information	Remarks and references to Appendices
OULTERSTEENE	30/4/16	7 p.m.	Sent an officer to get in touch with Brigade Headquarters. Found a reserve point for such in Brigade area. Got in touch with Brigade Supply Officer. Sent Supply wagon to Supply Point with orders to obtain our rations & the Rifles and Munition Divisional train. Took charge of 15 beds. Sent message to A.D.M.S. Returned in reply to Appendix 1, Appendix 11.	* Appendix I attached. * Appendix II attached. + Appendix III
			+ Message from No. 8 K.O.R.L. complied with. Received during day message from A. & B.M.G. 25th Division. This message Received at 5.45 p.m. Message from A. & B.M.G. 25th Division. 9 orderlies ordered F.A. with 4 sections. 1 orderer one section to not clear & ordered F.A. with 4 sections. A section to remain.	* Appendix IV
			Proceed BAILLEUL & one to ARMENTIERES & A section to remain. Notified D.A.D.M.S.†	† Appendix V
			Received a counter order at 8.32 p.m. Issued the necessary orders.	O Appendix 6.

Army Form C. 2118

WAR DIARY
or
INTELLIGENCE SUMMARY.
(Erase heading not required.)

Folio 4.

Place	Date	Hour	Summary of Events and Information	Remarks and references to Appendices
OULTERSTEENE	9/10/15	9 p.m.	Nothing to record. Twenty eight patients returned to Divisional train today.	
"	10/10/15	9 p.m.	Blanket supper returned to Divisional train today. Total no. of Patients treated in 78th Field Ambulance rest station during the week ended 10/8, 1 discharged to unit 141, transferred to C.C.S. 36, remaining 58.	
"	12/10/15	9 p.m.	Visited Sanitary exhibition at BAILLEUL. Also saw various patterns of incinerators made from food tins & biscuit tins visited B section & A.D.M.S. visited rest.	
"	13/10/15	9 a.m.	Sent my Sanitary Sgeant & Carpenters to visit and make notes at the Sanitary exhibition. Sent H.Q.S. & D.G.S. burials wagons to PONT DE NIEPPE to draw fuel for the continuation of stove tests.	
"	14/10/15	9 p.m.	Pte Meese transferred to 25th Divisional Ammunition subpart today with him a surgical haversack & water bottle. Pte Collins went to a clearing hospital having shown symptoms of delirium, unconfid. has examined by a Medical Board today.	

Army Form C. 2118.

Folio 5.

WAR DIARY
or
INTELLIGENCE SUMMARY.
(Erase heading not required.)

Place	Date	Hour	Summary of Events and Information	Remarks and references to Appendices
OULTERSTEENE	7/9/15	9 p.m.	Total number of patients admitted to rest station during the week = 103. Discharged to duty 31. Transferred to C.C.S. 15. Remaining 57.	
BAILLEUL	8/9/15	9 p.m.	Proceeded to BAILLEUL rest station with A section tent sub-division to join the rest station. B section Bearer sub-division re-called to OULTERSTEENE. The staff of the rest station now consists of A & B tent sub-divisions excepting 12 men of the Bearer sub-divisions of A & B to act as guards.	
"	10/9/15	9 p.m.	One officer & 20 men of A section tent sub-division joined the 73rd Field Ambulance at ARMENTIERES for four days instruction in advanced dressing station routine. A similar party for a similar training joined the 73rd Fd. Ambulance at PONT DE NIEPPE.	
"	11/9/15	9 p.m.	Lieut. one heavy draught horse & one mule from Divisional train to replace casualties.	

Army Form C. 2118.

WAR DIARY
or
INTELLIGENCE SUMMARY.

(Erase heading not required.)

Febr 6.

Instructions regarding War Diaries and Intelligence
Summaries are contained in F. S. Regs., Part II.
and the Staff Manual respectively. Title pages
will be prepared in manuscript.

Place	Date	Hour	Summary of Events and Information	Remarks and references to Appendices
BAILLEUL	28/10/15	9 p.m.	Both parties returned from the advanced dressing station without incident. Total No. of patients admitted to rest station during the week 146. Discharged to unit 33 Transferred to C.C.S. 11 remaining 100.	
"	29/10/15	9 p.m.	One Officer and 20 men proceeded to 73rd F.A. a similar party to 76th F.A. for instruction in advanced dressing station work.	
"	30/10/15	9 p.m.	Both the above parties returned safely. Total No. of patients admitted to rest station during the week 165. Discharged to duty 47. Transferred to C.C.S. 11. Transferred to other hospitals 13 remaining 95.	
"	1/11/15	9 p.m.	Lieut Alexander & 20 men have this day proceeded to manage the Divisional Baths at PONT DE NIEPPE.	

"A" Form.
MESSAGES AND SIGNALS
Army Form C. 2121

Appendix 1

| TO | A.D.M.S. | 25" | division | NIEPPE |

| Sender's Number | Day of Month | In reply to Number | |
| * | Thirtieth | No 1 | AAA |

Motor ambulances and motor cycles have not yet joined one When are first from brigade. area to be cleared to. ends.

From O C 77' Field Ambulance
Place OULTERSTEENE
Time midday

"C" Form (Duplicate).   Army Form C. 2123.

MESSAGES AND SIGNALS.

No. of Message ....

| | Charges to Pay. £ s. d. | Office Stamp. |

Service Instructions. YBE

Office Stamp: ZGF 30/9/15

Handed in at .... Office .... m. Received 6.58 p.m.

TO   O C 77 Field Ambulance
      Outterstene

Sender's Number	Day of Month	In reply to Number	AAA
M2	30		

Keep sick for the present if possible otherwise evacuate to clearing hospital BAILLEUL

FROM   ADMS
PLACE & TIME   25th Divn

77 A.7.a.
Vol. 2

121/7635

35th Kinnaird

Nov 15.

Nov 1915

77th Field Ambulance.
Army Form C. 2118.

WAR DIARY
or
INTELLIGENCE SUMMARY.
(Erase heading not required.)

Vol. 7

Place	Date	Hour	Summary of Events and Information	Remarks and references to Appendices
BAILLEUL	7/11/15	9 p.m.	No. of patients admitted to rest station during the week = 919. Discharged to duty 31. Transferred to ARQUES for the treatment 2. Transferred to 2/1st Div. rest station at CAESTRE = 2. Evacuated to C.C.S. = 11 remaining 53.	
"	8/11/15	9 a.m.	The remainder of the Field Ambulance moved today to OUSTERSTEENE to a farm about 3½ miles south east of BAILLEUL's railway station. All transport less two motor ambulances one G.S. waggon one water cart brought into the lines at BAILLEUL.	
"	13/11/15	9 p.m.	Admitted during past week 103 discharged to duty 22, sent to C.C.S. 12 divisional Rest Station 1 remaining 63. Transferred to Arques 5 to 50th Divisional Rest Station.	
"	20/11/15	9 p.m.	Admitted 151. discharged to duty 95, sent to C.C.S. 30 of which Cases dental cases 2 & vegetative vision for treatment at Arques remaining 26.	

H.G. Kenny
Major R.A.M.C.

WAR DIARY or INTELLIGENCE SUMMARY

77th Field Ambulance.
Folio 8.

Army Form C. 2118

(Erase heading not required.)

Place	Date	Hour	Summary of Events and Information	Remarks and references to Appendices
BAILLEUL	27/11/15		The detachment have fixed up accommodation for 30 slight cases at the farm 3½ miles S.W. of BAILLEUL Station. No. of patients admitted to the rest station during the past week = 146. Discharged to duty 42. Sent to C.C.S. 15. Remaining 83.	
"	28/11/15		10 more men sent to join Lieut ALEXANDER at the Divisional Baths at NIEPPE.	
"	30/11/15		Horse standings & shelters now completed & all horses under cover & in dry standings.	

H.B. KELLY
Major RAMC.

77ᵗʰ F.a.
Vol: 3

12/
7935

25ᵗʰ/12/

Dec 1915

Army Form C. 2118.

WAR DIARY
or
INTELLIGENCE SUMMARY.

(Erase heading not required.)

77th Field Ambulance

Instructions regarding War Diaries and Intelligence Summaries are contained in F.S. Regs., Part II. and the Staff Manual respectively. Title pages will be prepared in manuscript.

Place	Date	Hour	Summary of Events and Information	Remarks and references to Appendices
BAILLEUL	5/1/16	9/m	Five hundred R.A.M.C. arrived today as reinforcement to replace 3 men sent to base sick & 2 men transferred to other units	
"	6/1/16	11 a	Admitted to this unit station during the past week 158, returned to duty 41 sent to C.C.S. 21. Remaining 96.	
"	9/1/16	11 a	9 Z Cleared 7. of this unit sent to No 3 C.C.S. suffering from measles	
"	10/1/16	11 a	Admitted during the past week 134. returned to duty 36 sent to C.C.S. 19 (16 scabies) Remaining 79.	
"	12/1/16	9 a.m	Lieut Steele my transport officer transferred to another division. Have today joined for duty.	
"	13/1/16	9 a.m	Lieut Rennall attached at detached to H.S. Lake. Same as I.B here in place of no made over for me.	

H O Kelly
Major A.M./Mitchison
O.C. 77 F.M.M. Ambulance

Army Form C. 2118.

WAR DIARY
or
INTELLIGENCE SUMMARY.
(Erase heading not required.)

77th Field Ambulance

Instructions regarding War Diaries and Intelligence Summaries are contained in F. S. Regs., Part II. and the Staff Manual respectively. Title pages will be prepared in manuscript.

Place	Date	Hour	Summary of Events and Information	Remarks and references to Appendices
BAILLEUL	19/10/16	9 a.m	No. of patients evacuated to this unit taken during the past week = 156. Returned to duty 24. Sent to CCS 18. Remaining 104.	
"	20/10/16	9 a.m	Sergt-Major W. Chisholm R.A.M.C. having been granted a temporary commission as Hon Lieut of detail that Sermy, proceeded on 8 days leave to ENGLAND preparatory to Sergt TINNEY R.A.M.C.	
"	21/10/16	9 a.m	Orders received for to relieve 9th Wercs in charge of the Divisional Baths. Lieut RANKIN has proceeded to take up his duty with the 9th Scott. Fus.	
"	22/10/16	9 a.m	Lieut W. S. COX R.A.M.C. struck off unit also having proceeded on 14 days sick leave to UK	
"	23/10/16	9 a.m	At 10.60 a.m the men sent to join the 9th Worcs today to report to A.D.M.S at MERVILLE	

W. Hollis
Major RAMC

Army Form C. 2118.

WAR DIARY
or
INTELLIGENCE SUMMARY.

77 E Field Ambulance   L Coy 11

(Erase heading not required.)

Instructions regarding War Diaries and Intelligence Summaries are contained in F.S. Regs., Part II. and the Staff Manual respectively. Title pages will be prepared in manuscript.

Place	Date	Hour	Summary of Events and Information	Remarks and references to Appendices
BAILLEUL	30/9/15	9/—	The total nr. of patients admitted to the Ambulance from 30/9/15 to 30/9/15 = 1620 of whom 132 are remaining today. Including the remaining figures from the start this gives 1488 cases disposed of. Of this number 1435 have been returned to duty going as follows:— Of 722 94 returned to duty. Of the 413 cases evacuated to C.C.S. 94 were 8 natal cases which need merely sent on for treatment & should return to duty in due course. If we deduct these 94 cases it gives us 319 cases evacuated & no cases our knowledge of returns to duty to 77.11. We really of 6 sgm cleared from it only costs not cases admitted & discharged to duty.	H.O.S ReRy Major WrRogers

77th 7a.
Vol. 4

25th Div

FF 1941

77 F A

January
5

Army Form C. 2118.

WAR DIARY 77th Field Ambulance
or
INTELLIGENCE SUMMARY.
(Erase heading not required.)

Folio 12.

Instructions regarding War Diaries and Intelligence Summaries are contained in F. S. Regs., Part II. and the Staff Manual respectively. Title pages will be prepared in manuscript.

Place	Date	Hour	Summary of Events and Information	Remarks and references to Appendices
BAILLEUL	2/1/16	9p.m.	Number of patients admitted to this rest station during the past week = 144. Remaining 102. To duty 16. Base for eye treatment 3. To C.C.S. 22 to 9th Div. rest station.	
"	5/1/16	4p.m.	Lieut. F.J. COLLINS. R.A.M.C. reported for duty.	
"	7/1/16	5.45a.m	Left for 9 days leave.	
"	17/1/16	9p.m.	Returned from leave. No of patients admitted to this rest station during week ending 15/1/16 = 165. Returned to duty 27 cases to C.C.S. 34. Sent to Base 5 to Argues 1. No of Dental cases submitted in. To cast to C.C.S. = 25. Remaining 98.	
"	23/1/16	9p.m.	One officer & 30 N.C.O.s & men with equipment left today for PRADELLES. This Coy to advance party from this Field Ambulance for new quarters.	

H.O. Kelly
Major RAMC

WAR DIARY
INTELLIGENCE SUMMARY

Feb 13.
77th Field Ambulance

(Erase heading not required.)

Army Form C. 2118.

Place	Date	Hour	Summary of Events and Information	Remarks and references to Appendices
BAILLEUL	25/1/16	9 p.m.	Advance party from 27th Field Ambulance consisting of 2 officers & 30 N.C.O & men with equipment arrived today from OUTERSTEENE to take over this unit station. Total admissions during the past week = 128. Sent up to duty 30. Sent to C.C.S 17. To base 1. To Ayres 1. Remaining 77 No. of cases of Frostbite cases evacuated to base. Total = 8.	
BAILLEUL	26/1/16	9 p.m.	Field Ambulance moved by route march to PRADELLES. today, the move took place without incident. We have fairly warm dormitory stations here for rest of our men. No 15 c.c.s HAZEBROUCK is not our nearest for evacuation. No 12 c.c.s HAZEBROUCK & the stationary evacuation for cases other than Scabies & teeth are sent to No 52. c.c.s HAZEBROUCK.	

H.A.Colquhoun
Major 77th Field Ambulance.
O.C 77

Army Form C. 2118.

WAR DIARY
or
INTELLIGENCE SUMMARY.
(Erase heading not required.)

77th Field Ambulance
Mar 14.

Place	Date	Hour	Summary of Events and Information	Remarks and references to Appendices
PRADELLES	31/1/16	4p.m	Lieut COLLARD & 30 men of this ambulance reported from the Divisional Baths at NIEPPE today	
"	4/2/1			

H.B. Kelly
Lieut-Col. R.A.M.C.
O.C. 77th Field Ambulance

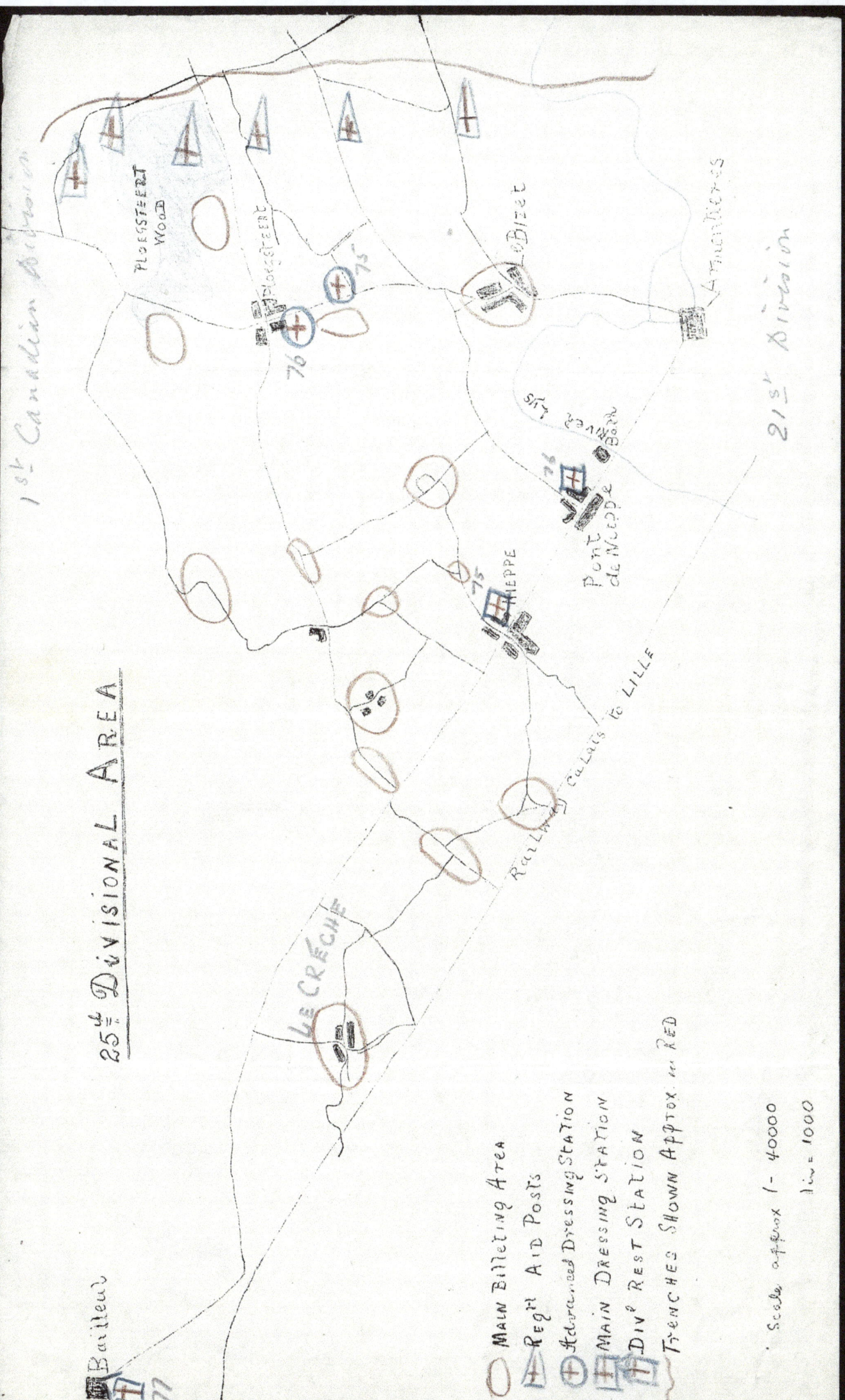

Feb 1916

44th Field Ambulance

Army Form C. 2118.

WAR DIARY
or
INTELLIGENCE SUMMARY.
(Erase heading not required.)

Abor B.
77 L Field Ambulance.

Instructions regarding War Diaries and Intelligence Summaries are contained in F.S. Regs., Part II. and the Staff Manual respectively. Title pages will be prepared in manuscript.

Place	Date	Hour	Summary of Events and Information	Remarks and references to Appendices
PRADELLES	11/9/15	1/30 pm	Two officers H.S. O.R. The whole vehicle & two motor ambulances, 13 horse left this by route march for VOLKERINCKHOVE then set out for WATTEN. Artillery from the camp where 3am tonight to WATTEN. Artillery have gone for two days practice. Several artillery have gone for two days practice. The detachment have today returned from VOLKERINCKHOVE. No incident of importance. No men fell out either going or returning. The distance was 20 miles.	
PRADELLES	13/9/15	9 pm	Lieut E.S. BISSELL. R.A.M.C. (Temporary) arrived for duty.	
"	24/9/15	9.1 pm	Lieut CASSING. R.A.M.C. left for company duty with 8th South Lancs.	
"	27/9/15	10 am	Lieut Knight left to take over charge of 10th Cheshire Regt. Lieut T.O. WHITE reported for duty.	

H.B. Wright Lt
Lieut in Ch of Offices

Army Form C. 2118.

WAR DIARY
or
INTELLIGENCE SUMMARY.
(Erase heading not required.)

77th Field Ambulance
Folio 16.

Place	Date	Hour	Summary of Events and Information	Remarks and references to Appendices
PRADELLES	28/6	9/30am	4 men of this Ambulance left today on transfer to a railway construction company.	
"	29/6	9/hr	Capt MONTGOMERY. R.A.M.C. of this unit left today for duty on the Lines of Communication. The R.A.M.C. personnel of this unit today received the 1914 pattern Infantry equipment. Old equipment handed in at withdrew.	

H.B Kelly
Lieut- Col R.A.M.C.

March 1916

5

17 June

Vol. 6

Army Form C. 2118.

WAR DIARY
or
INTELLIGENCE SUMMARY.

77th Field Ambulance
Folio 17.

(Erase heading not required.)

Instructions regarding War Diaries and Intelligence Summaries are contained in F. S. Regs., Part II. and the Staff Manual respectively. Title pages will be prepared in manuscript.

Place	Date	Hour	Summary of Events and Information	Remarks and references to Appendices
PRADELLES	9/3/16	9.30 a.m.	The Ambulance moved today to join the 7th Infantry Brigade in the OUTERSTEENE area. Route STRAZEELE — MERRIS — OUTERSTEENE. Moved off at 12.30 p.m. Took over S.A. HAZEBROUCK	
OUTERSTEENE		9 p.m.	Took over billets in OUTERSTEENE from 73rd Field Ambulance. The Division is under orders to move to a new area tomorrow. For the purposes of the move this Ambulance will act under the orders of the G.O.C. 7th Infantry Brigade. Received at 9 p.m. "Starter" orders for Brigade for tomorrows move. Made the following reference map sheet 27 & 36.A 1/40,000 ———— Starting point East coming F.S.C. 1/2 and S.W. of OUTERSTEENE. This ambulance will pass starting point in rear of Brigade at 9.24 a.m. Route VIEUX BERQUIN — LA COURONNE — NEERHOUCK — MERVILLE — ROBECQ.	H.A. Kelly Col. 77 Field Ambulance

WAR DIARY
or
INTELLIGENCE SUMMARY.

(Erase heading not required.)

Army Form C. 2118.

77th Field Ambulance
Septr. 18

Place	Date	Hour	Summary of Events and Information	Remarks and references to Appendices
OUTERSTEENE	1/9/16	9½ a.	Septinster P.26 & P.27. (BUSNES. Exclusive.) We have ambulances will move with the ambulance. The motor ambulances will follow motor an officer and tent takers in the rear of the horse ambulances. Very unsafe to open with straggling, bringing ground have been arranged in rear of March at which places the motor ambulances will call on route.	
P. 26 from '36.B.	1/9/16	9½ a.	March accomplished without incident. Forty four stragglers picked up. All the cleaned this evening to No. 39 C.C.S. ST. VENANT. Arranged with Brigade-Major 1st Infantry Brigade to collect such tomorrow morning before Brigade moves out to continue its march. The orderly hand arranged. Received further orders & found the time for tomorrow march	

H.B. Kelly Lt. Col.
O.C. 77 Field Ambulance.

WAR DIARY
or
INTELLIGENCE SUMMARY.

Army Form C. 2118.

Mar 19. 77th Field Ambulance

Place	Date	Hour	Summary of Events and Information	Remarks and references to Appendices
P.26. Reference 36.S.W.	10/3/16	11 p.m.	Starting point LILLERS. CHURCH. This ambulance will form starting point at 11.4 A.M. September VALHUON. Route LILLERS – BURBURE – PERNES – VALHUON. Reference HAZEBROUCK. 5A 1/100,000. LENS. 1/100,000.	
VALHUON	11/3/16	9 a.m.	March completed without incident. Nineteen sick collected at the wayside during point before starting; all these evacuated to No. 32. C.C.S. ST. VENANT. Five sick picked up on line of march St. of these 8 were sent to No. 6. C.C.S. LILLERS & the remainder were sent to again their units on arrival at Villaines.	

H.G. Kellog
Lt. 77th Field Ambulance

WAR DIARY
INTELLIGENCE SUMMARY

Army Form C. 2118.

Folio 20.
77th Field Ambulance

Place	Date	Hour	Summary of Events and Information	Remarks and references to Appendices
VAL HON	15/3/16	4 p.m.	Received orders to march independently to MAISNIL-ST-POL reference LENS map	
		11 p.m.	Starting at 10 a.m.	
MAISNIL-ST-POL	16/3/16	9½ a.m.	Arrived at 1 p.m. without incident. Opening up temporary dressing station for trailing sick of Brigade area. We are sharing the work at FOUY-EN-TERNOIS, MAZIERES, PENIN, F=SOFFINE, AVENDOINGT & F= PART OF IT, TERNAS, BUNEVILLE. Lieut regarding evacuation sick sent to No 30. C.C.S. at AUBIGNEY. We are classed by No 24. M.A.C. Infections cases are sent to Highland C.C.S. at NUEUX, DIEABES. Transport provided by No 24. M.A.C. Dental cases are treated at 75th Field Ambulance at BAILLEUL-au-CORMAILLES. Dentist attends each Tuesday. (Map referred to all above LENS 1/100,000.	

H.S. Kelly Capt.
77th Field Ambulance

Army Form C. 2118.

WAR DIARY
or
INTELLIGENCE SUMMARY.
(Erase heading not required.)

Folio 21.
77th Field Ambulance

Instructions regarding War Diaries and Intelligence Summaries are contained in F. S. Regs., Part II. and the Staff Manual respectively. Title pages will be prepared in manuscript.

Place	Date	Hour	Summary of Events and Information	Remarks and references to Appendices
MAISNIL ST OUR.	16/3/16	9 p.m.	Obtained slight of medical stores in at FREVENT (No 15)	
"	18/3/16	4 p.m.	Lieut. C. PENTLAND. RAMC from Irish Rifles reported for duty	
"	20/3/16	9 a.m.	Lieut. C. PENTLAND. RAMC. proceeded for temporary duty with 2 Batteries of R.F.A. to AVERDOINGT.	
"	23/3/16	4 p.m.	Infectious cases now to be transferred to 43 Field Ambulance at LIGNEREUIL. Map sheet 51.C. S. 21. L.	
"	24/3/16	9 p.m.	3 Officers 57 O.R. sent to No 32 c.c.s. to await also two motor ambulances	
"	26/3/16	9 p.m.	We are now evacuating our sick to No 43. c.c.s. at FREVENT.	

H.G. Kethro
Lt. R.C. O.C./MC

25th Div.

No 777 F. Amb.

April 1916.

COMMITTEE FOR THE
MEDICAL HISTORY OF THE WAR
Date 9 - JUN. 1916

Army Form C. 2118.

WAR DIARY
or
INTELLIGENCE SUMMARY
(Erase heading not required.)

Feb 22
77th Field Ambulance Vol 7

Place	Date	Hour	Summary of Events and Information	Remarks and references to Appendices
MESNIL ST POL	1/4/16	9am	Nothing to record. Weather fine.	
"	2/4/16	9pm	Nothing to record. Weather continued fine. LIEUT. PENTLAND R.A.M.C. rejoined for duty at 6 p.m.	
"	3/4/16	9pm	Nothing to record. Weather continued fine.	
"	4/4/16	9pm	Nothing to record. Weather continued fine.	
"	5/4/16	9pm	Nothing to record.	
"	6/4/16	9pm	Seven reinforcements arrived from the base.	
"	7/4/16	9pm	Lieut Morris Niven of this ambulance joined 25th D.A.C. for temporary duty. Capt Aldren A.A.M.C. proceeded to 30 C.C.S. for temporary duty vice First white A.A.M.C. recalled.	
"	8/4/16	9pm	Nothing to record. One H.D. have died of colic.	

H.E. Kelly
Lieut-Col comm.

WAR DIARY or INTELLIGENCE SUMMARY.

Army Form C. 2118.

Feb. 23.

77th Field Ambulance

Place	Date	Hour	Summary of Events and Information	Remarks and references to Appendices
MESNIL	12/4/16	9 p.m.	Sergt. GLOVER. of this unit transferred today to No 43. C.C.S. at FREVENT.	
MESNIL	13/4/16	9 p.m.	Staff-Sergt. CHAPMAN. R.A.M.C. joined for duty today from 43. C.C.S. Our section at 30 C.C.S. has been relieved & has proceeded to VILLERS CHATEL. Hour to await main body of Ambulance	
MESNIL	16/4/16	9 p.m.	Hour to await main body of Ambulance One section moved to TINQUETTE.	
MESNIL	18/4/16	9 p.m.	One section from TINQUETTE march to relieve the 1/2 North Midland Field Ambulance & to establish main dressing station at ACQ.	
ACQ	19/4/16	9 p.m.	One section from VILLERS. CHATEL moved to ACQ. Arriving station at MINT-ST-ELOY.	

W. McCann
O.C. 77 Field Ambulance

WAR DIARY or INTELLIGENCE SUMMARY

Army Form C. 2118.

79th Light
Ambulance

Folio 24

Place	Date	Hour	Summary of Events and Information	Remarks and references to Appendices
ACA	20/4/16	9 a.m.	Our remaining section moved from MESNIL to TINQUETTE.	
"	21/4/16	9 a.m.	One section for TINQUETTE moved to ACA & joined main dressing station. The system of evacuation in this line is by trollys at night. There trollys run close to Regimental aid posts. Two men from our trollys full service to Regimental aid posts. The trollys are met at MINT ST-ELOI by motor ambulances & conveyed direct to main dressing station at ACA. Pt. ambulance is clearing from left & centre sector of the four Regimental aid posts one in the line & two in nearby farm houses from the ambulance are picked up each and put in the line. We also have a post with wheeled stretcher in BETHUNE Road Wholly French ...	

Army Form C. 2118.

WAR DIARY
or
INTELLIGENCE SUMMARY.
(Erase heading not required.)

77th Field Ambulance

Place	Date	Hour	Summary of Events and Information	Remarks and references to Appendices
ACD	29/4/16 9am		Night cases regularly removed by day are conveyed from regimental aid post to an post on BETHUNE ROAD & thence to advanced dressing station at MONT-ST-ELOY. A new scheme for evacuation is being drawn up & will be reported on later.	
ACD	30/4/16 4pm		Lieut ALEXANDER. RAMC. transferred to A.E. Lieut HARTLEY. same. Joined for duty with this Ambulance	

M. Kelly
Lieut Colonel
77 Field
Ambulance
I.C. 77
Ambulance

25th Div.

No 77 F. Amb.

Mar 1915

COMMITTEE FOR THE
MEDICAL HISTORY OF THE WAR
Date 26 JUN 1915

Army Form C. 2118.

Vol 8

WAR DIARY
or
INTELLIGENCE SUMMARY. Feb 25. 77th Field Ambulance
(Erase heading not required.)

Place	Date	Hour	Summary of Events and Information	Remarks and references to Appendices
ACQ.	25/2/16	4pm	Lieut HARTLEY. R.A.M.C. rejoined 1st North Midland Field Ambulance. Lieut KENNEDY. R.A.M.C. from same joined for duty. The following Medical arrangements came into force night of 25th – 26th. This ambulance is clearing left & centre sector of the line. L = left sector. C = centre & R = Right. L.a. = Aid post for 8th holding Regiment and posts will be allotted right " " " " " a.c. = " " " " " S.a. = " " " " " in support of L sector. & Kimberley for the sector C & R. A notice will be put up outside each Aid post thus: [Aid post L.C.] Four Field Ambulance bearers will be stationed in each Regimental aid post. L.B. R.B. L.P. & R.P. Hartley Lieut-Col R.A.M.C. O.C. 77th Field Ambulance	

WAR DIARY
or
INTELLIGENCE SUMMARY.

(Erase heading not required.)

Army Form C. 2118.

Feb. 27. 77th Field Ambulance

Place	Date	Hour	Summary of Events and Information	Remarks and references to Appendices
A.C.C.	25/16	9pm	This Ambulance will establish an advanced dressing station staffed by 2 officers & 30 other ranks on the night 2/3rd in day-out-at the junction of the BOYAU CENTRAL & BETHUNE ROAD. The remainder of the staff of one officer + 2 motor ambulances will be maintained at MINT ST. ELOY. Four bearers will be detailed by this Ambulance to meet of the A.D.P. POSTS: R.C., L.L., R.P. & L.P. respectively. Evacuation routes: (a.) Direct from aid posts by TROLLEYS at night. (b.) By hand to advanced dressing station & thence by trolley out right or to trench via CARDUROY BATH or BOYAU CENTRAL night or by trench via CARDUROY BATH or BOYAU CENTRAL to FLEET ST. F.H.O. where cars will be in readiness. Information in FLEET ST. F.H.O. where cars will be in readiness. M/Ulle Te- same. N.C.S. 77th Field Ambulance	

WAR DIARY
or
INTELLIGENCE SUMMARY.

Army Form C. 2118.

Feb. 28. 77th Field Ambulance

Place	Date	Hour	Summary of Events and Information	Remarks and references to Appendices
ACQ	25/16	9 p.m.	(E.) An alternative route may be used from Advanced Dressing Station if shelled whether along BETHUNE RD. to LA TARGETTE, thence to cross roads in F.10.d. where cars can rest until O.i/c. Advanced Dressing Station will supply fresh cat MAIN ST. ECOY where cars are to meet cars. <u>Communication.</u> O.C. 77th Field Ambulance will have a relay today at St. Eloi. H.Q. and to Orlay at T.8.c.c. H.Q. Unit can communicate direct with Advanced Dressing Station (the quickest method of obtaining assistance.) If further assistance is required O.i/c. of Advanced Dressing Station can telephone through to 77th Field Ambulance to O.C. Field Ambulance. H.Q. 62nd Headquarters can also communicate with Field Ambulance. Noble Alex. Lt. Col. R.a.m.c. O.C. 77th Field Ambulance	

Army Form C. 2118.

WAR DIARY
or
INTELLIGENCE SUMMARY.

(Erase heading not required.)

Folio 24. 77 L/Gilly Ambulance

Place	Date	Hour	Summary of Events and Information	Remarks and references to Appendices
ACQ	2/5/16	9½a	Through 77th Field Ambulance on who commenced with Field Ambulance either about of sickly or through the A.D.M.S. all messages should give exact information of number of cases to be evacuated. Sick for unit at MONT-ST-ELOY & BOIS-DES-ALLEUX proceed to advanced post of this Ambulance at MONT-ST-ELOY. Sick for unit at FREVIN CAPELLE & CAPELLE FERMONT are collected by this Ambulance at G.D.M. Daily by Motor Ambulances. Discharges to duty are sent to refilling point. The 77th Field Ambulance has opened a D.R.S. at VILLERS-CHATEL with accommodation for 18 Officers. No H.Q., C.C.S & D.R.S. are at AUBIGNY. The hours admit all Officers.	W W G P Grice MBE O.C. 77 Field Ambulance

Army Form C. 2118.

WAR DIARY
or
INTELLIGENCE SUMMARY.
(Erase heading not required.)

771st Field Ambulance   Feb 31.

Place	Date	Hour	Summary of Events and Information	Remarks and references to Appendices
ACD	2/5/16	3pm	X mobile X-Ray Unit at 30 CCS.	
	3/5/16	9pm	Capt LESCHER & Lieut KENNEDY & 30. C.C. have proceeded to occupy advanced dressing station. Capt. McELNEY & 11 O.R. to MONT-ST-ELOY.	
"	4/5/16	9pm	4 privates arrived as reinforcements.	
"	8/5/16	9pm	One H.D. horse no 29 shot having had his leg broken by a kick from A.D. horse sent away to 2nd Echelons	
"	10/5/16	9pm	Capt McELNEY with relief party proceeded to advanced dressing station. Lieut PENTLAND to MONT-ST-ELOY.	
"	11/5/16	9pm	A considerable number of wounded being passed through, 128 last night.	

H.A. Kelly
Lieut Col comg

Army Form C. 2118.

1 / 77 Field Ambulance

WAR DIARY
or
INTELLIGENCE SUMMARY.

Feb 31. 77 Field Ambulance

(Erase heading not required.)

Instructions regarding War Diaries and Intelligence Summaries are contained in F. S. Regs., Part II. and the Staff Manual respectively. Title pages will be prepared in manuscript.

Place	Date	Hour	Summary of Events and Information	Remarks and references to Appendices
ACQ	23/5/16	9 p.m.	Heavy fighting took place on 21–22. Total casualties admitted here from 12 mn–21 to 9 p.m. 22 = 329. All the tents had to be used by hand or conducted walking to MONT-ST-ELOY, the Forty-five having ten floor up in many places. Eighteen hand from 75th Field Ambulance & 24 from 78th Field Ambulance had to be retained to assist. 75th Field Ambulance working from NEUVILLE-ST-VAAST who reported in the work of clearing the centre sector or the supply of 14/20 we hand hand in over the Left or R sector of the R sector of Souchez Field Ambulance of the 47 L. Division.	
	30/5/16	9 p.m.	One section of this Field Ambulance moved to TINQUETTE by route march starting at 8.30 p.m.	

Willally Kent–of mine
O.C. 77 Field Ambulance

COMMITTEE FOR THE
MEDICAL HISTORY OF THE WAR
Date 5 AUG 1915

No. 77 F.G.

June 1915.
5/

Vol 4

Army Form C. 2118.

WAR DIARY
or
~~INTELLIGENCE SUMMARY.~~
(Erase heading not required.)

Flan 32. 77th Field Ambulance

June

Place	Date	Hour	Summary of Events and Information	Remarks and references to Appendices
TINQUETTE	1/6/16	9 p.m.	On night 31st May/June 1st we withdrew from centre sector at 8 p.m. having handed this sector over to 1/2nd Highland Field Ambulance of 51st Division.	
	2/6/16	9 p.m.	On night 1–2nd June the remainder of this Ambulance moved to TINQUETTE by route march starting at 9 p.m. we are collecting sick from units in our Brigade area stationed in the following places. MONCHY-BRETON. HERLIN-LE-VERT. GUESTREVILLE. CHELERS. TINQUETTE. TINQUES. BETHENCOURT. 75th Field Ambulance is at BAILLEUL-AUX-CORNAILLES. & 76th at VILLERS CHATEL with a section at MINGOVAL. 76th are still acting as a Divisional rest station.	
	5/6/15	9 a.m.	Proceeding on leave, handing over command of this Ambulance to Captain F.J. Fowler A.D.M.S.	

H.O. Kelly
Lieut Colonel

Army Form C. 2118.

WAR DIARY
or
INTELLIGENCE SUMMARY.

77th Field Ambulance. Feb 33.

(Erase heading not required.)

Instructions regarding War Diaries and Intelligence Summaries are contained in F.S. Regs., Part II. and the Staff Manual respectively. Title pages will be prepared in manuscript.

Place	Date	Hour	Summary of Events and Information	Remarks and references to Appendices
TINCQUETTE	5/5/18	1 pm	Pte RANDELL A.E. & four O.R. transferred to 8 L.N.Lines for extra duty. Strength unchanged.	
	10/6/18	2 pm	Enemy shelled in this area forenoon. D Company & stretcher division transported well. Quite number of hostile equipment.	
	13/		Divisional field day. 77th & 75th FA. first took part. 77th Adv-Amb went 7th Brigade 78th Division attached from Divisional Mounted Brigade in Ground reserve. Attached to village & took up 10 am. ADS formed ½ mile in rear. Bearers efficient indeed. The brigade & all normal right & for net communication with M.O. of battalion by sentry two bearers to each M.O. one carrying pickets kits. Arrangements thus worked very well. Weather showers for first four days.	

M.M. Kelly Lieut-Col
wune
O.C. 77th Field Ambulance

Army Form C. 2118.

WAR DIARY
or
INTELLIGENCE SUMMARY. 77th Field Ambulance. Folio 34.
(Erase heading not required.)

Instructions regarding War Diaries and Intelligence Summaries are contained in F. S. Regs., Part II. and the Staff Manual respectively. Title pages will be prepared in manuscript.

Place	Date	Hour	Summary of Events and Information	Remarks and references to Appendices
TINCQUETTE	14/6/16	12 noon	Returned from leave.	
CANTELEUX	17/6/16	9 p.m.	The ambulance moved by route march today to CANTELEUX vide AVERDOINGT — SARS, LEZ, BUZ — REBREUVIETTE — MONTLEBLOND. The march completed without incident. We are attaching ourselves to our Brigade viz for unit it's BONNIERES. BEAUVIR. REMAGINIL. BRUY. (map reference LENS sheet 1:100000)	
FIENVILLERS	18/6/16	12 noon	On night 17/18th June. This ambulance moved to FIENVILLERS by route march starting after dark & arriving before dawn. (LENS sheet 1:100000). We are moving north of GEZAINCOURT. DONSUEVILLETTE. AUTHEUX. FIENVILLERS. BURLES. (7 Brigade group). Also R.A. Troops etc. BONNEVILLE PREFFERS. MONTRELET.	

H.B.Kelly.
Lieut-Col. R.A.M.C.
O.C. 77th Field Ambulance

WAR DIARY
or
INTELLIGENCE SUMMARY.

Army Form C. 2118.

No 35. 77th Field Ambulance

(Erase heading not required.)

Place	Date	Hour	Summary of Events and Information	Remarks and references to Appendices
PERNOIS	20/6/16	9 p.m.	On night 18-19/June this ambulance moved to PERNOIS. We are collecting sick from PERNOIS, HALLOY-LES-PERNOIS & CANAPLES, also from FIEFFES, BONNEVILLE & MONTRELET.	
BERNEUIL	25/6/16	9 p.m.	On night 24-25/June this Ambulance moved to BERNEUIL. Capt. B.M. COLLARD & 23 O.R. from this unit left to reinforce No 44 C.C.S. at PUCHVILLARS.	
TOUTENCOURT	28/6/16	9 p.m.	Moved here	
HARPONVILLE	30/6/16	9 p.m.	Arrived at 6 p.m. today. Lieut HEGARTY to report to 76th Field Ambulance for duty with a party unit in 32nd Division.	
CONTAY	24/6/16	1 a.m.	Received orders at 9.45 p.m. to proceed to CONTAY.	

H.O. Kelly
Lieut-Colonel
O.C. 77th Field Ambulance

25th Division

No 77 Field Ambulance

COMMITTEE FOR THE
MEDICAL HISTORY OF THE WAR
Date   31 Aug 1916

July 1916

WAR DIARY or INTELLIGENCE SUMMARY

VOLUME VI 10 July
77th Field Ambulance Folio 36.
Army Form C. 2118.

Place	Date	Hour	Summary of Events and Information	Remarks and references to Appendices
VADENCOURT	3/7/16	a.m.	Received orders to take over the Forward collecting station at VADENCOURT from 97th Field Ambulance and the tent division and the 10th Divisional trains. Motor and horse ambulances supplied by 2nd Field Ambulance and to be responsible for the evacuation of the wounded from the 32nd and 49th Divisional Areas. Ambulance cars motor were at CONTAY arriving the tent division supplying Evacuation teams from arrival to wounded in empty supply & ammunition trains from convoy to No 1 & No 34 C.C.S. at PUCHEVILLERS. As wounded were the ambulance drivers were evacuated to CONTAY & PUCHEVILLERS. LIEUT RIDDELL left at 11 a.m. LIEUT HEGARTY arrived from the line.	
VADENCOURT	4/7/16	9.30 a.m.	Tent division proceeded to VADENCOURT 13 O.R. rejoined from H.C.C.S. 1 Officer & 11 O.R. transferred from H.C.C.S. to 97 C.C.S. at BEAUCOURT to duty	A.B. Kelly Lieut Colonel

Army Form C. 2118.

WAR DIARY
or
INTELLIGENCE SUMMARY.
(Erase heading not required.)

77th Field Ambulance Folio 37

Place	Date	Hour	Summary of Events and Information	Remarks and references to Appendices
VADENCOURT	13/7/16	9/m	Two N.C.O's & 12 privates ordered to proceed to WARLOY to assist the 76th Field Ambulance. The 92nd Field Ambulance ordered to relieve these men. Ambulance. This they are unable to do, my seven N.C.O's men being available. Have reported to A.D.M.S. 25th Division, I do not consider my remaining staff sufficient to cope with an emergency. We are now receiving sick officers and wounded from 32nd, 23rd, 12th, 49, 19, & 85 various cdn. troops. Wire from Capt B.M. COLLARD. R.A.M.C. informs me he together with 11. O.R.s of this Field Ambulance are now on a hospital train at ACHEUX. The distribution of this Ambulance is now 1 Officer & 11. O.R.s a hospital train, 14 O.R.s at WARLOY with the 76th Field Ambulance, 3 Officers 82 O.R.s all motor ambulances 3 horse ambulances + 2 G.S. waggons country 78th Field Ambulance 1 Officer & 11 O.R.s motor establishment remains at VADENCOURT for the reception of two cyclists. H.O. Kelly Lt Col ramc	

Army Form C. 2118.

WAR DIARY
~~INTELLIGENCE SUMMARY~~.

Folio 38. 77th Field Ambulance.

(Erase heading not required.)

Place	Date	Hour	Summary of Events and Information	Remarks and references to Appendices
VADENCOURT	15/7/16	11.30am	The fourteen O.R's sent to assist the 76th Field Ambulance at WARLOY, returned at 10.15 p.m. 8 reinforcements arrived, 7 sent up immediately to the Lewis division who have had five men wounded & one with some they left.	
VADENCOURT	16/7/16 9am		Received orders from A.D.M.S. 25th Division that we could be relieved by an Ambulance of the 48th Division the next day, also that our transport would rejoin at 7 a.m. 17/7/16. Bearer division at 12 noon. The personnel attached to 27 C.C.S. would rejoin or relieve by a similar party from the 48th Division.	
"	17/7/16 3pm		Handed over to the 1/1st/3rd South Midland Field Ambulance. Bearer division & transport rejoined. Received orders to march to BEAUVAL. Sick & wounded admitted.	

nil. 7a.m. 18/7/16 = 0.45

H.B. Kelley Major
Temp/Lt. Colonel
O.C. 77 Field Ambulance

Army Form C. 2118.

Instructions regarding War Diaries and Intelligence
Summaries are contained in F. S. Regs., Part II.
and the Staff Manual respectively. Title pages
will be prepared in manuscript.

WAR DIARY
or
INTELLIGENCE SUMMARY.

77th E Field Ambulance.
Folio 89.

(Erase heading not required.)

Place	Date	Hour	Summary of Events and Information	Remarks and references to Appendices
BEAUVAL	24/7/16	7.0 p.m	Received wire from 7th Infantry Brigade that this ambulance would move today. Details later.	
		12.30 p.m	Orders to march out 2 p.m. to WARNICOURT WOOD. Lieut BISSELL sent on as billetting officer.	
		2 p.m.	Ambulance arrived & are billetted at L24.d.8.8. about 57.D. we are to collect sick from our own brigade. There are four small huts here each capable of accommodating 20 sick. Fitted up for receiving. Personnel in tents or bivouacs. Capt B.M. COLLARD & 11 O.R. regard which as the march	
WARNICOURT WOOD	29/7/16	7.30 p.m.	Received orders to take over the Post this far for the 29th Division, but one officer & 6 O.R.'s immediately to report to the 2/2nd London Field Ambulance at ACHEUX & turn the wire are officers & O.R. sent to do duty.	

A.C.C.S. BEAUVAL for duty.

H.C. Walts
Lieut Col A.C.M.S.
I.C. 77 E Field Ambulance

2353 Wt. W2544/1454 700,000 5/15 D.D. & L. A.D.S.S./Form/C. 2118.

Army Form C. 2118.

WAR DIARY
or
INTELLIGENCE SUMMARY.

77th Field Ambulance. Feby 1916

(Erase heading not required.)

Place	Date	Hour	Summary of Events and Information	Remarks and references to Appendices
ACHEUX.	23/2/16	9 p.m.	This Ambulance moved to ACHEUX & took over the Field Ambulance Walking station also the left collecting station. The station of Veterinary Medical officer & M.O. to German prisoner camps. One section complete sent to take over the front line. Reference 57 F.D. an advanced dressing station is at MESNIL. Q.29. a collecting post in dugouts at Q.16. d.2.9. with a collecting post at HAMEL Q.23. and a car stand near dug out a collecting post of COINERS. Q.29. L.3.5. We are doing the right & left half of centre sector. The 3rd field ambulance the right & left half of right sector we also to our collecting post at Q.16.d.2.9. and feet of right half of right sector is close to HAMEL. Evacuation from Q.16.d.2.9 at MESNIL is by Trolly from to HAMEL. HAMEL to COINERS by wheel stretcher & there by car to MESNIL. from MESNIL to ACHEUX by motor	

O.C. 77th Field Ambulance.

Army Form C. 2118.

WAR DIARY
or
INTELLIGENCE SUMMARY. No. 41. ACHEUX.

(Erase heading not required.)

Instructions regarding War Diaries and Intelligence Summaries are contained in F.S. Regs., Part II. and the Staff Manual respectively. Title pages will be prepared in manuscript.

Place	Date	Hour	Summary of Events and Information	Remarks and references to Appendices
ACHEUX	23/7/16	9.p.m.	Evacuation from ACHEUX of 9 train to BEZAINCOURT or of motor convoy	
"	27/7/16	7.30pm	Received orders to move main dressing station to BERTRANCOURT.	
BERTRANCOURT	29/7/16	11 a.m.	Moved here today. At 12 noon. Dressing & messing room & the newly staff to receive sick & wounded at ACHEUX until night of a message from me to divert sick & wounded to our new station. At 4.0 p.m. we were ordered up to receive 128 lying cases passage to A.D.S. to divert all cases to BERTRANCOURT.	
"	30/7/16	9 p.m.	Nothing of importance to record.	

H. O. Shelly
Lieut. H.A.? [?]
77th [?] Field
O.C. 77 [?]
[?] Ambulance

25th Div

74th Field Ambulance

August 1916

51

COMMITTEE FOR THE
MEDICAL HISTORY OF THE WAR
Date -9 OCT.1916

WAR DIARY or INTELLIGENCE SUMMARY

Army Form C. 2118

77th Field Ambulance

Place	Date	Hour	Summary of Events and Information	Remarks and references to Appendices
BERTRANCOURT	4/8/16	7.30 p.m.	Received R.A.M.C. order No 274 GHQ for 6, ordering us to take over the right & centre sectors of the line at present served by M. et F. de Et Division on right of 6/7 August. This ambulance (Field Ambulance) & Station on right of 6/7 August. This ambulance not to take over RED. HOUSE. Q.1.d.1.2. at an advanced dressing station, & take over from 62nd Field Ambulance the following posts at Upper Factory & cases. K.33. c.2.4. & STIRLING STREET K.34. C.4.8. and K.34. a. 5.5. Relief to be completed from east part at Q.4.a.4.5. and K.34. a. 5.5. Relief to be completed by 7th August midnight. The F Ambulance will be down CHEEROH. & 6th Avenue to the Upper Factory hence by wheel stretcher to RED. HOUSE, and on by car via COURCELLES to BERTRANCOURT, and to return via BEAUCOURT and 2nd RED. HOUSE & advanced dressing station of 62nd Field Ambulance	
"	5/8/16	4 p.m.	Visited RED. HOUSE & advanced dressing station of 62nd Field Ambulance	

H.P. Nally
Lieutenant Colonel R.A.M.C.
O.C. 77 Field Ambulance

Army Form C. 2118

WAR DIARY
or
INTELLIGENCE SUMMARY.

(Erase heading not required.)

Folio 43. 77th Field Ambulance

Instructions regarding War Diaries and Intelligence Summaries are contained in F. S. Regs., Part II. and the Staff Manual respectively. Title pages will be prepared in manuscript.

Place	Date	Hour	Summary of Events and Information	Remarks and references to Appendices
BERTRANCOURT	6/8/16	11.4p	The taking over by the 18th Field Ambulance completed	
"	7/8/16	7.30pm	Rear advanced line taken over	
"	9/8/16	7.3pm	Received R.A.M.C. order No. 31. That 74th Inf Brigade would be relieved on night of 10/11th August by a brigade of 19th Division. This Field Ambulance to be relieved by No. 3 Field Ambulance. A.D.S. & collecting posts to be relieved by 10 p.m. Main dressing station by 12 noon. On relief this Field Ambulance to march to BUS-LES-ARTOIS.	
BUS-LES-ARTOIS	10/8/16	11a.m	Relief completed & move to BUS-LES-ARTOIS completed.	
"	15/8/16	7.30/-	Received R.A.M.C. order No. 33 to march to PUCHEVILLERS, under orders of Brigade on 15/8/16.	
PUCHEVILLERS	16/8/16	12.mn	March to PUCHEVILLERS completed. We are going up to receive horses and...	

2353 Wt. W3544/1454 700,000 5/15 D. D. & L. A.D.S.S./Forms/C. 2118.

Army Form C. 2118

WAR DIARY
or
INTELLIGENCE SUMMARY.

Folio H. 77th Field Ambulance.

(Erase heading not required.)

Instructions regarding War Diaries and Intelligence Summaries are contained in F.S. Regs., Part II. and the Staff Manual respectively. Title pages will be prepared in manuscript.

Place	Date	Hour	Summary of Events and Information	Remarks and references to Appendices
PUCHVILLERS.	17/8/15	7.30 p.m.	The 77th attached C.O. 75th Field Ambulance at 2.15 p.m. O.S.C. left at 5 p.m. Rest of Division destination not yet ascertained. No word received so far.	
"	17/8/16	10.45 p.m.	Received R.A.M.C. order No. 35. stating 23rd Division will relieve 49th Division. The 75th Field Ambulance to relieve 1st West Riding Field Ambulance in the front line. The 76th & 77th Field Ambulance will act as many and have to collect sick from H.Qrs of 49th Division stationed in their area. Three sections will have to report to O.C. 75th Field Ambulance at FORCEVILLE at 8. a.m. 19th August. Two Officers & one horse sub-division from this Field Ambulance to report to O.C. 75th Field Ambulance at BLACK-HORSE Bridge at 7 p.m. 18th August. (Majority of 57.D. W.C.a.C.)	
"	18/8/16	4.30 p.m.	Bearer party left.	

H.B. Kelly
Lieut. Col. O.O. R.M.C.
O.C. 77th Field Ambulance

Army Form C. 2118

WAR DIARY
or
INTELLIGENCE SUMMARY.

(Erase heading not required.)

July 45. 77th Field Ambulance

Instructions regarding War Diaries and Intelligence Summaries are contained in F. S. Regs., Part II. and the Staff Manual respectively. Title pages will be prepared in manuscript.

Place	Date	Hour	Summary of Events and Information	Remarks and references to Appendices
PUCHEVILLERS	19/8	9 p.m.	3 Sanitary Ambulances left at 7 a.m. to join 73rd Field Ambulance. Capt. COHEN: R.A.M.C. reported for duty from No. 4 C.C.S. BEAUVAL. (rejoining) We are now attached to 49 Division for supplies.	
"	21/8	9 p.m.	Capt. COHEN to 25th Divisional Train for temporary duty. 2D.O.R. to 44 C.C.S. for duty.	
"	25/8	9 p.m.	Received R.A.M.C. order No 36 Copy No 8. to take over the Corps rest station at LOUVENCOURT & Officers Hospital move to be completed at 11 a.m. 26/8/15. Advance party to be sent on receipt of orders. Advance party left at 9.30 a.m.	
LOUVEN COURT.	26/8	9 a.m.	Took over Corps rest station & Officers Hospital. Received orders to take over main dressing station at CLAIRFAYE FARM. in addition.	

M. Welby Lt Col RAMC
O.C. 77 F Ambulance

2353 Wt. W3541/1454 700,000 5/15 D.D.&L. A.D.S.S./Forms/C. 2118.

Army Form C. 2118.

WAR DIARY
or
INTELLIGENCE SUMMARY.

Feb 48. 77th Field Ambulance

(Erase heading not required.)

Place	Date	Hour	Summary of Events and Information	Remarks and references to Appendices
LOUVEN-COURT.	27/2	9 p.m.	Have taken over the main dressing station at CLAIRFAYE FARM. Detached parties have not reported yet, i.e. 9 squads in tents 20 O.R. 44 C.C.S. 8 O.R. 4 C.C.S. for tent sub-division from 76th Field Ambulance is working at CLAIRFAYE.	
"	28/2	9 a.m.	9 squads rejoint from tents, also 20 O.R. from 44 C.C.S.	
CLAIRFAYE FARM.	31/2	9 p.m.	Headquarters of this Field Ambulance moved here today. Evacuation is by light railway from ACHEUX for sitting cases, lying cases by M.A.C.	

H.O. Kelly CC ROMC
Lieut. Col. the field
77 Ambulance
O.C. 77 Ambulance

Confidential

War Diary (Medical)

77th Field Ambulance

September 1916

Volume XII

Army Form C. 2118.

WAR DIARY
or
INTELLIGENCE SUMMARY

(Erase heading not required.)

Folio 47. 77th Field Ambulance.

Place	Date	Hour	Summary of Events and Information	Remarks and references to Appendices
CLAIRFAYE FARM.	2/9/16	9p.m.	Received S.B. 840 Secret from A.D.M.S. 25th Division re Medical arrangements for an attack at 5.10 a.m. 3/9/16. Three Field Ambulances to G.S. waggon from 75th & 77th Field Ambulances to report here 10 a.m. 3/9/16 to assist in evacuation of slightly wounded to ACHEUX tramway siding. This Field Ambulance to be prepared to send one Tent Sub-division to amt 75th or 76th Field Ambulance if the Tent Sub-division to amt. Only 128 wounded admitted, no one Officer evacd to amt.	
"	3/9/16	9p.m.	W.S. Train 1964. M.A.C. started by later. Received notes for Officers & waggons to rejoin their units.	
"	5/9/16	9a.m.	Received Divnl Orders No 34. That we will hand over CLAIRFAYE FARM to an Ambulance of 11th Division, the 108th by 12 noon on 7th or completion of relief, details of 77th Field Ambulance to proceed to LOUVENCOURT.	

W.H. Poole Lt Col
O.C. 77 Field Ambulance

Army Form C. 2118.

WAR DIARY
or
INTELLIGENCE SUMMARY. *77th Field Ambulance*
(Erase heading not required.)

Place	Date	Hour	Summary of Events and Information	Remarks and references to Appendices
CLAIRFAYE FARM.	5/9/16	9 p.m.	All personnel & cars at present detached to other Field Ambulances will rejoin their units by 11 a.m. 7th September. On 9th Sept 77th Field Ambulance less one section will remain at LOUVENCOURT, more to be completed by 12 noon, will move to RAINCHEVAL.	
"	6/9/16	9 p.m.	Received correction to Memorandum No 39. 77th Field Ambulance will remain at LOUVENCOURT, and collect sick from 5th Brigade at RAINCHEVAL & ARQUEVES.	
"	7/9/16	9 p.m.	Marched over CLAIRFAYE FARM to 53rd Field Ambulance by 12 noon. 76th Field Ambulance took over - also marched to LOUVENCOURT. 78th Field Ambulance which moved left at BEAUVILLERS to join 78th Field Ambulance. Fine today.	

M. Kelly
Lieut Col RAMC
O.C. 77th Field Ambulance

Army Form C. 2118.

WAR DIARY
or
INTELLIGENCE SUMMARY.

Folio A.9. 77th Field Ambulance

(Erase heading not required.)

Instructions regarding War Diaries and Intelligence Summaries are contained in F.S. Regs., Part II. and the Staff Manual respectively. Title pages will be prepared in manuscript.

Place	Date	Hour	Summary of Events and Information	Remarks and references to Appendices
LONGUEAU SRT.	7/9/16	9/6am	Orders for my surplus Sergt-Major issued to proceed to join my O.C. Sergt to proceed to join 6th Cavalry Field Ambulance forthwith. Received last night 11 O.R. 11 reinforcements.	
"	8/9/16	9/- am	Sergt Major F. RICHARDSON. R.A.M.C. left this Field Ambulance this morning to join the 6th Cavalry Field Ambulance	
"	9/9/16	9/- am	Received orders that Division would move tomorrow. Field Ambulance to move under orders of A.D.C. Brigade. This Field Ambulance to have different entraining station at LONGUEVAL. Carried on in the officers hospital & dispersed station until the carried on in the officers hospital it was decided to send no sisters with the unit. Unit then constituted it was detached to send no sisters with the Brigade with motor transport & one horse ambulance & one lusitania motor ambulance.	
"	10/9/16		One section moved to LONGUEVILLETTE.	

M McCoy Lieut-Col RAMC
O.C. 77th Field Ambulance

Army Form C. 2118.

WAR DIARY
or
INTELLIGENCE SUMMARY.
(Erase heading not required.)

Folio 30. 77th Field Ambulance

Place	Date	Hour	Summary of Events and Information	Remarks and references to Appendices
LONGUE-VILLETTE	17/7/16	9/a.m	One Section moved to BEAUMETZ.	
BEAUMETZ	18/7/16	9/a.m	One Section moved to DONQUEVERELLE FARM, we are collecting sick from Brigade Area.	
DONQUEVERELLE FARM	19/7/16	11/a.m	The two sections from LONGUEVILLETTE arrived this evening.	
DONQUEVERE ALE FARM	20/7/16	11/a.m	Received R.A.M.C. Operation order No 40 stating division will move tomorrow under G.O.C.3 Brigade.	
"		3.10 pm	Received 7th Inf Brigade order No 152. 77th Ambulance to move to LONGUEVILLETTE tomorrow via LONGVILLERS - BERNAVILLE - FIENVILLERS. Starting point, road junction on main CANDAS-LONGVILLERS road 700 yds S.S.E of the CRAMONT. Time 7.2 a.m	Mobility limit to MMC. O.C. 77 Field Ambulance

Army Form C. 2118.

WAR DIARY
or
INTELLIGENCE SUMMARY. Folio St. 77th Field Ambulance

(Erase heading not required.)

Place	Date	Hour	Summary of Events and Information	Remarks and references to Appendices
LONGUEVILLETTE	25/9/16	9/am	March completed at 2 p.m. today. Two men of the Field Ambulance fell out en route of march.	
ARQUEVES	26/9/16	9/am	The Brigade continued its forward today. This Field Ambulance arrived at 9 a.m. we are motor ambulances, no billets being allotted to us. We are allotting Brigade work, the regiment being distributed at ARQUEVES & RAINNEVAL. All sick are being transferred to the C.C.S. at LOUVENCOURT at present in charge of the 73rd Field Ambulance.	
ARQUEVES	28/9/16	9/am	The D.I. Infantry Brigade Fourth Division is at HEDAUVILLE being much reduced by G.A.C. 5th Infantry Brigade to one motor convoy.	
HEDAUVILLE	29/9/16		Received preliminary orders M.C. under that 25th Division will take over the line from the 1st Division in front of LES BOEUFS. Orders that S.P. this ambulance will take over at present over from 77 Field Ambulance & CLAIRFAYE FARM for SICK and walking wounded. A.D.S. at V.S.& A.T. Collecting post V.S.&A.T. cars are coming to front on Tramway at V.S.&A.T. from hey on Tramway at V.S.&A.T. from hey	

WAR DIARY
INTELLIGENCE SUMMARY

(Erase heading not required.)

Army Form C. 2118.

Place	Date	Hour	Summary of Events and Information	Remarks and references to Appendices
HEDAUVILLE	29/9/16	11 a.m.	We landed in Ford cars & set up AVELUY CHATEAU. at 8 a.m. 30/9/16. We sent to the Field amb HEDAUVILLE CHATEAU in control of the Field ambulance. One field amb sent along to the 3T at X.6.C.7.9. moved up to TARA RAVINE Evening one moved down to AVELUY CHATEAU.	
HEDAUVILLE	30/9/16	9 a.m.	Proceeded with Off to Vlg 2 advanced dug outs & many of our Lt. R.A.P's arranged shelters for wounded & planned way of evac. in HEDAUVILLE for the night. Passed R.A.M.C. into Bn HQ. and lay on cars & stretcher bearers at BAZENTIN & received A.A.M.C. units & officers ordering not to attack till 2nd oct BAZENTIN-LE-PETIT was taken by H.Q. Feb L. Fat. Two hund. men to move to one hole captured by H.Q. the two day. Moved fore on pm EAST at B. same C.	Billeting party to move up to field Ambulance.

WAR DIARY
or
INTELLIGENCE SUMMARY

Army Form C. 2118.

Place	Date	Hour	Summary of Events and Information	Remarks and references to Appendices
BAZENTIN	1/9/16	9pm	Visited A.D.S. there a Fd Ambulance of 2 officers & 110 A.R. left the line.	
"	2/9/16		Put POSTLAND & RUSSELL signed ambulance stay for forward zones only. Front zones ADS to have half a section of ambulance for evacuation post Nos. 51 & 52. Left forward empire from a reserve post Nos. 51 & 52. POZIERES. We are using Nos 53 & 54 for sight wounded. Road from R.22.a.8.5 to R.34.c.4.8. to the Quarry. Nos. 49 & 27 — R.27.a.5.9 — R.33.a.5.7 — R.33 x.2.1. Thence S.W. Railway Cutting Road No. 2 SAP 4 INT. Road. Several M.O.R.C. orders & A.D.M.S. WEST CATERPYE wood for a 9/9/16 but they expect not to start RUPPRIV. (39 Division) will not be sent to NOS centres at MORTON/ 9 nearly 75 miles from Rail to F.A.D. not for the sick field Ambulance which obtains our F.A.D. Battalion	

Army Form C. 2118.

WAR DIARY
or
INTELLIGENCE SUMMARY.
(Erase heading not required.)

Nov. 54.
77 F. Field Ambulance

Place	Date	Hour	Summary of Events and Information	Remarks and references to Appendices
BOUZINCOURT	2/10/16	9.0 a.m.	Brigade Operation orders No. 11 received from MARLEY. (Special orders issued)	
BOUZINCOURT	3/10/16	9 a.m.	Received 73 Infantry Brigade order No. 18. That the Front on night of 2/3 October will extend to Front as far East as forty-three inclusive. No right boundary will then be Twenty-three road to R.28. N.S.8. Thence to R.34. T.8.7. — 0.24. N.5.7. cents away (inclusive) — NO 4. AVENUE — OVILLERS — ALBERT ROAD (exclusive) — NO 4. AVENUE — OVILLERS — ALBERT ROAD. Before 37 D. coming to this extension the new system of Boundary connected up the Field Ambulance (RAMC refer to HQ.) will be right Brigade to use Road (a.) Through advanced dressing station established today in POZIERES (open to Trunnion coming on ALBERT — POZIERES. ROAD.) Horse from here to use ALBERT to BOUZINCOURT. (b.) Through Point 77 (OVILLERS. ADS) to AVELUY. CHATEAU (c.) Through Point 77 (OVILLERS. ADS) to AVELUY. CHATEAU also available will all by Motor Ambulance from M.A.C. sent from M.A.C. and Ambulance will by Motor BOUZINCOURT / POZIERES. Road. Four 77. HEAVYS Remained in reserve at BOUZINCOURT. Reported not will be posted to BOUZINCOURT to carry over to C.C.S. Reported not but in case one are installed at Hqrs. 28. c.2.1. (e.) R.34. N.C.4. Evacuation from medical A.D.S. cottage from POZIERES to A.D.S. POZIERES. by is by hand from (a.) by tramway to A.D.S. POZIERES.	

H. O. Whitty, Lieut - Col. A.M.S.
O.C. 77th Field Ambulance

Army Form C. 2118.

WAR DIARY
or
INTELLIGENCE SUMMARY.

(Erase heading not required.)

77th Field Ambulance
folio 53.

Instructions regarding War Diaries and Intelligence Summaries are contained in F. S. Regs., Part II. and the Staff Manual respectively. Title pages will be prepared in manuscript.

Place	Date	Hour	Summary of Events and Information	Remarks and references to Appendices
BOUZINCOURT	7/10/16	9 a.m	Visited A.D.S.	
"	8/10/16	9 p.m	System of evacuation working smoothly but owing to wetting & heavy state of the ground, the work of the stretcher bearers is most strenuous & fatiguing.	
"	10/10/16	9 p.m	Received orders to hand over BOUZINCOURT today at 3 p.m. to the 76th Field Ambulance. This Ambulance to take over 76th during ALBERT day out. Move completed & we are forced up to relieve cars at Gun Car from OVILLERS now run by Ford cars to Main Lambsarm & ALBERT. BAPAUME road. All evacuation for OVILLERS & POZIERES has now through the new dressing station.	
NORTH CHIMNEY ALBERT.	15/10/16	11 a.m	The new P.O. is being completed for OVILLERS to R.28 & cars will now be demanded by Tel line.	H.W.Kelly Captain RAMC Tpt O.C. 77th Field Ambulance

2353 Wt. W2544/1454 700,000 5/15 D. D. & L. A.D.S.S./Forms/C. 2118.

Army Form C. 2118.

WAR DIARY
or
INTELLIGENCE SUMMARY.
(Erase heading not required.)

Instructions regarding War Diaries and Intelligence Summaries are contained in F. S. Regs., Part II. and the Staff Manual respectively. Title pages will be prepared in manuscript.

Folio 36.   77th Field Ambulance

Place	Date	Hour	Summary of Events and Information	Remarks and references to Appendices
NORTH CHIMNEY. ALBERT.	18/10/16	9 p.m.	Received A.D.M.S. order No. 57 that 74th Brigade will attack REGINA TRENCH at Zero on 19/10/16. This Field Ambulance will clear H and R.23.a.3.3. at R.22.a.3.6.	
"	19/10/16	9 p.m.	Attack postponed 24 hours.	
"	20/10/16	9 p.m.	Attack postponed 24 hours.	
"	21/10/16	9 p.m.	Attack commenced at 12.5 p.m.	
"	22/10/16	9 p.m.	Wounded practically all cleared at 11 a.m. A.D.M.S. order No. 59 that the Division would be relieved on 22/4/5 issued last night. 74th Brigade were to be handed over to 18th Division. This Field Ambulance to hand over its collecting post at MIERES CEMETERY to 55th Field Ambulance, the A.D.S at X.8.b.79, & Quarry to 59th Field Ambulance. The main dressing station at ALBERT to 55th Field Ambulance.	

Walter L Seth Lt Col
O.C. 77th Field Ambulance

Army Form C. 2118.

WAR DIARY
or
INTELLIGENCE SUMMARY. File F. 77th Field Ambulance

(Erase heading not required.)

Instructions regarding War Diaries and Intelligence Summaries are contained in F. S. Regs., Part II. and the Staff Manual respectively. Title pages will be prepared in manuscript.

Place	Date	Hour	Summary of Events and Information	Remarks and references to Appendices
ALBERT	28/9/16	9pm	On the 23rd notified the Field Ambulance of impending move to orders of G.O.C. 7th Infantry Brigade. Received 7th Infantry Brigade order No. 186. This Ambulance to move to VAL DE MAISON, via HEDAUVILLE, VARENNES, HARPONVILLE. DUTENCOURT. Starting point ROAD JUNCTION V.12. C.7.6. time 6.45. a.m.	
VAL DE MAISON.	23/9/16	9 p.m.	March completed at 3 p.m.	
"	24/9/16	11 a.m.	Received 7th Infantry Brigade order No. 187. This Ambulance to move to LONGUEVILLETTE. Starting point VAL DE MAISON. Hour 9.a.m.	
"	"	2 p.m.	March completed.	
"	25/9/16	9/16	Ambulance rested today	
"	26/9/16	9 p.m.	Ambulance rested today	

Wetherby Park Lt Col R.A.M.C.
O.C. 77th Field Ambulance

WAR DIARY
INTELLIGENCE SUMMARY

Army Form C. 2118.

Field Service. 77th Field Ambulance

Place	Date	Hour	Summary of Events and Information	Remarks and references to Appendices
LONGUENESSE	25/10/16	9 p.m.	Received extract from 25th Division G.64. dated 25/10/16. That the division will move to Northern Area to join 2nd Army on 29th & 30th insts. Field Ambulances to move under orders of G.O.C. Brigades. Received 7th Infantry Brigade orders re same, & allotting forty country of one officer and N.C.O. & troops with large system & 7 to be dropped at 8 a.m. on 27/10/16 from Doullens North Station. The remainder of the Ambulance will move by train from Doullens North at 11.30 a.m. on 30/10/16. Transport to be at station 3 hours & personnel 1½ hours before train starts, a very trying heavy party will accompany the transport. Sent two officers to reconnoitre the roads & approaches to station. Received orders for Motor Ambulances to proceed by road to Doullens: ST. POL — AUXI — ST HILAIRE — AIRE — HAZEBROUCK — LE BEARD — CAESTRE. Transport to proceed by road to FLETRE, Route Doullens: ST. POL — AUXI — ST HILAIRE — AIRE — HAZEBROUCK — LE BEARD — CAESTRE.	
	28/10/16	9 a.m.	Ambulance on trek.	

H.O. Welby Capt. R.A.M.C.
O.C. 77th Field Ambulance

Army Form C. 2118.

WAR DIARY
~~INTELLIGENCE SUMMARY.~~

Hqrs. 59. 77th Field Ambulance

(Erase heading not required.)

Instructions regarding War Diaries and Intelligence Summaries are contained in F. S. Regs., Part II. and the Staff Manual respectively. Title pages will be prepared in manuscript.

Place	Date	Hour	Summary of Events and Information	Remarks and references to Appendices
LONGUEVILLETTE	29/10/16	9/1 am	72 Hby to rest	
PONT DE NIEPPE	30/10/16	10.10 am	Arrived by train at BAILLEUL & proceeded to PONT DE NIEPPE. Received R.A.M.C. order No. 50.A. On 1st November the 77th Field Ambulance will relieve the 23rd Field Ambulance in the right half of the line & take over the main dressing station at PONT DE NIEPPE. Advanced dressing Station at BURNT OUT BREWERY, & Post at MOTOR CAR CORNER, relief to be completed at 12 noon.	
"	31/10/16	9 am	2 Officers & 57 O.R. proceeded to Advanced line.	

H.O. Kelly
Lieut. Colonel
O.C. 77th Field Ambulance

160/86.

25th Div.

74th Field Ambulance

Nov. 1916

Army Form C. 2118.

Vol 14 / 77 2nd Field Ambulance

WAR DIARY
or
INTELLIGENCE SUMMARY. Folio 60. 77 2nd Field Ambulance

(Erase heading not required.)

Place	Date	Hour	Summary of Events and Information	Remarks and references to Appendices
PONT DE NIEPPE.	1/11/16	9 p.	Relief of 23rd Field Ambulance completed at 12 noon. Lieut BISSELL. R.A.M.C. sent for temporary duty with 19th Durhams.	
"	6/11/16	9 p.	Advanced dressing station party relieved.	
"	8/11/16	9 p.	Lieut BISSELL. R.A.M.C. left for England, has expired, he has been relieved by Capt BOYCE. Lieut LAWSON. R.A.M.C. from 75th Field	
"	9/11/16	9 p.	Lieut PENTLAND evacuated sick to C.C.S. Ambulance joined for temporary duty.	
"	13/11/16	9 a.m	A.D.S. party relieved today.	
"	14/11/16	9 a.	Lieut & Q.M. DONNELLY joined ambulance today from England. Capt Lowther proceed to A.D.S. in relief of Capt McClary rejoined H.Q.	

W Mally
Lieut-Col comd.
77 2nd Field Ambulance
O.C. 77 2nd Field Ambulance

Army Form C. 2118.

WAR DIARY
or
INTELLIGENCE SUMMARY. *No. 61. 77th Field Ambulance*
(Erase heading not required.)

Instructions regarding War Diaries and Intelligence Summaries are contained in F. S. Regs., Part II. and the Staff Manual respectively. Title pages will be prepared in manuscript.

Place	Date	Hour	Summary of Events and Information	Remarks and references to Appendices
PONT DE NIEPPE.	15/4/16	9p.m	The following work is at present in hand viz. Boarding up + half plastering all other huts, digging more extensive drains all round, supply of latrines both, digging more extensive drains all round, supply of latrines both, fitted a detached building incinerator, making roads + pathways, digging drains + cement floors, straightening + waterproofing A.D.S., making latrines + pathways at A.D.S. Troops were given, baths, either by parties being sent in trucks to B.H.Q. or in huts either for troops in the line. Iron walls of cemented are owing to x x x of trench etc. being the officiating of the general right + removal of the ambulance being the new emergency of improving the buildings + keeping the men employed at improving the buildings	
"	16/4/16	9p.m	Lieut. LAWSON R.A.M.C. left for England on expiry of contract. No reinforcement arrived from the base.	

H.S. Welly
Lieut. Col. R.A.M.C.
O.C. 77 Field Ambulance

Army Form C. 2118.

WAR DIARY
or
INTELLIGENCE SUMMARY.

(Erase heading not required.)

WO 62. 77th Field Ambulance

Place	Date	Hour	Summary of Events and Information	Remarks and references to Appendices
PONT DE NIEPPE	27/11/16	9 p.m.	Erected A.D.S. & Bastin car corner Captain HARVEY R.A.M.C. from 75th Field Ambulance joined for temporary duty.	
"	28/11/16	9 p.m.	A.D.S. & Regimental aid post relieved today.	
"	29/11/16	9 p.m.	Capt. BYRNE. R.A.M.C. returned from temporary duty with 10th Cheshires.	
"	22/11/16	9 a.m.	Lieut STERLING. R.A.M.C. joined the unit from ENGLAND.	
"	29/11/16	9 p.m.	Capt. HARVEY. R.A.M.G. returned to 75th Field Ambulance	
"	30/11/16	9 p.m.	Capt. WILL. R.A.M.C. joined for duty. 3 O.R.'s from base details joined for duty.	

H.B.Kelly
Lieut Col R.A.M.C.
O.C. 77th Field Ambulance.

140/190.

25th Div.

41st Field Ambulance

Dec 1916

COMMITTEE FOR THE
MEDICAL HISTORY OF THE WAR
Date 31 JAN. 1917

Army Form C. 2118.

WAR DIARY
or
INTELLIGENCE SUMMARY.   77th Field Ambulance

(Erase heading not required.)

Instructions regarding War Diaries and Intelligence Summaries are contained in F. S. Regs., Part II. and the Staff Manual respectively. Title pages will be prepared in manuscript.

Vol 5

Place	Date	Hour	Summary of Events and Information	Remarks and references to Appendices
PONT-DE-NIEPPE	1/12/16	9/10 am	Lieut PAUL R.A.M.C. attached to report for temporary duty with 13th The Kings.	
"	2/12/16	9 pm	Lieut STERLING R.A.M.C. with 39 O.R.'s went as relief party to A.D.S.	
"	3/12/16	9 am	Nothing to record.	
"	7/12/16	9 pm	Relief party proceeded to A.D.S. 39 O.R.'s arrived as reinforcement.	
"	8/12/16	9 pm	Captain WILL R.A.M.C. proceeded to A.D.S. in relief of Captain BOYCE	
"	9/12/16	9 pm	Proceeding on leave	
"	10/12/16	9 pm	Capt. McELNEY R.A.M.C. returned from leave. LIEUT. STIRLING R.A.M.C. proceeded for temporary duty as M.O. i/c 8th L.T.M. Batt.	
"	13/12/16	9 pm	Capt BARTLETT R.A.M.C. joined for duty	
"	14/12/16	9 am	Lieut FAIRCLOUGH R.A.M.C. joined for duty	

H.E. Kelly Major
Lieut-Col
O.C. 77th Field Ambulance

2353 Wt. W3144/1454 700,000 5/15 D.D.&L.   A.D.S.S./Forms/C. 2118.

Army Form C. 2118.

WAR DIARY
or
INTELLIGENCE SUMMARY.
(Erase heading not required.)

Folio 64. 77 Field Ambulance

Place	Date	Hour	Summary of Events and Information	Remarks and references to Appendices
PONT-DE-NIEPPE	15/10/16	9pm	Nothing to record.	
"	16/10/16	9½am	A Section proceeded to A.D.S. & regimental aid posts. B. Section took over the hospital duties at Main Dressing Station. C. section in reserve.	
"	17/10/16	9½am	Nothing to record.	
"	18/10/16	9½am	Nothing to record.	
"	19/10/16	9½am	Nothing to record.	
"	20/10/16	9½am	Nothing to record.	
"	21/10/16	9½am	B section proceeded to take over advanced line today. C section took over the duties in connection with the hospital. A section in reserve & available for guards, working parties etc.	
"	25/10/16	9½am	Lieut Sterling A.A.M.C. proceeded to M.O. 9/c 1st Wilts whilst M.O. on leave.	
	28/10/16	9.30 am	C section relieved B. out in line. A Section took over duties in hospital from C section.	Abraham Leslie Capt R.A.M.C. O.C. 77 Field Amb.

WAR DIARY
or
INTELLIGENCE SUMMARY.
(Erase heading not required.)

Army Form C. 2118.

Folios 64 & 65.
77th Fld Amb

Place	Date	Hour	Summary of Events and Information	Remarks and references to Appendices
[Wissant]	29/8/16	8.30 am	"B" Section Tent subdivision, in accordance with orders 25 2/10 CCS ADMS 25th Div, proceeded to WALLON CAPPEL where they are to billet night 29/30. On 30/7/30 they are to billet in LUMBRES + billet there night 30/31/8. On 31st they march to their destination and occupy artillery camp near WISSANT. They are to form a small divisional hospital for the sick of the 2nd army Artillery Camp, starting point when S.19.b.9.9 (Junction B Rue d'Occident + Rue de CASSEL). BAILLEUL 10.20 am under orders OC 173rd Bgde RFA who will arrange billets + ration - after see 29th while on the march. OC detachment will on arrival report to OC 2nd Army Artillery Camp who will provide billet + hospital accommodation. Tent Subdivision consisted of CAPT BARTLETT RAMC in charge + CAPT BOYLE RAMC with 19 RAMC NCOs + men. 12 NCOs + men A.S.C. 3 motor ambulances, two GS wagons, 1 lumbar wagon + one water cart.	

Abraham Leather
a/ADMS
v.d.c. 77
25 Div [?]

Folio E3 66
77 Field Amb.

Army Form C. 2118.

WAR DIARY
or
INTELLIGENCE SUMMARY.
(Erase heading not required.)

Instructions regarding War Diaries and Intelligence
Summaries are contained in F. S. Regs., Part II.
and the Staff Manual respectively. Title pages
will be prepared in manuscript.

Place	Date	Hour	Summary of Events and Information	Remarks and references to Appendices
Imphal	30 Jan	2.0 pm	Visited ADS, MOTOR CAR CORNER, No 5 + No 6 posts.	

Abraham Lescher
Capt RAMC
i/c OC 77 FA

25

14/9/42

25th Div

74th Field Ambulance

Jan. 1917

COMMITTEE FOR THE
MEDICAL HISTORY OF THE WAR
Date 13 MAR. 1917

Army Form C. 2118.

Folio 87 77 Field Ambulance

WAR DIARY
or
INTELLIGENCE SUMMARY.

(Erase heading not required.)

Place	Date	Hour	Summary of Events and Information	Remarks and references to Appendices
PONT de NIEPPE	3rd Jan		A Section relieved C Section in line. B section took over duties in hospital.	
	Jan 9th		B section relieved A section in line. C Section took over duties in hospital.	
PONT DE NIEPPE.	12/1/17. 9/pm		Returned from leave today	
"	13/1/17. 9pm		Capt WILL. R.A.M.C. detailed for permanent medical charge of 13th Cheshire Regiment. Capt COHEN. R.A.M.C. to rejoin this Ambulance from 13th Cheshire Regiment.	
"	14/1/17. 9am		Lieut STARLING. R.A.M.C. to 8th Beds for temporary duty. Capt CARR. R.A.M.C. to 8th South Lancs for temporary duty.	
"	15/1/17. 9am		Lieut Fairclough U.S.M.C. reported for duty	

A.B. Kelly Lt-Col R.A.M.C.
O.C. 77th Field Ambulance

Army Form C. 2118.

WAR DIARY
or
INTELLIGENCE SUMMARY.   Folio 68.   77th Field Ambulance

(Erase heading not required.)

Instructions regarding War Diaries and Intelligence Summaries are contained in F. S. Regs., Part II. and the Staff Manual respectively. Title pages will be prepared in manuscript.

Place	Date	Hour	Summary of Events and Information	Remarks and references to Appendices
PONT DE NIEPPE	21/1/17	9 a.m.	A.D.S. just changed today. Weather very foggy & cold. Nothing to record.	
"	22/1/17	9 a.m.	Nothing to record.	
"	23/1/17	9 p.m.	Nothing to record.	
"	25/1/17	7 a.m.	Sgt Paul. name. sent to A.D.S. to relieve First Earnshaw R.A.M.C. sent for temporary duty with 2nd South Lancs.	
"	28/1/17	9 a.m.	Sgt Cohen. R.A.M.C. to 3rd Worcesters for temporary duty.	
"	31/1/17	9 a.m.	Nothing to record	

H.B. Kelly
Lieut-Colonel name
I.C. 77th Field Ambulance

140/199

25th Div.

74th Field Ambulance

Feb. 1917

COMMITTEE FOR THE
MEDICAL HISTORY OF THE WAR
Date 4 APR. 1917

Army Form C. 2118.

WAR DIARY
or
INTELLIGENCE SUMMARY.

(Erase heading not required.)

Vol 17

77th Field Ambulance

Place	Date	Hour	Summary of Events and Information	Remarks and references to Appendices
PONT-DE-NIEPPE	1/2/17	9 a.m.	Nothing to report	
"	2/2/17	9 a.m.	Tent Sub-Div Nurse sent to a few days course of Sanitation at HAZEBROUCK.	
"	5/2/17	9 a.m.	Capt. Cotter came to A.D.S. in relief of Capt. McCleary reported this a.m.	
"	7/2/17	9 a.m.	Nothing to report. Visited A.D.S. & Bath in error.	
"	8/2/17	9 a.m.	Relief party proceeded to A.D.S. Estaires	
"	11/2/17	9 a.m.	Capt. McElroy R.A.M.C. & Capt. Cotter R.A.M.C. of this unit placed on sick list. Visit Sterling R.A.M.C. to A.D.S.	
"	12/2/17	9 a.m.	Capt Paul, R.A.M.C. proceeded to Sanitary class at Hazebrouck. Had Capt. McKee at Field Battery at my request. Capt. Teesdale R.A.M.C. at main dressing station. A.D.S.	
"	15/2/17	9 a.m.	Nothing special to report	

H.O.Kelly
Lieut-Col. R.A.M.C.
O. C. 77th Field Ambulance

Army Form C. 2118.

WAR DIARY
or
INTELLIGENCE SUMMARY.

(Erase heading not required.)

Feb. 70. 77th Field Ambulance

Instructions regarding War Diaries and Intelligence Summaries are contained in F. S. Regs., Part II. and the Staff Manual respectively. Title pages will be prepared in manuscript.

Place	Date	Hour	Summary of Events and Information	Remarks and references to Appendices.
PONT DE NIEPPE	16/2/17	9 a.m	Received orders to be prepared to send one heavy sub-division one motor ambulance one horsed ambulance to assist 75th Field Ambulance at the same time tomorrow the 17th inst. The 7th Infantry Brigade are carrying out a raid.	
PONT DE NIEPPE	19/2/17	9 a.m	Received extract from 25th Division order No. 172. that the 25th Division will be relieved between the 20th & 28th February by the New Zealand Division.	
"	20/2/17	9 a.m	Received R.A.M.C. Order No.55. This Field Ambulance to be relieved by No.1 New Zealand Field Ambulance New Zealand Division on 24/2/17 — 23/2/17. Relief to be completed by 11 a.m on 25/2/17. On completion of relief this Field Ambulance will march to FLETTRE. Ref S.A HAZEBROUCK. under orders of G.O.C. 7th Infantry Brigade, & occupy the Chateau.	
FLETTRE	25/2/17	9 a.m	Ambulance moved by route march to FLETTRE Feb 24 & Headquarters up to receive sick of the Brigade Group.	

H.W. Kelly
Rank or name
O.C. 77th Field Ambulance

Army Form C. 2118.

WAR DIARY
or
INTELLIGENCE SUMMARY. 77th Field Ambulance.

(Erase heading not required.)

Place	Date	Hour	Summary of Events and Information	Remarks and references to Appendices
FLETRE	27/1/18	9pm	We have accommodation for 50 patients here. Medical arrangements remain the same as when at PONT-DE-NIEPPE.	
"	28/1/18	9 p.m.	Nothing special to report. Route marches/physical drill & Lectures the order of the day	

H.O. Kelly
Lieut-Col A.A.M.C.
O.C. 77th Field Ambulance

140/2042

26th Div.

77th Field Ambulance

COMMITTEE FOR THE
MEDICAL HISTORY OF THE WAR
Date 11 MAY 1917

Army Form C. 2118.

WAR DIARY
or
INTELLIGENCE SUMMARY.

(Erase heading not required.)

Folio 72. 77th Field Ambulance

Vol / 8

Place	Date	Hour	Summary of Events and Information	Remarks and references to Appendices
FLETRE	1/3/17	9 p.m.	Nothing to record	
"	4/3/17	9 p.m.	Capt COHEN. R.A.M.C. sent as M.O. to the 25th Division ReinfC	
"	7/3/17	9 p.m.	Capt MILLAR. R.A.M.C. joined for duty from the 16th Division.	
"	10/5/17	9 p.m.	Received orders to prepare to move to a new area. All patients transferred to No 12. C.C.S. HAZEBROUCK.	
"	11/3/17	9 p.m.	Received orders at 10 a.m. that the 9th Inf Brigade group would proceed on 11/3/17. to the area WALLON. CAPPEL. — EBLINGHEM— LYNDE—SERCUS. Starting point Ref sheet 27. Belgium & FRANCE, CAESTRE — Road junction W. 3. a. 4.5. The unit will pass starting point at 11:10. Billetting parties will not wait at U. 22. L.S.O. and conduct them to their destination. In accordance with above the unit moved to & Billetted at LYNDE. We have no accommodation for patients & are transferring to No. 10. G. H. ST OMAR.	

H. Kelly

Temp Lt Colonel.

O.C. 77th Field Ambulance

2353 Wt W3511/1454 700,000 5/15 D.D.&L. A.D.S.S./Form/C. 2118.

Army Form C. 2118.

WAR DIARY
or
INTELLIGENCE SUMMARY.   Folio 73.   77 E. Field Amb

(Erase heading not required.)

Place	Date	Hour	Summary of Events and Information	Remarks and references to Appendices
LYNDE	13/3/17	9 a.m.	Received training. Nothing to record.	
"	15/3/17	9 a.m.	Detachment reported today.	
"	18/3/17	9 a.m.	Lieut. Stirling R.A.M.C. proceeded as M.O. i/c 112th Brigade R.F.A.	
"	18/3/17	9 a.m.	Received 7th Inf Brigade order No. 218. That the Brigade Group would move on 19th inst to the area of BORRE.	
BORRE 19/3/17		9 a.m.	This unit proceeded by route march to BORRE today.	
"	20/3/17	9 a.m.	Received 7th Inf Brigade order No. 219. That the Brigade Group would march tomorrow the 21st to the OUTERSTEENE area.	
OUTERSTEENE 21/3/17		9 a.m.	This unit arrived OUTERSTEENE at 12.30 p.m. today.	

H.A. Kelly
Lieut-Col R.A.M.C.
O.C. 77th Field Ambulance

Army Form C. 2118.

WAR DIARY
or
INTELLIGENCE SUMMARY.

(Erase heading not required.)

77th Field Ambulance

Instructions regarding War Diaries and Intelligence Summaries are contained in F. S. Regs., Part II and the Staff Manual respectively. Title pages will be prepared in manuscript.

Place	Date	Hour	Summary of Events and Information	Remarks and references to Appendices
OUTERSTEENE	22/3/17	9 p.m.	Received 7th Inf. Brigade Order No 220 that the 7th Inf. Brigade group would march tomorrow to the LA CRECHE & NEUVE EGLISE area, rep. STA. HAZEBROUCK	
STEENJE	23/3/17	12 noon	Field Ambulance arrived and are in billets.	
"	24/3/17	9 p.m.	We are allotted beds at the D.R.S. staffed by 2nd New Zealand Field Amb. Sent to No 5th C.C.S. HAZEBROUCK Sittis to No 2 Australian C.C.S. Eye cases to No 1st C.C.S. Specials to No 8 C.C.S. BAILLEUL, Injuries sent to No 1 C.C.S. BAILLEUL.	
"	28/3/17	9 a.m.	Lieut. M. J. RYAN, R.A.M.C. joined from leave.	
"	31/3/17	9 a.m.	Nothing to record.	

H. C. Kelly Lieut-Colonel
O. C. 77 Field Ambulance

140/086

25th Div.

17th F.A.

COMMITTEE FOR THE
MEDICAL HISTORY OF THE WAR
Date −6 JUN. 1917

Army Form C. 2118.

WAR DIARY
or
INTELLIGENCE SUMMARY.

(Erase heading not required.)

Felix H. 77th Field Ambulance

Vol 19

Place	Date	Hour	Summary of Events and Information	Remarks and references to Appendices
STEEN-JE	1/4/17	9pm	Nothing to record	
"	2/4/17	9.30am	Received extract from Divisional order no 176, one tent sub-division of this Ambulance to march under orders of G.O.C. 75th Infantry to immediate south of New Zealand Division with headquarters at ROMARIN. Also from A.D.M.S. to send today an advance party of 2 officers & 20 other ranks to take over the Divisional Rest Station NE. DE. MNEE. BAILLEUL to arrive by 12 noon. Main body this tent sub-division should move on Tuesday 3/4/17 move to be completed by 12 noon.	
		9am	Advance party took over D.R.S. arriving at 11.30am	
BAILLEUL	3/4/17	9pm	Main body arrived at 11 a.m. at O. no 176 cancelled.	
"	4/4/17	9pm	Nothing to record.	
"	5/4/17	9pm	Nothing to record.	

H.G. Kelly Lieut-Colonel
O.C. 77th Field Ambulance

Army Form C. 2118.

WAR DIARY
or
INTELLIGENCE SUMMARY. *Flip 70.* 77th Field Ambulance

(Erase heading not required.)

Instructions regarding War Diaries and Intelligence Summaries are contained in F. S. Regs., Part II. and the Staff Manual respectively. Title pages will be prepared in manuscript.

Place	Date	Hour	Summary of Events and Information	Remarks and references to Appendices
BAILLEUL	6/4/17	9/a.m	Nothing to record.	
"	12/4/17	9/a.m	Nothing to record	
"	13/4/17	9/a.m	1 N.C.O. + 20. O.R.s rejoined Headquarters from cooking party	
"	14/4/17	9/a.m	Lieut. RYAN. R.A.M.C. to No. 53. C.C.S. for temporary duty.	
"	15/4/17	9/a.m	O.C. No. C.O. + 11 men took over the Gum boot station.	
"	21/4/17	9/a.m	Received R.A.M.C. order No 63. 76th Field Ambulance will send an advanced party on 22/4/17. to take over the 25th Divisional Rest Station Rue de Mrc. Party should arrive by 12 noon. Main body will march in on the 23/4/17 Move to be completed by 12 noon. 76th Field Ambulance will on being relieved, take over the Left main trossing station at I/R.C. + 5.	
"	23/4/17	12 noon	Move completed this Ambulance is now at I/R.C. + 5. There is a certain amount of road & construction work to be done as the	

H.C. Kelly Lieut-Col
A.A.M.C.

O.C. 77th Field Ambulance

WAR DIARY
or
INTELLIGENCE SUMMARY.

Army Form C. 2118.

77th Field Ambulance

Feb. 77.

(Erase heading not required.)

Place	Date	Hour	Summary of Events and Information	Remarks and references to Appendices
T.19.c.4.5. Sheet 28.	24/4/16	9 p.m.	We are engaged in preparing this dressing station as a Corps main dressing station. During our occupation of this S.R.S. at the Rue de Paris, BAILLEUL we admitted 275 and 137 are returned fit for duty & 42 evacuated to C.C.S.	
	25/4/16	9 p.m.	Pte. GEC BETTS of this unit transferred to the R.E. by order.	
"	27/4/16	9 p.m.	Nothing to record. Received extract from D.O. No. 180 dated 20/4/17. S.M.O. will close at BAILLEUL at 12 noon, and open at RAVELSBURG (S.16.d.45.50) on April 28th. The location of the 2nd Australian Supply Column is Sheet 36. A.17. C.V.R.	
"	28/4/16	9 p.m.	Capt. W. PAUL R.A.M.C. rejoined this ambulance from the laundrology.	
"	29/4/16	9 p.m.	Received 25th Division: g.113/7 dated April 29. That the 25th Division will be withdrawn to rest & concentrate in the MERRIS area by Sept. on 1st May. Instructed as to movement & billeting will be issued later. This ambulance has one tent sub-division to proceed under orders of A.D.M.S. 75th Infantry Brigade. This ambulance to march to OUTTERSTEENE starting at 8.35 a.m. 30/4/17 to meet to collect sick from 7th, 8th, 73rd Infantry Brigade Groups.	

H.S. Kelly Lieut a.r.m.
O.C. 77th Field Ambulance

Army Form C. 2118.

WAR DIARY
or
INTELLIGENCE SUMMARY.

(Erase heading not required.)

77th Field Ambulance. A.D.M.S. 1st Corps 77.

Place	Date	Hour	Summary of Events and Information	Remarks and references to Appendices
OUTERSTEENE	30/4/17	12 Noon	Field Ambulance moved in billets at OUTERSTEENE. Working party of 20 men withdrawn from NEUVE EGLISE. A.R. Kelly Lieut-Col R.A.M.C. I.O. 77th Field Ambulance	

14/2/16

25th Div.

No. 77. F.A.

May 1917

COMMITTEE FOR THE
MEDICAL HISTORY OF THE WAR
Date 10 JUL 1917

Army Form C. 2118.

WAR DIARY
or
INTELLIGENCE SUMMARY.   77th Field Ambulance
(Erase heading not required.)

Place	Date	Hour	Summary of Events and Information	Remarks and references to Appendices
OUTERSTEENE	1/5/17	12 noon	Received intimation of H.Q. 182 that the Division will be in Army Corps from May 2nd inclusive & will be ready to move at 36 hours notice. The Division will consist of the combined N.Z. ANZAC Corps.	
"	2/5/17	11:30 am	Received extracts from 23rd Sectional Order No. 183. The 7th Infantry Brigade and 110th Brigade R.F.A. will proceed to Henny Area on May 4th. It will be employed by the M.G.C. Light Trench Mortar Battery, 201st My A.S.C. & one section 77th Field Ambulance. The ration of 77th Field Ambulance will march under order of O.C. 7th Infantry Brigade.	
"	4/5/17	8.30 am	C. Section of this Field Ambulance proceeded by route march with 7th Infantry Brigade to the TROUVES training areas.	
"	7/5/17	8 am	Capt. F. G. LESCHER. R.A.M.C. proceeded on leave of absence to PARIS.	HS Kelly Lieut Col acting O.C. 77th Field Ambulance

Army Form C. 2118.

WAR DIARY
or
INTELLIGENCE SUMMARY.   Folio 80.   77th Field Ambulance

(Erase heading not required.)

Place	Date	Hour	Summary of Events and Information	Remarks and references to Appendices
OUTTERSTEENE	8/5/17	1 p.m.	Received R.A.M.C. order No. 64. 77th Field Ambulance will move into the left main dressing station at Sheet 28. T.19.d.4.5. on 11th May 1917. Move to be completed by 12 noon.	
"	9/5/17	9 a.m.	Received a continuation of R.A.M.C. order No. 64. 77th Field Ambulance will collect sick from 74th Infantry Brigade. Visit of Lt. S.T. BEARD. R.A.M.C. arrived for duty from England.	
"	10/5/17	6 p.m.	Received a communication from A.D.M.S. 25th Division that sick evacuated from New Zealand Division to 25th Division will be received at left main dressing station at Pom Erley.	
"	11/5/17	12 noon	Arrived at 2nd Lieut Loft Main Dressing Station at T.19.R.4.5. Sect 28.	
"		6 p.m.	On tent sub-division of 2nd New Zealand Field Ambulance arrived for duty. As carried cart & transport sent to these officers at STRAZEELE for duty.	

W. Mayberry, Lieut A/Adjutant
O.C. 77th Field Ambulance

Army Form C. 2118.

WAR DIARY
or
INTELLIGENCE SUMMARY.

(Erase heading not required.)

Field F.A. 77th ½ Field Ambulance

Instructions regarding War Diaries and Intelligence Summary are contained in F.S. Regs., Part II. and the Staff Manual respectively. Title pages will be prepared in manuscript.

Place	Date	Hour	Summary of Events and Information	Remarks and references to Appendices
T.M. Sept. Coly Farm Dressing Station WESTHOF	13/5/17	4 p.m.	We are engaged in supplying this dressing station & receiving sick & wounded from New Zealanders & 25th Division.	
"	14/5/17	12 noon	Received orders to send one G.S. limbered wagon to report to GILES FARM at S.12.a.4.1. at 10 a.m. on the 16th inst. taking rations for the 17th. Fresh wagon will be replaced by a G.S. wagon supplied by D.D.M.S. 77. We got three one G.S. through from Canadians have just reported for duty. We are engaged in fitting this dressing station as a café near dressing station & a café collecting station. The Corner at Cote 60 dug-outs & the castle 750 walking cases.	
"	17/5/17		Received R.A.M.C. motor No. 65 to hold 12 men & 12 horses in readiness to be sent on	
"	19/5/17	9 p.m.	Passed through to form a Motor Ambulance Convoy under Headquarters. Received R.A.M.C. motor No. 66. The 7th Infantry Brigade will relieve the 75th Infantry Brigade in the WULVERGHEM Sector by 3 a.m. May 24th. On completion of relief 75th Infantry Brigade will move in the RAVELSBURG area. The 75th Field Ambulance will continue to collect sick from 75th & 7th Infantry from Battalions in the line. This Ambulance to collect from 75th & 7th Infantry Brigades. (Ref. Sheet 28. S.W. 1/20,000.)	

H.E. Kelly Lieut RAMC

Army Form C. 2118.

WAR DIARY
or
INTELLIGENCE SUMMARY.

(Erase heading not required.)

Army Form C. 2118.

77th Field Ambulance. Folio 87.

Place	Date	Hour	Summary of Events and Information	Remarks and references to Appendices
WESTHOF DRESSING STATION.	20/5/17	3.0 pm	The section of this Field Ambulance which was away with 7th Infantry Brigade returned today. This ambulance will collect sick from 7th & 8th Infantry Brigades. We also received sick & wounded from the New Zealand Division serving with Corps.	
"	21/5/17	12 noon	3 O.R.'s from Graves Registration Unit attached to this Corps main dressing station for duty.	
"	23/5/17	9 am	Capt. MILLAR. R.A.M.C. of this unit transmitted sick to No. 7 General Hospital MALASSISE. Lieut RYAN returned for duty from 53 Casualty Clearing Station.	
"	24/5/17	11 am	Received orders to send 12 N.C.O.'s & 12 Privates to report to D.A.D.S. at 5 p.m. on Saturday 26/5/17. Capt R BARTLETT. R.A.M.C. reported from Temporary duty with 6th L.S.W Borderers. Capt OWEN left for 14 days leave. Lieut RYAN takes temporary M.O. to 2nd S.A.C. 2nd Infantry Corps took over 2 tent sub-divisions from New Zealand Division serving with John Cowan, making the personnel for the Corps Main dressing station 6 tent sub-divisions & 12 additional N.C.O's Privates & O.R.'s detailed to Corps wounded on 26/5/17.	
"	25/5/17	9 am	H.B. Kelly. Lieut Col. O.C. 77th Field Ambulance	

Army Form C. 2118.

WAR DIARY
or
INTELLIGENCE SUMMARY.   Feb 28.   77th Field Ambulance

(Erase heading not required.)

Place	Date	Hour	Summary of Events and Information	Remarks and references to Appendices
F.M.hq45	28/5/17	9/p.m.	Lieut ARNOT. R.A.M.C. joined for duty. Lieut sub-division from No 1 Field Ambulance NEW ZEALAND. Division due on 25/5/17 has not yet joined. He returned reported from this light Main Draining Station are:— Daily state by Division to each A.D.M.S. " " " A.D.M.S. " " In duplicate to D.M.S. " " In duplicate of D.M.S. Received roll by Sisters daily A.36. Wire sick evacuations from noon to noon. Wire sick evacuations admitted from midnight to midnight	
"	31/5/17	11a.m.	Received A.D.M.S. 2S. Division No S.B. 629. Instrns arranged in the event of offensive [...] Instructor. Inspector of Ambulances on 1 occurs. [...] One into division. This Ambulance fully equipped will be at HM.Lopez Main Dressing Station. For M.O's & 118 beds or more. H.G. Why Lieut-Colonel c.o. 77th Field Ambulance	

2353 Wt. W2514/1454 700,000 5/15 D.D.& L.   A.D.S.S/Form/C. 2118.

Army Form C. 2118.

WAR DIARY
or
INTELLIGENCE SUMMARY. Feb 63. 77th Field Ambulance
(Erase heading not required.)

Instructions regarding War Diaries and Intelligence
Summaries are contained in F.S. Regs., Part II.
and the Staff Manual respectively. Title pages
will be prepared in manuscript.

Place	Date	Hour	Summary of Events and Information	Remarks and references to Appendices
T.14.b.4.5 Sheet 28	21/5/17	1pm	All surplus cars will be at disposal of No. 75th Field Ambulance officials for clearing the line who will send them at sheet 28. T.20. c. 7.1. Ford car posted at sheet 28. T.15. b.5.5. 77th Field Ambulance will send 3 horse ambulance & 3 G.S. waggons from each ambulance at sheet 28. T.15. a.7.6. H.B.Alley Lieut-Col comm. O.C. 77th Field Ambulance	

140/7230

No. 77 7.a.

June /5/

COMMITTEE FOR THE
MEDICAL HISTORY OF THE WAR
Date - 7 AUG. 1917

WAR DIARY
or
INTELLIGENCE SUMMARY

Army Form C. 2118.

July 87 77th Field Ambulance

Place	Date	Hour	Summary of Events and Information	Remarks and references to Appendices
T.M. 4.5. Sheet 28	1/9/17	11 am	Received R.A.M.C. order No. 64 dated 1/9/17. The 7th Infantry Brigade will be relieved on the WINNEZEELE sector on night 2/3 June on completion of relief the 7th Infantry Brigade will move into camp at RAVELSBERG. This Field Ambulance will collect sick from 7th Infantry Brigade & carry them direct to the 76th Field Ambulance D.R.S. BAILLEUL. The evacuations from the sector at present are sent to 7th Field Ambulance BAILLEUL. This unit is supplying escorts to No. 1. New Zealand Field Ambulance at S.16. Sheet 28. Sick who is admitted to C.C.S. There are to be evacuated by motor Ambs. My cars at present to convey sitters it will be the motor Amb. after to return to duty in a few days cases it will return to no.1 New Zealand Field Ambulance.	

H.G. Roby Capt

o.c. 77th Field Ambulance

Army Form C. 2118.

WAR DIARY
or
INTELLIGENCE SUMMARY.   Feb 8.5. 77th Field Ambulance
(Erase heading not required.)

Instructions regarding War Diaries and Intelligence Summaries are contained in F.S. Regs., Part II. and the Staff Manual respectively. Title pages will be prepared in manuscript.

Place	Date	Hour	Summary of Events and Information	Remarks and references to Appendices
T.M.L.4.5.	3/6/17	10 a.m.	Received orders from A.D.M.S. 25th Division to send one G.S. waggon complete to report to reinforcement coy. M.T.R.T.D.C.G/E.	
			Received from D.D.M.S. 2nd Anzac Corps an amended list of returns which required from this C.M.D.S.	
T.M.L.4.5.	4/6/17	5 pm	one section of 1st NEW ZEALAND Field Ambulance reported for duty.	
T.M.L.4.5. 6/	6/6/17	9/-	3 horse ambulances & S.J.S. waggon handed under orders of 76th Field Ambulance for conveyance of sitting wounded cases to this C.M.D.S. from the collecting posts.	
			Bearer division proceeded to bivouac near R.A.Ps. main over D O.C. 75th F. Amby.	
		7.30	Attack on MESSINES RIDGE. Started at 3/10 a.m. on morning of 7 inst.	
T.M.L.4.5	7/6/17	12 noon	Since that time 187 Officers & 7822 O.R.s passed through this C.M.D.S. This figure includes 7 enemy officers & 356 O.R.s. Evacuation to hospital & 1 sitting cases was by the 14 M.A.C. and lying cases by Motor Lorries. All arrangements worked smoothly.	

H.O.W By Lieut. Col.
O.C. 77th Field Ambulance

Army Form C. 2118.

WAR DIARY
or
INTELLIGENCE SUMMARY.
(Erase heading not required.)

Folio 86. 77th Field Ambulance

Place	Date	Hour	Summary of Events and Information	Remarks and references to Appendices
T.19.d.4.5.	10/6/17	6/p.m.	Nothing to report, not many casualties coming in. Beard returned	
"	11/6/17	6/p.m.	Received R.A.M.C. order No. 74. The 25th Division will relieve the 4th Australian Division in the battle front between the BLAUEPOORTBEEK on the north & the LA. DOUVE river on the south on night 12/13 June. 76th Field Ambulance will take over the front line. 77th Field Ambulance will take over the D.R.S. 78th Field Ambulance Reserve division will be in reserve in C.M.D.S. This Field Ambulance will collect sick of 7th Infantry Brigade as now in the R.A.M.C. order No. 72. France around NEUVE EGLISE.	
"	12/6/17	9/a.m.	Received 2nd ANZAC [Speedway] MEDICAL. D.D.M.S. 1103/17 that operations will be returned on the afternoon of June 14th. The arrangements for evacuation of Cy. Posts having station will be as for the 7th inst.	
"	13/6/17	9/p.m.	Received R.A.M.C. order No. 73. From 25th Division I.C. 77th Field Ambulance will send 3 Horse Ambulances & Leinster House. By 12 noon 14/6/17 to report to A.C. 78th Field Ambulance 5. Lieutenant & 2 Inds. to report to A.C. 78th Field Ambulance HANDAHER FARM by 11 a.m. All have horse lines under 2 Officers to report to A.C. 78th Field Ambulance HANDAHER FARM by 11 a.m. [illegible] A.O. Kelly Lt Col [illegible] O.C. 77 Field Ambulance	

Army Form C. 2118.

WAR DIARY
or
INTELLIGENCE SUMMARY.

Files 89. 77th Field Ambulance

(Erase heading not required.)

Instructions regarding War Diaries and Intelligence Summaries are contained in F. S. Regs., Part II. and the Staff Manual respectively. Title pages will be prepared in manuscript.

Place	Date	Hour	Summary of Events and Information	Remarks and references to Appendices
T.19.b.4.5.	18/6/17	9 a.m.	Received D.D.M.S. Second ANZAC 10.3/17. This C.M.D.S. will cease to function as such at noon today. All personnel will join their units. This Field Ambulance will take over the C.M.D.S. N.2 Field Ambulance station in the K of the 25th Division. N.C. return will be rendered as usual to A.D.M.S. Stores in accordance with above orders. The personnel of No. 1, 2, 3, & 4 New Zealand Field Ambulances rejoined their units. Four Ambulances joined from 78th Field Ambulance rejoined from 76th Field Ambulance.	
T.19.b.4.5.	19/6/17	9 a.m.	One officer & all ranks left Hyères & one N.C.O. rejoined from 76th Field Ambulance	
"	19/6/17	9 p.m.	Received R.A.M.C. order No. 74. This Field Ambulance will collect sick from 7th Infantry Brigade.	
"	20/6/17	9 a.m.	Proceeding on leave & handing over the command of the Ambulance to Capt. F.G. LESCHER. R.A.M.C.	

H.C. Vatt
Lieut-Col. R.A.M.C.
O.C. 77th Field Ambulance

WAR DIARY
or
INTELLIGENCE SUMMARY.
(Erase heading not required.)

Army Form C. 2118.

Folio 88 77th Field Ambulance

Instructions regarding War Diaries and Intelligence Summaries are contained in F.S. Regs., Part II. and the Staff Manual respectively. Title pages will be prepared in manuscript.

Place	Date	Hour	Summary of Events and Information	Remarks and references to Appendices
T19.6.4.5 June 28	21/6.		Remainder of teams returned from 76th F. Amb.	
"	22/6.	2 pm	In accordance with A.D.M.S. order no 75 3 bearers over the dressing station to 00 no 9 Aust Fld Amb.	
			The relay was completed by 2 pm.	
"	22/6.	2.10pm 8.30	7th Bde order no 251 Alteryal Orders to march night 23/24 to SWARTEN BROEK area, under orders G.O.C. 7th Inf Bde	
LE TIR ANGLAIS Sth HAZEBROUK	24/6.	2.30 am	Billeted in SWARTEN BROEK area — Collect sick which on orders of the march from 7th Bde group.	
"	24/6.	12.30 pm	Received 7th Bde Order no 252. We are to march night 24/25th to HAVERSKERQUE area.	
HAVERSKERQUE	25/6	2.30 am	Billeted in HAVERSKERQUE	
"	25/6	1.45 pm	Received Orders 7th Bde order no 253 march night of 25/26th to LIGNY-LEZ-AIRE area	
AUCHY AU BOIS	26/6	2.45 am	Billeted at AUCHY-AU-BOIS in above area.	
"	26/6	3.0 pm	Received 7th Bde order no 254 march night of 26/27 to COYECQUE area.	

Capt R.A.M.C.
77 Fld Amb

Army Form C. 2118.

folio 89. 77 Field Amb

WAR DIARY
or
INTELLIGENCE SUMMARY.

(Erase heading not required.)

Place	Date	Hour	Summary of Events and Information	Remarks and references to Appendices
COYECQUE.				
27/5/17	27/5/17	2:30 am	Billeted in COYECQUE.	
			Hospital established for collection of Bde sick	
"	27/6	2:0 pm	Lt Ryan RAMC reported to OC 186 Coy RE to take permanent charge of medical care of Divisional REs.	

Confidential

War Diary

Medical

77th F. Ambulance

July 1917

WAR DIARY
INTELLIGENCE SUMMARY

Army Form C. 2118.

77th Field Ambulance

Place	Date	Hour	Summary of Events and Information	Remarks and references to Appendices
COYECQUE	2/7/17	3 p.m.	Returned from leave & took over command of 77th Field Ambulance from Lieut. ARNUT. R.A.M.C. joined from temporary Medical charge of 10th Welsh Regt.	
"	7/7/17	9 a.m.	Received R.A.M.C. Order No. 76. The 7th Infantry Brigade will move up to the line and by rail on 7th July & relieve a Brigade of the 8th Division in the forward area and in the line on the night July 8th & July 9th/10th. The 77th Field Ambulance will accompany 7th Infantry Brigade & will take over the front line medical arrangements from Field Ambulance in line. Details to be arranged between the O.C.'s Field Ambulances concerned.	
"	5/7/17	2 p.m.	Received an Amendment to R.A.M.C. Order No. 76. That move of Field Ambulance with Brigade is cancelled.	
"	"	8 p.m.	Received an Amendment to R.A.M.C. Order No. 76. The Field Ambulance will now move with the Brigade. Capt. R. J. McELNEY. R.A.M.C. proceeded on leave of absence to United Kingdom.	

H.B. Kelly, Lieut-Colonel
O.C. 77th Field Ambulance

WAR DIARY
or
INTELLIGENCE SUMMARY

Army Form C. 2118.

77th Field Ambulance 1st Lot Gp.

(Erase heading not required.)

Place	Date	Hour	Summary of Events and Information	Remarks and references to Appendices
COYECQUE	5/7/17	9 p.m.	Received 7th Infantry Brigade Order No. 2575. This Field Ambulance will move under orders of G.O.C. 7th Infantry Brigade. Dismounted personnel will be conveyed by Bus to STEENBECQUE. Buses will arrive at COYECQUE at 10 a.m. Mounted portion will march from Cross Roads just N.E. of Church in DELETTE. Starting time 9.54 a.m. 2nd. THEROUANNE - MAMETZ - AIRE - BUSSCHEURE. Destination STEENBECQUE. (Reference) 5.A. HAZEBROUCK. Billetted here.	
STEENBECQUE	6/4/17	5 p.m.	Ambulance arrived & is billetted here.	
		9 p.m.	Received 7th Infantry Brigade Order No. 256. The Brigade will continue its march tomorrow. Dismounted portion by Bus leaving at 10 a.m. To road Junction L.17.L.30. (Reference) 27. N.E. 1/20,000. Horse & mounted & march to Field Ambulance camp at L.21.L.2.5. in the case of this Ambulance, Transport will proceed by road.	
L.21.L.25.	7/7/17	7 p.m.	Field Ambulance arrived. Capt. Boyce. proceeded to H.Q. Kelly Post - Lynne Sheet 28. O.C. 77th Field Ambulance	

Army Form C. 2118.

WAR DIARY
or
INTELLIGENCE SUMMARY. 77th Field Ambulance

(Erase heading not required.)

Place	Date	Hour	Summary of Events and Information	Remarks and references to Appendices
62d.2.5. Sheet 28.N.W.	8/7/17	4pm	Received 7th Infantry Brigade order No. 257. The 7th Infantry Brigade will relieve the 25th Infantry Brigade 8th Division in the sector between the YPRES-ROULERS railway in the North & a line drawn from I.18.d.48.68 — I.18.c.99.45. Northern edge of ZILLEBEKE LAKE in the South. For details from the neighbourhood of YPRES on night of July 8/9th & more forward on to the neighbourhood of YPRES on night of July 9/10th. Then these Bdy take is completed by remaining or night of July 9/10. For arrangement with O.C. No. 24 Field Ambulance first Battalions advance parties into all A.D.S.'s & R.A.P.'s at S.A.A. this morning.	
"	9/7/17	3am	Sent main body to take over lines of the Ambulance. All 28. The following is now the distribution. Headquarters. Sny at R.39.a.5.9. A.D.S. Canal Bank I.13.c.7.8. A.D.S. MENIN ROAD T.4.a.9.6. R.A.P. Infantry Hme I.16.d.7.8. R.A.P. Railway road I.11.c.6.3. A.D.S. Zillebeke I.14.c.7.3. W.C. Kelly Captn RAMC O.C. 77th Field Ambulance	

Army Form C. 2118.

WAR DIARY
or
INTELLIGENCE SUMMARY.   Feb. 93.   77th Field Ambulance

(Erase heading not required.)

Place	Date	Hour	Summary of Events and Information	Remarks and references to Appendices
Sheet 28. H.29.a.5.9.	9/7/17	6 h.m.	Railway Wood R.A.P. is reached by Ambulance Cars either by cart track leading to A.D.S. MENIN ROAD out to a point where cart track joined with the Railway & thence by Railway to R.R. Fire corner & by wheeled carrier to MENIN ROAD A.D.S. Half-Way House R.A.P. evacuated by Ambulance bearers to the ZILLEBEKE Road, thence to Hell Fire corner, & by wheeled carrier to MENIN ROAD. A.D.S. LILLE GATE. A.D.S. clear throughout. Canal Bank A.D.S. clear throughout.	
"	10/9/17	9 p.m.	Military Medal awarded to Sergt. W. Green, A.S.C. M.T. for his work at Menin Ridge in driving his car to bring down wounded, though on being dismounted dump.	
"	11/9/17	9 p.m.	Nothing to record. We are finishing an elephant dug out at MENIN ROAD. & making good the road at Headquarters.	

H.B. Kelly Lieut - ce comm
o.c. 77th Field Ambulance

Army Form C. 2118.

WAR DIARY
or
INTELLIGENCE SUMMARY.

Feby. 1917.   77th Field Ambulance

(Erase heading not required.)

Instructions regarding War Diaries and Intelligence Summaries are contained in F.S. Regs., Part II and the Staff Manual respectively. Title pages will be prepared in manuscript.

Place	Date	Hour	Summary of Events and Information	Remarks and references to Appendices
H.24.a.5.7.	16/7/17	9 p.m.	2 horse Ambulance wet flown into a ditch today. No casualties but waggon destroyed.	
"	20/7/17	9 p.m.	A fire occurred outside MENIN ROAD Aid post last night, a dump of petrol & gun shells & timber being ignited. The personnel worked hard & extinguished the flames after 2½ hours.	
"	22/7/17	9 p.m.	A fire occurred again at A.D.S. owing to hostile shelling, a dump of stoo-stretchers destroyed & A.D.S. had to be abandoned. Received R.A.M.C. orders No. 82. To hand over the line to 24th Field Ambulance on night 23/24 relief to be completed by 8 a.m. on completion of relief the Field Ambulance will move at H.26.d. sheet 28. & Transport will move to sheet 28. H.20.a. 5.5.	
"	24/7/17	8 a.m. 9 a.m.	Relief complete. Transport at H.20.a 5.5. & Bivouac at H.26d.	

M. Kelly ℓℓ Major
Temp. O.C. 77th
O.C. 77 Field Ambulance

2353 Wt. W2544/1454 700,000 5/15 D.D.&L. A.D.S.S./Forms/C. 2118.

Army Form C. 2118.

WAR DIARY
or
INTELLIGENCE SUMMARY.

Feb 15. 77th Field Ambulance

(Erase heading not required.)

Place	Date	Hour	Summary of Events and Information	Remarks and references to Appendices
H.26.d.	24/7/17	2 p.m.	Sent 8 mules to Divisional Pack Transport Coy. And two clerks to Coy't Main dressing station at DICKEBUSH.	
			Sent one clerk sub-driver & Capt Bayne & Capt Paul to Coy't main dressing station.	
"	25/7/17	10 a.m.	DICKEBUSH.	
			Capt COHEN. R.A.M.C. struck off the strength and sent to Heavy Artillery. This leaves us with 3 officers at present to undertake a difficult scheme through and the division in projected offensive.	
			Received R.A.M.C. order No. 82. When 7th Inf. Brigade moves forward its Field Ambulance will move forward with them. We are forwarding a mobile hand transport section composed of 4 mules & men and 2 G.S. wagons from 75th Field Ambulance. Received R.A.M.C. order 84. It is not now proposed this Ambulance moves as was originally the orders 85 & 84. cancel R.A.M.C. order No. 85. 78th Field Ambulance will relieve us for 75th & 78th Infantry Brigade. 75th Field Ambulance from 7th Brigade.	

Wakelly Smith
Lieut
O.C. 77th Field Ambulance.

WAR DIARY
or
INTELLIGENCE SUMMARY

H.Q. 77th Field Ambulance

Army Form C. 2118.

Place	Date	Hour	Summary of Events and Information	Remarks and references to Appendices
Neb at	28/7/17	9 a.m.	In bivouac. Awaiting orders	
"	31/7/17	9 a.m.	Awaiting orders.	

H.C. Kelly
Lieut. Col. R.A.M.C.
O.C. 77th Field Ambulance

Volume 23

Confidential

War Diary

Medical 77th Field Ambulance

25th Division

August 1917.

Army Form C. 2118.

WAR DIARY
or
INTELLIGENCE SUMMARY.   Feb. 17.   77th Field Ambulance.
(Erase heading not required.)

Place	Date	Hour	Summary of Events and Information	Remarks and references to Appendices
H.26.d.	1/8/17	5.30am	Received R.A.M.C. order No. 91. The 25th Division will take over from the 7th Division. This Field Ambulance will move Headquarters to CHATEAU HENDRIQUES H.27.c.5.7. & take over from the 24th Field Ambulance the following posts:— (a) Walking wounded Collecting Post H.24.b.4.4. (b) Advanced Dressing Station CANAL DUG. OUTS. I.13.d.0.3. (c) Collecting Post BIRR. CROSS ROADS I.17.F.2.8. & advanced Relay Post Right Brigade. All reliefs to be completed by 4 p.m. 1st August. The above order complied with. The advanced relay post is in HOUSE CHATEAU Wood. Found also a Regimental aid Post established by troops previously attached to Regiment. A park of motor ambulances has been established at MENIN ROAD A.D.S. somewhere near BIRR-X-ROADS is N.F. Motor Ambulance.	

H.O. Kelley
Lieut. Col. R.A.M.C.
O.C. 77th Field Ambulance.

Army Form C. 2118.

WAR DIARY
or
INTELLIGENCE SUMMARY.

Feby 98. 77th Field Ambulance

(Erase heading not required.)

Place	Date	Hour	Summary of Events and Information	Remarks and references to Appendices
H.Qs.S.9.	6/9/17	11 am	Received R.A.M.C. Frontier order No. 91. The 25th Division will operate at an early date The Black line — J.8.c.65.30 — J.8.c.55.72. — J.8.a.41.55. — J.8.a.35.85. — J.2.e.1.0. — J.7.c.d.75.55. Reference sheet 28. N.W. 1/40,000. The O.C. 76th Field Ambulance will be responsible for the evacuation from the Front line. This Field Ambulance will establish & maintain wounded collecting Posts at advanced dressing station CANAL-DUG-OUTS, & be responsible for picking up wounded found along road to Walking wounded Collecting Posts including stretcher loads along road & stored at CANAL-DUG-OUTS & stretcher along road to Loading Point at approximately J.14.a.8.6. Route BIRR-CROSS-ROADS — MENIN-GATE — YPRES Motor Lorries to WATER-GATE to point J.14.c.7.0. along F. track to CANAL DUG-OUTS. Camel DUG-OUTS to loading Point J.14.a.8.6.	

H.E. Kelly
Lieut. ? R.A.M.C.
O.C. 77th Field Ambulance

Army Form C. 2118.

WAR DIARY
or
INTELLIGENCE SUMMARY.

(Erase heading not required.)

Folio 93. 77th Field Ambulance.

Place	Date	Hour	Summary of Events and Information	Remarks and references to Appendices
H.Q. at 54 Sheet 28.N.W.1 1/40,000	7/8/17	7pm	Received orders to reduce our ride to 5. Lie & the Wounded now to the Divisional Artillery.	
"	8/8/17	4.30am	Flagged out the route for walking wounded cases as directed in R.A.M.C. order No 91. Zero will be 4.45 a.m. 8/8/17. Operations postponed.	
"	9/8/17	1.30am		
		11am	Received information that operations would take place some time tomorrow.	
"	10/8/17		Received R.A.M.C. operation order No 92. The 25th Division will be relieved in the left sector II Corps on 10th 11th & 12th August. This Field Ambulance will hand over walking wounded collecting post & canal dug out to 24th Field Ambulance & opening an wounded collecting post to be completed by 8 p.m. CHATEAU HENDRICQUES will be handed over & LANDROVER FARM taken over. The horse personnel attached to 75th Field Ambulance will rejoin unit & relieve this Field Ambulance will retail 1 M.O. C.O.R. & 60 O.R. to be attached to form a collecting post at STEENVOORDE in addition to LW & 75 & Infantry Brigade Bearer Divisions. H.B. Kelly Lieut. Col. R.A.M.C.	

WAR DIARY or INTELLIGENCE SUMMARY

Army Form C. 2118.

(Erase heading not required.)

Army Form C. 2118.

Instructions regarding War Diaries and Intelligence Summaries are contained in F.S. Regs., Part II. and the Staff Manual respectively. Title pages will be prepared in manuscript.

Summary: From 11th 77th Field Ambulance

Place	Date	Hour	Summary of Events and Information	Remarks and references to Appendices
CHATEAU HENDRICQUES	11/8/17	1pm	A.D.M.C. Hendon visit cancelled.	
"	12/8/17	7pm	Received R.A.M.C. Standing Order No. 94. The 78th Field Ambulance will take over the southerly portion of that part of the MENIN ROAD A.D.S. which lies North of the Roman Road, from us at J.7.a.55 & I.12.d.5.1. relief to be completed on 13th August. Received Standing Order No. 95. The 3 Divn. will be relieved by 55th & 8th Divisions on the nights of 12th/13th & 13th/14th August. This Field Ambulance will hand over walking wounded collecting post & Advanced Dressing Station camel day-ends to 24th Field Ambulance. Relief to be completed by 10 a.m. on 14th August. This Field Ambulance will also hand over CHATEAU HENDRICQUES. Proceed to LANDHOUWER Farm. This Field Ambulance will form a collecting post at STEENVOORDE & collect from 7th & 14th Infantry Brigades.	
"	13/8/17		Relief completed at 8 p.m.	

H.B. Kelly,
Lieut-Col. R.A.M.C.
O.C. 77th Field Ambulance

Army Form C. 2118.

WAR DIARY
or
INTELLIGENCE SUMMARY.
(Erase heading not required.)

Feb 10. 77th Field Ambulance

Instructions regarding War Diaries and Intelligence Summaries are contained in F. S. Regs., Part II. and the Staff Manual respectively. Title pages will be prepared in manuscript.

Place	Date	Hour	Summary of Events and Information	Remarks and references to Appendices
LANROUVER FARM Sheet 28 C.21.	14/8/17	8 p.m.	Capt. F.E. LESCHER & Capt. B. BARTLETT of this Unit proceeded on leave. Cpl. A. WHITLOW awarded Military Medal. 25 Reinforcements arrived during last 3 days. Our Total Battle casualties during the past fortnight have been 9 killed & 28 wounded.	
"	15/8/17	9 p.m.	Received R.A.M.C. order No. 96. The 76th Field Ambulance will move on 16 August to STEENVOORDE. The detachment of this Field Ambulance will join from STEENVOORDE. This Field Ambulance will take over collecting from 75th Brigade at DOMINION CAMP at C.23.d.5.5.	
"	19/8/17	1.30 a.m.	Received R.A.M.C. orders No. 97 & No. 98. Received R.A.M.C. order No. 97. The 25th Division Artillery will be withdrawn into the STEENVOORDE & ECKE area on 17/8/17. This Field Ambulance will proceed to STEENVOORDE & join 1st Brigade as a Temporary Suffolk & relieve Brigade with this Unit next to clear of RENINGHELST by 8.15 a.m.	
"	"	11.30 a.m.	arrived STEENVOORDE.	
"	"	8 p.m.	Received a warning order that the 7th Brigade would probably move to DOMINION Camp at C.23 on 19/8/17.	

H.E. Kelly Capt R.A.M.C.
O.C. 77th Field Ambulance

Army Form C. 2118.

WAR DIARY
or
INTELLIGENCE SUMMARY. *Feb/12 77th Field Ambulance*
(Erase heading not required.)

Place	Date	Hour	Summary of Events and Information	Remarks and references to Appendices
STEENVOORDE	18/8/17	4pm	In billets resting.	
		7pm	Received R.A.M.C. order No 98. The 7th Infantry Brigade and Field Coy R.E. & Field Ambulance will move to DRANOUTRE AREA on March 19th. This Field Ambulance will arrange for collection of sick on march on completion of move this Field Ambulance will collect from 74th Infantry Brigade. Received R.A.M.C. Order No 99. The 74th Brigade Group will move on 21st August to STEENVOORDE WEST AREA.	
"	19/8/17	7pm	Lieut ARNOTT. R.A.M.C. & two Horsed Ambulances accompanied 7th Brigade on March & returned on completion of March, 29 men fell out on line of march & were conveyed to their destination.	
"	20/8/17	3.30pm	General cleaning of equipment & inspection of gas helmets etc.	

H.B. Kelly Lieut-Col RAMC
O.C. 77th Field Ambulance

Army Form C. 2118.

WAR DIARY
or
INTELLIGENCE SUMMARY.

Folio 103. 77th Field Ambulance

(Erase heading not required.)

Place	Date	Hour	Summary of Events and Information	Remarks and references to Appendices
STEENVOORDE	22/8/17	1 p.m	Received notice that 7th Infantry Brigade will move by march route from DOMINION lines to STEENVOORDE. E. Coln on August 23rd. Route via RENINGHELST and AZEELE. Head of Column to enter RENINGHELST at 8 a.m. This Field Ambulance to arrange for collection of sick on line of march. Received order to send a Medical Pair for duty with 2nd Army Prisoner of War cage. OC Marren served for duty.	
"	23/8/17	5.30am	Two horse Ambulances & Capt R. McElroy proceeded to RENINGHELST to meet & accompany 7th Infantry Brigade on line of march.	
"	"	10 a.m	First draft n.c.o.s proceeded for duty with 5th Army Prisoner of War cage	
"	"	2 p.m	11 Reinforcement O.R.s arrived	
"	24/8/17	5 p.m	OC Marren proceeded to convalescent camp at MILLAIN	

H.G. Willoughby Kent—Lt. Col.
O.C. 77th Field
Ambulance

Army Form C. 2118.

WAR DIARY
or
~~INTELLIGENCE SUMMARY.~~ Folio 104. 77th Field Ambulance

(Erase heading not required.)

Place	Date	Hour	Summary of Events and Information	Remarks and references to Appendices
STEENVOORDE	26/8/17	5/pm	Capt F. Tucker came returned from leave. The G.O.C. inspected the Ambulance, and informed employer units.	
"	28/8/17	12 n/n	Lieut REDMOND. U.S.A. O.R.M.C. joined the Ambulance.	
"	28/8/17	6 p.m	Capt R. McELNEY. R.A.M.C. & Lieut REDMOND. U.S. O.R.M.C. Lent to 2nd Corps Moters Whining station in relief of Capt BOYCE & Capt DAVY, who have rejoined the unit. Received a warning order that 7th Infantry Brigade & 20 Bg. R.S.C. will be placed at the disposal of 23rd Division & will be employed to move on August 30th This Field Ambulance will act as Horsed division 1. 2. Ambulance with 7th Infantry Brigade. The Divn Trans with 1 officer will report on arrival to O.C. 77th Field Ambulance at A.D.S. MENIN ROAD from whose they will be distributed.	
"	29/8/17	7.15pm	Received an order to send an M.O. to the Lewillaine Sgte for temporary duty. Received further orders that the Lewinn shirker would now be bury at work & from 30/8/17.	F.B. Kelly Capt R.a.m.C. V.C. 77th Field Ambulance

Army Form C. 2118.

WAR DIARY
or
INTELLIGENCE SUMMARY.

(Erase heading not required.)

Feby W.D. 77th Field Ambulance

Place	Date	Hour	Summary of Events and Information	Remarks and references to Appendices
STEENVOORDE	30/6/17	12.30am	Received 7th Infantry Brigade T.1016. The party of one officer & 40 o.rs of 77th Field Ambulance will proceed to Frust starting at K.33.d. central at 2.50 p.m. 30/6/17.	
"	"	10.30am	Capt Boyce proceeded to join the Lot Wiltshire Regt for temporary duty.	
"	"	12 noon	Received 7th Infantry Brigade order No 273. The marching point will be K.33.d.8.2. at 3.15 p.m.	
"	"	3.15pm	The above division under command of Capt W. Paul, embarked.	

H.O. Kelly, Lieut-Colonel
O.C. 77th Field Ambulance

VOLUME 24.

SEPTEMBER 1917.

Confidential

"WAR DIARY"

MEDICAL

CONFIDENTIAL

77th FIELD AMBULANCE.

R. A. M. C.

COMMITTEE FOR THE
MEDICAL HISTORY OF THE WAR
Date -5 NOV. 1917

Army Form C. 2118.

WAR DIARY
or
INTELLIGENCE SUMMARY.
(Erase heading not required.)

No. 106. 77 Field Ambulance

Place	Date	Hour	Summary of Events and Information	Remarks and references to Appendices
STEENVOORDE	1/9/17	11 a.m.	Received R.A.M.C. O.O. 101. This Field Ambulance to march today under orders of O.C. 74th Brigade & take over WARATAH Farm from 22nd Field Ambulance on relief of march billet last from 74th Infantry Brigade in OUDERDOM area.	
"	1/9/17	7.30 p.m	Arrived WARATAH FARM. Hut 28. G.15.	
WARATAH FARM	2/9/17	2.15 am	Received R.A.M.C. order 102. This Field Ambulance to remain at WARATAH FARM.	
"	2/9/17		Received R.A.M.C. order 103. This Field Ambulance to hand over WARATAH FARM to 75th Field Ambulance & take over from 69th Field Ambulance 23rd Division the portion of the Corps Main Dressing Station Dickebush assigned to that ambulance & will act as the motor dressing station for the ambulance clearing the line.	
DICKEBUSH	4/9/17	12 noon	Arrived & took over.	

H.C. Kelly Lieut-Colonel
O.C. 77 Field Ambulance

Army Form C. 2118.

WAR DIARY
or
INTELLIGENCE SUMMARY.

(Erase heading not required.)

Files 107. 77th Field Ambulance

Instructions regarding War Diaries and Intelligence Summaries are contained in F.S. Regs., Part II. and the Staff Manual respectively. Title pages will be prepared in manuscript.

Place	Date	Hour	Summary of Events and Information	Remarks and references to Appendices
DICKEBUSH	4/9/17	7 p.m.	LIEUT. ARNOTT. R.A.M.C. rejoined from 5th Army Prisoners of War Cage & proceeded on leave. Capt Powell A & B Section Horses sub-sections & 10 O.C. rejoined this afternoon. We are collecting sick from the Brigade in Reserve	
"	5/9/17	11 a.m.	Capt BOYCE. R.A.M.C. rejoined.	
"	6/9/17	5 p.m.	Capt BOYCE. R.A.M.C. proceeded as Temporary Medical officer to 106th Field Coy R.E. Received orders that the Central Bureau would reopen at 12 noon of 7th inst. Two clerks from 75th & 76th Field Ambulance & 4 for the 47th Division joined.	
"	8/9/17	6 p.m.	Received R.A.M.C. Operation Order No. W.S. This Field Ambulance will be relieved by 12 noon 9th inst by an Ambulance of the 1st Australian Division.	
"	9/9/17	12 noon	Received Orders that on completion of relief by an Ambulance of the 1st Australian Division this Field Ambulance will march into VANSCHIER FARM.	

H.O. Kelly Lieut-Col.
O.C. 77th Field Ambulance

Army Form C. 2118.

WAR DIARY
or
INTELLIGENCE SUMMARY.
(Erase heading not required.)

No. 108. 77th Field Ambulance

Instructions regarding War Diaries and Intelligence Summaries are contained in F. S. Regs., Part II. and the Staff Manual respectively. Title pages will be prepared in manuscript.

Place	Date	Hour	Summary of Events and Information	Remarks and references to Appendices
VANSCHIER FARM.	9/9/17	3.30 p.m.	Relief by 1st Australian Field Ambulance completed & this Field Ambulance moved by march route to VANSCHIER FARM. The Unit has now joined the 7th Brigade Group & will march under orders of G.O.C. 7th Infantry Brigade.	
		8.9 p.m.	Received 7th Infantry Brigade Order No 277. The Division will be transferred by march route from the 2nd Army to the 1st Army 1st Corps. The Brigade Group will march to the First Army Area on the 10th, 11th & 12th inst, to CAESTRE, STEENBECQUE & BURBURE areas respectively. This Field Ambulance will march from G.21.c.5.7. to G.33.c.2.4. (Sheet 27) starting point, Road junction in main ABEELE-STEENVOORDE Road 1400 yds S.W. of Pint E in ABEELE. Route, Cross Roads ½ mile N.W. of BUESCHEPE CHURCH – GODEWAERSVELDE. Tail of convoy starting point 10.41 a.m.	
CAESTRE	10/9/17	6 p.m.	Arrived 2 p.m. Received march table for tomorrow. This Field Ambulance will move to THIENNES. Starting time 8.27 a.m.	H.S. Kirby Lieut-Col. i.c. 77 Field Ambulance

Army Form C. 2118.

WAR DIARY
or
INTELLIGENCE SUMMARY. *No. 108. 77th Field Ambulance*

(Erase heading not required.)

Place	Date	Hour	Summary of Events and Information	Remarks and references to Appendices
THIENNES	11/9/17	5 p.m.	Arrived this afternoon. Received march table for tomorrow. This unit moves to HURIONVILLE.	
HURIONVILLE	12/9/17	3 p.m.	Arrived HURIONVILLE. Billeted. Put up all accommodation tent & no place suitable for hospital purposes.	
"	13/9/17	4 p.m.	Attending Brigade sick.	
"	14/9/17	9 p.m.	Nothing to record.	
"	15/9/17	9 p.m.	Nothing to record. Capt. H. Bool A.A.M.C. sent for temporary duty to 9th Reserve Regt.	
"	16/9/17	9 p.m.	Nothing to record.	
"	17/9/17	9 p.m.	Nothing to record.	
"	18/9/17	9 p.m.	Tent Sub-divn. of this unit sent for temporary duty with 3rd Worcestershire Regt.	

H.B. Kelly
Lieut-Col.
O.C. 77th Field Ambulance

Army Form C. 2118.

WAR DIARY
or
INTELLIGENCE SUMMARY.

(Erase heading not required.)

Folder No. 77 ½ Field Ambulance

Place	Date	Hour	Summary of Events and Information	Remarks and references to Appendices
HURIONVILLE	25/9/17	9pm	Capt BARTLETT of this unit set out of 9th Mature Park in chief of Capt Paul who proceeded on leave to United Kingdom today. Capt Boyce of this unit sent off temporary duty with 1st Wiltshire Regt. Received R.A.M.C. order No 107. On receipt of 75th Infantry Brigade & 75th Field Ambulance to forward some. Field Ambulance has not moved.	
"	28/9/17	11am	Capt Bartlett rejoined.	
"	29/9/17	11am	Unit without movement.	
"	30/9/17	11am	Went round right sector of Divisional front with O.C. A.D.S. The A.D.S. is in town of LIEVIN. Reported that huts for the sick in rear were three huts one in allery, all require repairing. Requested one hut square for me in allery to Front Line. We require 60 N.C.O. & men will be sent to filled in LIEVIN probably on 2/10/17. To commence work on these huts, nothing more is attached to R.E.	

H.G. Kelly Capt
O.C. 77 ½ Field Ambulance

Volume 25   Confidential

War Diary

Medical

77th F. Ambulance

October 1917

Army Form C. 2118.

WAR DIARY
or
INTELLIGENCE SUMMARY.

(Erase heading not required.)

Feb. 111. 77 th Field Ambulance

Instructions regarding War Diaries and Intelligence Summaries are contained in F. S. Regs., Part II. and the Staff Manual respectively. Title pages will be prepared in manuscript.

Place	Date	Hour	Summary of Events and Information	Remarks and references to Appendices
HORSONVILLE	1/2/17	9pm	Received orders from A.D.M.S. to detail 1 officer & 60 O.R. to proceed on 2nd inst. from LILLERS by tram to NOEUX-LES-MINES. Four lorries 9.30 a.m. from NOEUX-LES-MINES. Party will proceed from LIEVIN to take forward billets in LIEVIN. Have been arranged by Four Major LIEVIN. Party will be attached to 105th Field Coy R.E. for returns from the 5th inst. This party will work on construction of rear advanced dressing stations.	
"	2/2/17	9pm	Capt. ARNOTT & 60 O.R. left for LIEVIN this morning.	
"	3/2/17	9pm	Received from A.D.M.S. a warning order that the 25th Division will relieve the 2nd Division in the CAMBRIN-FESTUBERT sector on or about 5th, 6th relief to be completed by 7th. The party of 1 officer & 60 O.R. to be by 6 a.m. or later the 7th from NOEUX-LES-MINES at 11 a.m. withdrawn from LIEVIN & will move by bus to their destination. Field ambulance will move order of 9.a.c. 7th Field on the 5th inst to BETHUNE following further instructions as to their destination. Field ambulance will march under orders of 25th Div. H.Q. Kelly Lieut-Colonel O.C. 77 Field Ambulance	

Army Form C. 2118.

WAR DIARY
or
INTELLIGENCE SUMMARY. Febo 118. 77th Field Ambulance

(Erase heading not required.)

Place	Date	Hour	Summary of Events and Information	Remarks and references to Appendices
HORNOYVILLE	3/10/17	1 pm	Received 7th Infantry Brigade order No 278. The Brigade group will march tomorrow to billets in BETHUNE & BEUVRY, & at night 5/6th the Brigade will relieve the 6th Infantry Brigade in the GIVENCHY sector. Billetting parties will meet staff Captain at BETHUNE church at 9.30 am	
BETHUNE	4/10/17	9 pm	Arrived in billet at 1.30 pm. Received R.A.M.C. order No 108. This Field Ambulance will take over from 5th Field Ambulance 2nd Division the evacuation of the GIVENCHY sector & 2nd half of CANAL SECTOR. Relief to be completed by 9 am on 6th October. This Field Ambulance will take over the MAIN DRESSING STATION. MESPLEUX FARM. (X.14.a.1.6.) of Sheet 36 & 36 c. 1/40,000. A.D.S. at TUNING FORK. F.S.A.6.0. LONE FARM. A.2.d.2.4. R.A.P.s at BARNTON ROAD A.2.b.2.4. HART'S REDOUBT. A.8.d.7.4. WINDY CORNER. A.8.c.8.4. PONTIFEX ROAD. A.14.2.R.1.	
"	5/10/17	9 pm	Capt. P. McELNEY & 14. O.R. proceeded at 2 pm today to take over the A.D.S. TUNING FORK, and evacuation from BARNTON ROAD R.A.P. Capt. BARTLETT & 9. O.R. left at 4 pm for the A.D.S. LONE FARM & evacuation. Capt. [?] & 3 recovery R.A.P.	McElney Capt-Lt 77th Amb. O.C. 77. 2nd Field Ambulance

Army Form C. 2118.

WAR DIARY
or
INTELLIGENCE SUMMARY.
(Erase heading not required.)

Army Book 113. 77 Field Ambulance

Place	Date	Hour	Summary of Events and Information	Remarks and references to Appendices
NESPLAUX FARM	6/10/17	9p.m.	Moved on to Main dressing Station this morning & took over at 9.a.m.	
			Visited Light Rest Station. MERVILLE.	
			Officers Rest Station. CHATEAU DEMUM. HAZEBROUCK — MERVILLE. Went	
			Supplies Medic Depot. REMIER. LE CLERE. (K.34.d.4.7)	
			Urgent cases to 33 C.C.S. BETHUNE. Ordinary cases to MERVILLE.	
			For L.C.S. CHEQUES. for Dysentry. 3n 57 WILLERS. for S.I.	
			No. 17. A.D.M.S. BETHUNE. No 3. Mobile Laboratory. MERVILLE.	
			Visited A.D.S.	
"	7/10/17	9p.m.	Visited A.D.S. Rue Farm & right Sector R.A.P.s	
"	8/10/17	9p.m.	Went round able time indenting for RAPs & A.D.S.	
"	9/10/17	9p.m.	Capt. PAUL R.A.M.C. sent for temporary duty at No. 57. C.C.S. MERVILLE	
				H.B. Kelly Port-Lemaye O.C. 77 Field Ambulance

Army Form C. 2118.

WAR DIARY
or
INTELLIGENCE SUMMARY. Folio 114. 77th Field Ambulance

(Erase heading not required.)

Place	Date	Hour	Summary of Events and Information	Remarks and references to Appendices
MESPLAUX FARM.	10/10/17	9am	Nothing to record.	
"	11/10/17	9am	Nothing to record.	
"	12/10/17	9am	Nothing to record.	
"	13/10/17	9am	Nothing to record.	
"	14/10/17	9am	Proceeding on 10 days leave. Handed over command to Captain F. GLESCHER RAMC.	

H.G. Kelly
Lieut-Colonel
O.C. 77th Field
Ambulance

WAR DIARY
or
INTELLIGENCE SUMMARY

Army Form C. 2118.

John 1/5, 77... Uuh

(Erase heading not required.)

Place	Date	Hour	Summary of Events and Information	Remarks and references to Appendices
MESPLAUX FARM	23/X	9 am	It is proposed to build a new RAP for the Batt: but in the line of the Right Brigade. The site in in SPOIL BANK A.15 C.7.9. had to be viewed by BETHUNE (combined chief) accordingly. Party are viewed at LONE FM. 1 N15 d 9.0 R.	1/5 4 RB Uuh
"	24/X	6.0 pm	Stationed 1 officer and a ADS & 4 other ranks at team with Bath and RAPs - fixed up at him accommodation at RB MDS.	
"	27/X	9 am	Working party of 4 men to help strengthen the RMP of the Reserve Battalion carre Biques (i.c 75 th Bde.) Recalled expn. car & bearers from him.	
"	31/X	12.30 am	Fire broke out in front of Barn where Equipment was stored about 12.30 am at MDS. Fire was stopped & finally put out about 1.45 am. No patients had to be moved. Bearers done their stuff. The roof of Barn destroyed & some medical equipment. Alarm & fire appliances worked well.	
		—	Wounded treated at MDS during month Officers 5 O.R. 34.	

M. Leschin
Capt RAMC (SR)
OC 77 FA

Volume 26   Confidential

War Diary

Medical

77th Field Ambulance

November 1917

Army Form C. 2118.

WAR DIARY
or
INTELLIGENCE SUMMARY.
(Erase heading not required.)

Page 116. 77th Field Ambulance

Instructions regarding War Diaries and Intelligence Summaries are contained in F.S. Regs., Part II. and the Staff Manual respectively. Title pages will be prepared in manuscript.

Place	Date	Hour	Summary of Events and Information	Remarks and references to Appendices
MESPLAUX. FARM.	2/11/17	7 p.m.	Returned from leave. H.B.Kelly Lieut-Col.A.M.C.	
"	3/11/17	6 p.m.	Lieut DAVIS. U.S.O.R. Joined on 1/11/17. for duty with this unit.	
"	5/11/17	6 a.m.	Visited LONE. FARM. A.D.S. & WINDY. CORNER & HERTS. REDOUBT. R.A.P.s	
"	7/11/17	6 a.m.	Visited TUNING. FORK. A.D.S.	
"	9/11/17	8.30 a.m.	Capt McELNEY of this unit proceeded on leave.	
"	11/11/17	11 a.m.	Visited A.D.S. LONE. FARM. & R.A.P.s	
"	12/11/17	8 a.m.	Visited A.D.S. LONE. FARM. & R.A.P.s	
"			Lieut Good sent to A.D.S. TUNING. FORK. Capt Boyer to temporary medical charge of 13th Welsh Regt.	

H.B.Kelly Lieut-Col.
O.C. 77th Field Ambulance.

Army Form C. 2118.

WAR DIARY
or
INTELLIGENCE SUMMARY.

Folio N°. 77th Field Ambulance

(Erase heading not required.)

Instructions regarding War Diaries and Intelligence Summaries are contained in F. S. Regs., Part II. and the Staff Manual respectively. Title pages will be prepared in manuscript.

Place	Date	Hour	Summary of Events and Information	Remarks and references to Appendices
13/11/17. MES PLANS FARM.	13/11/17	10 a.m.	Sergt-Major IVINS. proceeded to a 4 days course of instruction at 25th Divisional gas school. Pte BROADSMITH. a candidate for commission proceeded to 11th Lancashire Fusiliers for one months probationary course.	
"	17/11/17	2 p.m.	Lieut WATT. R.A.M.C. posted to this unit for temporary duty. Lieut REDMAND. U.S. M.O.R.C. posted to permanent charge of 10th & 63rd Cheshire Regt & struck off the strength of this unit.	

Army Form C. 2118.

WAR DIARY
or
INTELLIGENCE SUMMARY. folio 118 77th Fld Amb.

(Erase heading not required.)

Instructions regarding War Diaries and Intelligence Summaries are contained in F.S. Regs., Part II and the Staff Manual respectively. Title pages will be prepared in manuscript.

Place	Date	Hour	Summary of Events and Information	Remarks and references to Appendices
MESPLAUX FARM xx½ A.9.6 Ref. Carancourt BETHUNE 1/40,000	25/11	6 pm	Warning order from 7th Inf Bde Group — to act as this unit — that it would be relieved by the 127 Bde 42nd Divn on Nov 27th & will be transferred by stages to I Army training area	
"	26/11	7 am	Syllabus supplementary to Div Order No 249 received. Instr. the Bde Group are digging & filling places. Allotted on march.	
"	26/11	9 am	RAMC order No 110 received. We shall be transferred to I Corps at 6 am 29/XI. We are to hand over the Main Dressing Station MESPLAUX Fm XY9A.6.6, ADS TUNING FK F9.a.50 & ADS LONE FM A.7 d.4.3 & evacuation sgts routes for casualties from GIVENCHY & NORTHERN trenches half O Canal section to 1/3 EAST LANCS F.A. on Nov 27th. Relief to be complete by 3 pm 27 Nov, details to be arranged between OsC F Ambs concerned. On completion of relief this unit will march out under orders of GOC 7th Inf Bde Group. This unit is to collect sick from the 7th Bde group on afn Nov 27th.	

M Lochen
Capt. RAMC
a/OC 77 Fld Amb

Army Form C. 2118.

WAR DIARY
or
INTELLIGENCE SUMMARY.

Folio 119. 77 Fd Amb.

(Erase heading not required.)

Place	Date	Hour	Summary of Events and Information	Remarks and references to Appendices
MESPLAUX FARM BETHUNE (Contoured Sheet) X14 a 9.6.	24/11	10 am	Advanced party @ 10.30am + 12 OR from 1/3 EAST LANCS Fld Amb arrived. A party was sent to each from the two F.A. ADS, + a man was put in each Rg out post. Stretchers, Trench shoes etc were handed over.	
	"	4pm	7th Inf Bde order no 89.6 received. Units are ready on to march independently to their new billeting area. We are to march to ANNEZIN.	
			The signal works Scale equipment has been altered in the Div Sign at BETHUNE, together with the field function bearer March + improved stretchers etc.	
			A motor lorry has been ordered to report at the MDS the day of the move + to carry with the most during the move.	
			Our final destination in MAISNIL (Ref Hazebr. SA HAZEBROUK).	
	11	7.10 pm	Operation order no 23 from 1/3 EAST LANC F.amb received. They are billeted nights 26th/27th Nov at BETHUNE. Our party @ 1 Off + 16 men will march direct to ADS TUNING FK (contoured BETHUNE map F 8, a, 5.0), another party @ 1 Off + 2 1 OR will march direct to ADS LONE FM + take these posts over + relieve our men in the lines. The main body will march to MESPLAUX Fm. Their move will take place morning @ 27 Nov. A. Lindrew Capt. RAMC a/o/c 77 Fld Amb.

WAR DIARY
or
INTELLIGENCE SUMMARY.

(Erase heading not required.)

Army Form C. 2118.

Folio 120. 77 Fd Amb April

Instructions regarding War Diaries and Intelligence Summaries are contained in F.S. Regs., Part II. and the Staff Manual respectively. Title pages will be prepared in manuscript.

Place	Date	Hour	Summary of Events and Information	Remarks and references to Appendices
MESPLAUX FARM	26/IV	10 pm	Sent orders to OC ADSs that on relief of our posts, stretcher all our men were relieved & hurt returned	
N14.9.6 BETHUNE Central map			From the RAPs & dress post, they were to march out with the FA equipment & join us at ANNEZIN. Transport being sent up to them. March was not to be commenced before 2 am	
	27/IV	11.30 am	Men body of 1/5 EAST LANC FAmb arrived & took over. Our bearer store closed as first bearer of all patients in hospital transferred to the new Ambulance.	
		1.30 am	Then unit marched out to ANNEZIN. On march intervals between units 500 yds – between transport & unit & the end 100 yds.	
		2.30 am	7th Inf Bde order no 297 received on Nov 28th we are to march with the Bde group & billet at HURIONVILLE. R4 5A HAZEBROUCK.	
		5.30 am 6.0 am	Parties from #808 arrived. 7th Inf Bde orders the Bdy march time fixed for Bd & Nov. 26. arrived.	
ANNEZIN R9 5A HAZEBROUCK	28th	10.30 am	Marched to HURIONVILLE. The men had to march in form tonight to ease the march.	

J.W. Lindore Capt RAMC a/OC 77 Fd Amb

Army Form C. 2118.

Folio 121   77 Fld Amb

WAR DIARY
or
INTELLIGENCE SUMMARY.

(Erase heading not required.)

Instructions regarding War Diaries and Intelligence Summaries are contained in F. S. Regs., Part II. and the Staff Manual respectively. Title pages will be prepared in manuscript.

Place	Date	Hour	Summary of Events and Information	Remarks and references to Appendices
HURIONVILLE	26/XI	2.0 pm	The billeting officer & this unit reported that at MAISNIL where he had arrived, there was no accommodation for a hospital. Saw the Staff Capt. who said that we were to proceed to CAPELLE SUR LA LYS instead.	
HAZEBROUCK Aug 5 A	"	"	When Amb. in some accommodation.	
"	"	"	Sw Advp̃a came at LOCON at 12 noon & arrived at POMY at same hour.	
"	29/XI	8.30 am	Marched to CAPELLE-SUR-LA-LYS arrived 5 pm. Route was much near EUTEM, ST hR, BLEQUIDECQUES, LEPLESSES, ST HILAIRE, APPY-AVROIX, LIMAY, COHEM, BAVYST JULIEN. Collected sick from Bde on + began the march. Bde sick, WANDINE, CHATSAV.	
CAPELLE SUR LA LYS.	30/XI	9 am	Opened up a temporary hospital for sick & Bde troops.	
"	"	10.00	Copy of medical arrangements to 25th Div whilst in 1st army training area received. This unit collects sick of the Bde, & does medical & sanitary duties to the Div. Coy	

J. Leadun Capt DAMC o/c 77 Fld Amb

Army Form C. 2118.

WAR DIARY
or
INTELLIGENCE SUMMARY.
(Erase heading not required.)

Folio 122. 77 Fld Amb.

Place	Date	Hour	Summary of Events and Information	Remarks and references to Appendices
CALONNE SUR LA LYS	30/XI	10 a.m.	A.S.C. & 7th Bn. M.G. Coy at NOUVEAUVILLE & MAISNIL respectively. Evacuation of sick to 39 Stationary Hosp. Minor Sick to "A" Section 1st Corps Rest Station LABEUVRIERE & B Section FOUQUIERES. Officer to Officers hospital BERGUETTE. Scabies to 1st Corps Scabies hospital ALLOUAGNE. Dental cases 5 cases a day to No 6 CCS LILLERS. Injection cases to No 7 General MALASSISE. Eye cases to No 23 CCS LOZINGHEM every Monday. A.D.M.S. sees in/c(?) the Injured every Monday. Medical Stores will be drawn from No 17 Adv. Depot Medical Stores every Tuesday, will be Consolidated return submitted to A.D.M.S. previous Sunday.	

M Leston
Capt. O.C. (?)
af 0/77 Fld Amb

Volume 26   December 1917

77th Field Ambulance

R A M C

War Diary

Medical

Confidential

WAR DIARY
or
INTELLIGENCE SUMMARY.

(Erase heading not required.)

Army Form C. 2118.

Feb 1918. 77th Field Ambulance.

Place	Date	Hour	Summary of Events and Information	Remarks and references to Appendices
CAPELLE-SUR-LA-LYS	1/12/18	8/10 a.m.	Received warning order to prepare to move by road from 1st Corps area to the 3rd Army Area. Movement will commence about noon December 3rd. The Field Ambulance will need motor lorries of J.O.C. 7th Infantry Brigade.	
"	"	11.8 p.m.	Received 7th Infantry Brigade warning order No. L.	
"	"		Received 7th Infantry Brigade order No 298. That the Brigade Group will move to the BERGUENEUSE area tomorrow. This Unit will move to RECLINGHEM-BEAU- METZ Cross Roads 3/4 mile W.S.W. of Lu LAIRES-LISBOURG (Map refce).	
			MAZEBROUKE. S.A. LENS. 11.	
CREPY	3/14/18	7.45 a.m.	Arrived & billetted at CREPY.	
"	"	10 p.m.	Recd 7th Infantry Brigade warning order that the Brigade Group will return to HAVRANS tomorrow. Brigade order 3rd.	
"	5/12/18	12 noon	Recd 7th Infantry Brigade order No 299. This Unit will entrain at MARRANS at 3.8 p.m. Detrain No 7 & detrain at MIRAUMONT. H.A.Ridley Lieut Cuscar.	

Army Form C. 2118.

WAR DIARY
or
INTELLIGENCE SUMMARY.
(Erase heading not required.)

Sept 1914.   77th Field Ambulance

Place	Date	Hour	Summary of Events and Information	Remarks and references to Appendices
COURCELLES-LES-CAMPS	5/9/17	7:45am	Detrained at MIRAUMONT & proceeded by route march to COURCELLES-LES-COMPS. Assigned 7th Infantry Brigade & moving orders to be prepared to move at short notice.	
"	"	12 noon	Received 7th Infantry Brigade order No. 500. The Brigade group will march to BARASTRE. Wire laying. This unit will march at 3 pm to BARASTRE via BIHUCOURT — GRAND — BIEFVILLERS — BAPAUME — BARCOURT — HAPLINCOURT.	
BARASTRE	"	8:45pm	Arrived in camp at BARASTRE (map reference LENS 11.)	
"	8/9/17	9:45am	Received moving order from 7th Infantry Brigade to be prepared to move in Corps Reserve Locations HAVRINCOURT WOOD.	
"	9/9/17	12 noon	Received 7th Infantry Brigade I.B.S. 764/295. Until the Brigade will be prepared to attach to the Brigade of 3rd Division in support. Expect no further instruction from A.D.M.S. To notifying Brigade Surgeon in the meantime. No movement to take place unless until we receive the enemy.	

A.D.S.S./Forms/C.2118.

Army Form C. 2118.

WAR DIARY
or
INTELLIGENCE SUMMARY.
(Erase heading not required.)

Army Form C. 2118. 77th Field Ambulance

Place	Date	Hour	Summary of Events and Information	Remarks and references to Appendices
BARASTRE	8/12/17	3 p	Received orders to send one officer and one tent sub-division for duty at S.B. a.z.s. EDGEHILL near ALBERT. Lieut DAVIS, departed with C. section tent sub-division. Received a warning order that 7th Infantry Brigade will take over the line now held by the 9th Infantry Brigade (3rd Division) on the night of December 9/10th under orders of G.O.C. 3rd Division from point D.B. U.8.1 to C.12.a.4.3. This Field Ambulance will move with 7th Infantry Brigade & will be billeted in 3rd Division Area under 3rd Division & arrangements. A.D.M.S. 3rd Division is appointed for the Field Ambulance to whose accommodation of [illeg] 7th or 140th Field Ambulance. FAVREUIL (H.17c.) If necessary 75th Field Ambulance will move from the line to Brigade under present 3rd Division arrangement. Present move to be that of 7th Infantry Brigade, this unit move to FAVREUIL at 6h.a. 9/12/17. Received 3rd Division A.A.M.C.O. 69. This unit will be relieved by 140th Field Ambulance FAVREUIL. (Map sheet 57c) Hostilly Point - at HOME. O.C. 77 & Field Ambulance	

2353 Wt. W3514/7454 700,000 5/15 D D & L A.D.S.S./Form/C. 2118.

Army Form C. 2118.

WAR DIARY
or
INTELLIGENCE SUMMARY.
(Erase heading not required.)

Folio 126. 77th Field Ambulance

Place	Date	Hour	Summary of Events and Information	Remarks and references to Appendices
FAIREVIL	1/12/17	9 a.m.	Arrived & billetted with 142nd Field Ambulance 3rd Division.	
"	"		Received R.A.M.C. order No. 114. That at 8 a.m. on December the 10th the command of the front extending from S.21.d.5.3 to C.12.a.a.5 (S.W.) will pass to O.C. 23rd Division.	
"	"	Noon	To Toll of FAIREVIL allotting sick.	
"	10/12/17	12 noon	Divisional Headquarters moved today to the MONUMENT FAIREVIL (H.S.C.) Received R.A.M.C. order No. 115. That the 142nd Divisional Boundary will be extended Southwards to the following two lines Ref. 65Y, 6.5. N.8.0. Thence along HOBART AVENUE to C.18. a.6.9. This entire frontage will be taken over by 7th Infantry Brigade & will be cleared by 77th Field Ambulance.	

H.B. Kelly Lieut-Colonel
O.C. 77th Field
Ambulance

Army Form C. 2118.

WAR DIARY
or
INTELLIGENCE SUMMARY.

(Erase heading not required.)

Folio 127. 77th Field Ambulance

Instructions regarding War Diaries and Intelligence Summaries are contained in F. S. Regs., Part II. and the Staff Manual respectively. Title pages will be prepared in manuscript.

Place	Date	Hour	Summary of Events and Information	Remarks and references to Appendices
FAVREUIL	14/10/17	12 noon	Received R.A.M.C. order No. 116. This Field Ambulance will take over from 142nd Field Ambulance by 11 a.m. 15th Oct & form Divisional Main Dressing Station. B't Field Ambulance will remain in present billets.	
"	15/10/17	12 noon	Took over the Field Ambulance site at H.Q. FAVREUIL (Sheet 57c) & are going to accommodate 100 patients. Received R.A.M.C. order No. 117. That the 75th Field Ambulance will take over at 5pm with 1st Station BIHUCOURT. Tomorrow & 75th Field Ambulance will take over site with occupied by 77th Field Ambulance H.Q. (FAVREUIL.)	
"	16/10/17		Received in accordance to R.A.M.C. order No. 117. The 75th Field Ambulance will move to SAPIGNIES. This Field Ambulance has established a collecting post for Walk sick & wounded at VAUX en Tart.	

H.B.Kelly
Kant-Col. RAMC
O.C. 77th Field Ambulance

Army Form C. 2118.

WAR DIARY
or
INTELLIGENCE SUMMARY. Feb 128. 79th Field Ambulance
(Erase heading not required.)

Instructions regarding War Diaries and Intelligence Summaries are contained in F. S. Regs., Part II and the Staff Manual respectively. Title pages will be prepared in manuscript.

Place	Date	Hour	Summary of Events and Information	Remarks and references to Appendices
FAUREUIL	20/10/15	6 p.m.	Received orders that the M.O. at VAUX billeting post might be withdrawn.	
"	21/10/15	6 p.m.	Received R.A.M.C. order No. 116. to detail 1 medical officer & sufficient personnel to attend Loung Station VAUX (C. 26. d. 1. 9.) to meet 3rd Division Evacuate cases from left sector of 23rd Division front. It is now at this post is occupied the billeting post at VAUX I.1. a. 4.a. may be withdrawn.	
"	22/10/15	6 p.m.	One officer 16 A.R. detailed to N.O.S. VAUX (C. 26. d. 1. 9.) This A.D.S. is to operate with 3rd Division & to conform to an after Battalion or being closed by the route Evacuation is by tram to C.C.S.	
"	23/10/15	6 p.m.	Nothing to record for past 10 days.	

H. O. Kelly Lieut-Colonel
O.C. 79 Field Ambulance

25/

14/2/96

COMMITTEE FOR THE
MEDICAL HISTORY OF THE WAR
Date —4 MAR. 1918

No. 77 + a.

Jan. 1918

CONFIDENTIAL.

JANUARY, 1918.

WAR DIARY
MEDICAL.

77th Field Ambulance, R.A.M.C.

VOLUME

Army Form C. 2118.

WAR DIARY
or
INTELLIGENCE SUMMARY. Form 129. 77th Field Ambulance
(Erase heading not required.)

Instructions regarding War Diaries and Intelligence Summaries are contained in F. S. Regs., Part II. and the Staff Manual respectively. Title pages will be prepared in manuscript.

Place	Date	Hour	Summary of Events and Information	Remarks and references to Appendices
S.T.C. FAVREUIL	1/1/18	6 p.m.	Capt. F. LESCHER. R.A.M.C. returned from leave last night.	
"	4/1/18	10 p.m.	Capt. BOYCE. R.A.M.C. returned from leave.	
"	5/1/18		Capt. BOYCE R.A.M.C. to 3rd Worcestershire for temporary duty.	
"	7/1/18	3 p.m.	Capt. BOYCE. R.A.M.C. proceeded in temporary medical charge of 3rd Worcestershire Regt. Visited A.D.S. & all posts in Left Sector	
"	9/1/18		The New Year's Honour Gazette contained the following names of this Unit. Capt. R. BARTLETT awarded M.C. Mentioned in Dispatches:- LIEUT-COL. H. B. KELLY. D.S.O. Capt. N. BOYCE. Sergt-Major J. IVINS.	
"	12/1/18	3 p.m.	Capt. B. BARTLETT. R.A.M.C. proceeded as M.O. in temporary medical charge 13th Cheshires while M.O. is on leave.	
"	13/1/18	6 p.m.	Capt. BOYCE. rejoined.	
"	14/1/18	10 a.m.	Capt. ARNOTT. R.A.M.C. proceeded as M.O. in temporary medical charge 11th Cheshires while M.O. is on leave.	

H. B. Kelly Lieut-Col R.A.M.C.
I.C. 77th Field Ambulance

Army Form C. 2118.

WAR DIARY
or
INTELLIGENCE SUMMARY.
(Erase heading not required.)

Folio 131   77 Field Amb.

Place	Date	Hour	Summary of Events and Information	Remarks and references to Appendices
FAVREUIL	28/11/18		Personnel huts are being built outside huts sites N.W. & S.E. Revetments consisting of earth between frames made of rabbit wire, corrugated iron sheets each hut is built of 1¾ feet broad at top & 2 feet at base. Three are three feet deep. Such is piled round the huts against the corrugated iron, so as to make sort banks. At about 8 o'clock each night, all patients put their mattresses on the floor & sleep on them. In the alarm being given, the guard wake the Officers & men who take refuge in the trenches next to their huts. The orderly Officer Ward masters & orderlies see that patients who are well enough to do so the trenches. The remaining patients keep on the floors. The stables are protected by a wall 3 feet high all round. The stables about 3 feet wide of base. There are traverses 3 feet high 2 ft broad at base running down centre. Between each traverses running at right angles. Six horses are similar traverses.	
"	29/11/18	9 am	Capt. Paul returned from leave.	
"	"	11 pm	Capt Arnott reported from duty with 11th Cheshires	

J.H. Leslie
Capt RAMC

Army Form C. 2118.

WAR DIARY
or
INTELLIGENCE SUMMARY. Feb 1918. 77th Field Ambulance.

(Erase heading not required.)

Instructions regarding War Diaries and Intelligence Summaries are contained in F. S. Regs., Part II. and the Staff Manual respectively. Title pages will be prepared in manuscript.

Place	Date	Hour	Summary of Events and Information	Remarks and references to Appendices
FAIRESVIB	16/1/18	5.30am	Lieut FAIRBANKS. U.S.A. M.O.R.C. who has been attached to this unit for the past few days proceeded to rejoin his unit.	
"	17/1/18		Weather very inclement following on a severe period of frost it is now raining very heavily, rendering all camps & tracks in a bad condition & tending to affect the health of the troops.	
"	19/1/18	10a.m.	Proceeding to relieve A.D.M.S. who is proceeding on leave, handed over command of Ambulance to Captain F.G. LESCHER. R.A.M.C.	
"	21/1/18	10.am a.m.	Capt BEARD proceeded on leave to United Kingdom. Vaulx A.D.S + R.A.Ps.	H.A.Kelly Lieut-Col. RAMC
"	28/1/18		About 15-20 enemy aeroplanes flew over Corps round dropping bombs. nearest to this Camp 200 yds. - no damage done to us - But wound men & other units were killed & wounded. + many horses. We collected some of the wounded men. hyper. we have clear with full moon & days very fine. Our defences against hostile aircraft as any failure. Trenches 5 feet deep 2 ft broad at top & narrowing	J. Leacher Capt RAMC

Army Form C. 2118.

WAR DIARY
or
INTELLIGENCE SUMMARY.
(Erase heading not required.)

Instructions regarding War Diaries and Intelligence Summaries are contained in F. S. Regs., Part II. and the Staff Manual respectively. Title pages will be prepared in manuscript.

Place	Date	Hour	Summary of Events and Information	Remarks and references to Appendices
Veleu 13 2	29/1/-	9.30 pm	Hostile a/c recd by numerous machines. many bombs dropped on area. two first in area	77 Field Ambc
	30/1/	10 am	Camp, the nearest being 20 yds away. No damage done.	
	30/1	9 am	Visited ADS & RAP. A new ADS & RAP are being built at C.16.a.5.4 & C.11.b.1.1.	
	24/1/1	2 pm	Capt Boyce RAMC reported to Corps Musketry School for instr.	
	30/1	6 pm	Capt Bartlett RAMC reported from duty with 13th Cheshires.	
	30-		Hostile aeroplane came over but recd ammense recpn & co. No bombs dropped. Recn nil	
	31/1/18	11 am	Nyt very bright & cold. Moon sent at 10.15 am.	
		10 am	Weather frosty & cold.	

J.K. Leshum
Capt RAMC

Army Form C.2118.

WAR DIARY
or
INTELLIGENCE SUMMARY.
(Erase heading not required.)

Summary of Events and Information

To
Date. 28th Feb'y, 1918.

FOLIOS. 129 - 132.

W A R   D I A R Y .

M E D I C A L .

77th Field Ambulance.

COMMITTEE FOR THE
MEDICAL HISTORY OF THE WAR
Date — 8 APR 1918

Army Form C. 2118.

WAR DIARY
or
INTELLIGENCE SUMMARY.   Fla/133 77th Field Ambulance
(Erase heading not required.)

Place	Date	Hour	Summary of Events and Information	Remarks and references to Appendices
FAIRVEUIL	4/2/18	1 p.m.	Reported at 10 a.m. took over from A/A.D.M.S. & took over the command of this Ambulance	
"	5/2/18	11 "	Nothing to record.	
"	6/2/18		Lieut. DAVIS. U.S.A. M.O.R.C. to take int-division reprinted from 56. C.C.S. D.D.M.S. 4 cases reported to hospital.	
"	7/2/18	8.30 p.m.	Proceeding on 14 days leave. Handing over the command of the Ambulance to Capt F.G. Fenton. R.A.M.C. S.R.	

H.D. Kelly Lieut-Colonel
O.C. 77th Field Ambulance

Army Form C. 2118.

WAR DIARY
or
INTELLIGENCE SUMMARY.
(Erase heading not required.)

Folio 134. 77th Field Amb.

Place	Date	Hour	Summary of Events and Information	Remarks and references to Appendices
FAVREUIL	8/2	10 am	Went round the whole of evacuation routes with M.O.M.S. 2/5th Div & 6 Div.	
"	9/2		Capt BOYCE rejoined from duty at Div Mounting School.	
"			Received R.A.M.C. operation order no 119. as relief by 6th Div.	
"	11/2	2 pm	Adv Party from no 16 F.A. reported at A.D.S.	
"	12/2		Remainder of A.D.S. party from no 16 F. Amb. arrived at VAULX A.D.S. & took over from this field amb. Relief was completed by 4 pm & our party rejoined headquarters that evening.	
"		3 pm	Advanced party & main body of 16 F.A. reported at the Main Dressing Station FAVREUIL.	
"	13/2	10 am	Relief completed - this unit marched independent of Bde to COURCELLE-LE-COMTE, to occupy billets who were used by 1/3 Highland Fld Amb- up to 9a. We have had a holding party on same lines that Brigade has been in the ACHIET area since 10/2 & we have been collecting theirsick. A horse ambulance has been attached to the 112th Bde RFA for temporary duty. A holding party consisting of a corporal R.A.M.C. two privates. occupies the field amb site at G.9.C.8.2.	

H Leckie
Capt RAMC
o/c 77 Fld Amb.

Army Form C. 2118.

WAR DIARY
or
INTELLIGENCE SUMMARY.
(Erase heading not required.)

Folio 135   77th Fld Amb

Instructions regarding War Diaries and Intelligence Summaries are contained in F. S. Regs., Part II. and the Staff Manual respectively. Title pages will be prepared in manuscript.

Place	Date	Hour	Summary of Events and Information	Remarks and references to Appendices
COURCELLE LE COMTE STE A.D.S.O.Q.	14/2	9.0 am	from 7th Feb. This unit has opened up to receive sick of Scabies from 2.5th Div. Accommodation 70 beds. Serious sick & wounded go to 45+49 CCS ACHIET-LE-GRAND. Cases suitable for a rest station to CORPS REST STATION BIHUCOURT. Dental & Eye cases to 75 F Amb on Tuesdays & Thursdays for dental cases. Eye cases on Saturdays. Injections & Self inflicted wounds to 56 CCS EDGE HILL. EAR, NOSE & THROAT cases to 3rd CANADIAN Stationary hospital DOULLENS. Serious sick from Chinese Labour Corp to 56 CCS.	
"	15/2	7 pm	Capt Paul went as MO i/c (temporary) to 1st Bn WILTS.	
"	"	9 pm	CAPT BOYCE departed on 10 days special leave to U.K.	
"	"	10 am	20NS OR detailed for work at 49 CCS, 5 for No 3 CCS.	
"	20/2	9 pm	Capt ARNOTT returned from leave.	
"	"	6 pm	Attended Conference at ADMS's office	
"	21/2	10 am	Recontacted the line held by the 51st Div.	

JH Lescher
Capt RAMC
a/ OC 77 Fld Amb

Army Form C. 2118.

WAR DIARY
or
INTELLIGENCE SUMMARY.
(Erase heading not required.)

Folio 136   77 Fld Amb.

Place	Date	Hour	Summary of Events and Information	Remarks and references to Appendices
COURCELLE	22/2	12 noon	Inspection of hospital site by G.O.C. 25th Div. A nursing party is going to be stationed at the new camp G.9.d.3.2 (57c) to help treat a field ambulance section for 50 sick patients.	
	26/2	6 pm	Attended Conference of ADMS Office. VI the Corps front is to be extended we revealed going south the 7th Bde to occupy the left sector, & the 51st Div a the take part in a trench attack on some part of the corps front. Work is progressing at the new site — G.9.d.3,2. — A sectional hospital for the Corps is going to be built for 250 patients.	
	28h	11.30 am	Inspection of Ambulances by DMS, Third Army.	
	29/2	9 am	Work done here since occupation consists in fitting out this site for accomodation for 70 sick men, patients, making of baths, a disinfector chamber, improvement to huts existing buildings.	

J Fletcher
Capt RAMC
a/c.o 77 Field Am

Army Form C. 2118.

WAR DIARY
or
INTELLIGENCE SUMMARY.
(Erase heading not required.)

Folio 137 77 Fld Amb

Place	Date	Hour	Summary of Events and Information	Remarks and references to Appendices
COURCELLE	24/2	9 am	+ drainage system, wash etc, + starting drilling the new Field Corps Scabies hospital G9 c 8 2, as well as training the Scabies of the division, + the Bde rick training is also taking place	

R Lachun
Capt RAMC
o/c 77 Fld Amb

99th Field Ambulance.

Army Form C. 2118.

WAR DIARY
or
INTELLIGENCE SUMMARY.

(Erase heading not required.)

Confidential

Vol 30

Volume 30.

War Diary
Medical
77th Field Ambulance

March 1918

Date 9-4-18

Army Form C. 2118.

WAR DIARY
or
INTELLIGENCE SUMMARY.
(Erase heading not required.)

Folio 158. 79th Field Ambulance

Instructions regarding War Diaries and Intelligence Summaries are contained in F. S. Regs., Part II. and the Staff Manual respectively. Title pages will be prepared in manuscript.

Place	Date	Hour	Summary of Events and Information	Remarks and references to Appendices
COURCELLE LE-COMTE	2/3/18	8 pm	Returned from leave & took over command of the Field Ambulance	
"	3/3/18	5.30 pm	Attended a conference at A.D.M.S's office	
"	4/3/18	2.30 pm	Attended a lecture at H.Q. of School	
"	5/3/18	2.30 pm	Attended a lecture at H.Q. of Gas School	
"	6/3/18	2.30 pm	Attended a lecture at H.Q. of Gas School. We are at present constructing a light railed Hospital of 250 beds.	
"	7/3/18	10.30 am	Visited the Field Ambulance site at BEUGNY. In the event of active operations this Unit will establish a walking wounded collecting post there.	
"	8/3/18	10 am	Received orders to send 1 Officer & 17 other ranks to the Corps walking wounded station BEUGNY.	
"	10/3/17	10 am	The party arrived at 49 C.C.S. & joined	

H. A. Vickers
Capt. R.A.M.C

Army Form C. 2118.

WAR DIARY
or
INTELLIGENCE SUMMARY.

(Erase heading not required.)

Feb 18. 77th Field Ambulance

Instructions regarding War Diaries and Intelligence Summaries are contained in F. S. Regs., Part II. and the Staff Manual respectively. Title pages will be prepared in manuscript.

Place	Date	Hour	Summary of Events and Information	Remarks and references to Appendices
BUCHANAN CAMP. ACHIET-LE-GRAND.	12/3/16	10.45 a.m.	Moved from COURCELLES to BUCHANAN CAMP with a view to not being on a main road. Established Hospital & being near our Brigade group in the event of a move.	
"	13/3/16	10 a.m.	Divided BEUGNY where my tents sub-divided & erecting a camp. Nothing worth of note. Took my Senior N.C.O.'s round the different out-of sight spots. Visited BEUGNY.	
"	14/3/16	10 a.m.	Nothing to record. We are encamped according orders & in the meantime pushing on the work of finishing the Light Divisible Hospital & fitting up a working wounded Capt. Cluted at BEUGNY.	
"	19/3/16	12 noon		
"	19/3/16	6 p.m.	Received orders that the 77th Division will relieve the 6th Division in the Line on 21/3/16. This Field Ambulance will take over from the 13th Field Ambulance right of. the evacuation of Casualties from the right & centre Brigades viz 14 & 15. At LAS=NICOURT and the main tramway FAYREUIL from 12th Field Ambulance, refills to be completed by 6 p.m. 21/3/16. H.W. Kelly Lieut-Colonel O.C. 77th Field Ambulance	

2353 Wt. W2514/1454 700,000 5/15 B.D. & L. A.D.S.S./Forms/C. 2118.

WAR DIARY
or
INTELLIGENCE SUMMARY.
(Erase heading not required.)

Army Form C. 2118.

Folio 142. 77 Div. Amb.

Place	Date	Hour	Summary of Events and Information	Remarks and references to Appendices
On the March	21/3/18	2.30pm	Started to march to BEUGNY. On the march up I learned that there had already been observed & the whole Corps MDS for shelter & walking cases had been withdrawn behind FREMICOURT. At LOCK CAMP on the BAPAUME–CAMBRAI Road	
At LOCK CAMP	21/3/18	5.30pm	I then took over administration of C.M.W. & Sn. Evacuation was by them to Retirement centre BAPAUME, & thence by 149 M.A.C. Cars to C.C.S. There was to be a continuous service of Motor Ambns., each of 4 trucks. At this moment the train was working fairly speedily. I learnt that 74 Inf Bde. were holding the MORCHIES Rd line & were being cleared by 75th F.Amb. who had opened an ADS at BEUGNY & so the 7th Inf Bde. manned the CORPS LINE and were between FREMICOURT & BEUGNY. It was evident the casualties that the 75th F.Amb. cleared out looks after two Bdes. Reporting this to ADMS I received orders to evacuate the casualties of our own Bde. ie 7th Bde. I accordingly got into touch with Bde. Hdqrs; explored the battn. posns. each ma in his R.A.P.	

H. Leslie Major R.A.M.C. O.C. 77th F.A.

Army Form C. 2118.

WAR DIARY
or
INTELLIGENCE SUMMARY.

(Erase heading not required.)

Folio 140. 77th Field Ambulance

Instructions regarding War Diaries and Intelligence Summaries are contained in F.S. Regs., Part II. and the Staff Manual respectively. Title pages will be prepared in manuscript.

Place	Date	Hour	Summary of Events and Information	Remarks and references to Appendices
BUCHANAN CAMP. ACHIET-LE-GRAND	20/3/18	9.30 a.m.	An advance party of 1 Officer & 48 O.R.'s proceeded to take over line from 18th Field Ambulance with ADS equipment, & 40 abin. cart.	
"	21/3/18	4:30 am	Reg. Men. LENS.11. Intense enemy bombardment commenced; many shells falling in neighbourhood of our Camp & ACHIET-LE-GRAND. One man of our unit was killed.	
"	"	9 am	Orders that w.hdy of 6th Div by 25th was cancelled were received, & that IV Corps Medical Defence Scheme was to come into operation. So 2 Officers & 87 O.R. were sent for duty to 45 CCS	
"	"	2 pm	[to prepare to attempting...] Disposition of the Unit was as follows:—	
			1 Officer + 48 O.R at LAGNICOURT ADS	
			1 " + 17 O.R at BEUGNY	
			2 " + 87 O.R at 45 CCS	
			1 " 1 O.R at Div Signal School	
			1 " — Short of establishment	
			2 " " On leave	
			G.D " with transport & HdqtS at ACHIET-LE-GRAND	

M Beghin
Major RAMC
for O/C 77 F Amb.

Army Form C. 2118.

WAR DIARY
or
INTELLIGENCE SUMMARY.
(Erase heading not required.)

Folio 141   77 Field Amb.

Place	Date	Hour	Summary of Events and Information	Remarks and references to Appendices
BUCHANAN CAMP.	21/3/18		MO at COUIN with field amb. was advised to rejoin his Unit at once	Instructions to 2nd/1st & 3rd/1st DR.'s to
ACHIET LE GRAND		11 am	A message by motor cyclist was sent to A98 LAGNICOURT instructing M.O. + 4 BR.'s to	BEUGNY
			with cars + to report to O.C. C.W.W.D.S. (corps walking wounded dressing station) BEUGNY	
			This message was delivered about 12.30 pm under considerable difficulties by A/Sgt	
			BLECHMERE who had to pass through a considerable zone of shelling & machine gun	
			fire. When he left the A93, the enemy were in the valley on the left of the seventeen	
			road & were enfilading the roads with machine gun fire. A reply stated that as the	
			Bearers of the AB 6th Div (19 F. Ambs) had not been reinforced & that he had more wounded	
			than he could deal with, he would carry out the order as soon as he considered	
			circumstances justified him.	
	"	11 am	Word received that Capt. R.G. McELVEY MC RAMC OC C.W.W.D.S. had been	
			killed in action near BEUGNY.	
	"	2 pm	Orders attempt for this Unit to take over the C.W.W.D.S. BEUGNY	H. Leschen Major RAMC OC 77 F Amb.

2353 Wt. W2514/1454 700,000 5/15 D.D. & L. A.D.S.S./Forms/C. 2118.

Army Form C. 2118.

WAR DIARY
or
INTELLIGENCE SUMMARY.
(Erase heading not required.)

Folio 143. 77 Field Amb.

Place	Date	Hour	Summary of Events and Information	Remarks and references to Appendices
N° LOCH CAMP	20/3/18		and sent Squads of Bearers to be attached to each of regimental M.O.	
		7.0 pm	M.O.s of Divisional R.E.s & of Signal School joined this unit for duty	
			Some shelling round the camp	
	21	midnight	Many wounded of 5th of 25th & 19th have come in, the wounded F.A. to be sent to the boys	
			Stretcher cases from the CORPS.	
			All my personnel from the ADS at LAGNICOURT have rejoined with the exception of 1 officer (found to be a prisoner) & 4 OR. — CAPT ARNOTT RAMC	
			At 3.0 they are known to be somewhat demoralised they had all worked strenuously after Dr APS bringing in severely wounded men, when the enemy were within a few hundred yards from the ADS	
	22/3/18	6 am	Since 8.0 pm yesterday 7 PB cases wounded have been cleared by us	
			about 8 0 pm 21/3/18	
	11	11 am	Shelling pretty continuous near Camp. Visited M.O.s of 7th Bde. Helped the 1/2 Highland F.Amb. evacuate some of their stretcher cases, as they were getting congested.	

H. H. Leslie Major R.A.M.C.
O.C. 77 F.Amb.

Army Form C. 2118.

WAR DIARY
or
INTELLIGENCE SUMMARY.
(Erase heading not required.)

Iphr 14 f 77th Fiel Amb

Place	Date	Hour	Summary of Events and Information	Remarks and references to Appendices
N° LOCH CAMP	28/3/18		Cases awaiting evacuation. M.A.C. not working well. Been satisfactory. W. and Mickey use of empty returning lorries. Had it not been for these lorries the accumulation on the Turn would be monstrous. I sent 2 drunken motor ambulances to help O.C. 75 F.Amb with helpful and accumulation at his A.D.S. BEURRY. The 1/2 Highland Field Amb received orders to proceed to GREVILLERS. I reported to A.D.M.S. about the amb. clearing out Drunkets inasmuch as unable to cope with the shelter cases of other divisions, as well of those of the 7th Bde, to the	
"	"	4 pm	C.W.W. & St. they left an officer & a burying party. Shells now commenced to fall in close proximity to the Camp.	
"	"	5 pm	I located all remaining stretcher cases on a tramway came up about 5-6 pm & shifted my position to the opposite side of the road, & opened up my M.D.S. in the Church Army hut. I sent all the transport less two horse ambulances 1 A.P.S. limber 1 cooks cart & water cart & riding horses to join 7th Bde transport near GREVILLERS	

H. Lester Major R.A.M.C. ofc 77 F.Amb.

Army Form C. 2118.

WAR DIARY
or
INTELLIGENCE SUMMARY.
(Erase heading not required.)

Folio 145. 77 Fuld Amb

Place	Date	Hour	Summary of Events and Information	Remarks and references to Appendices
McLoch CAMP.	22/3		Under orders of the Quarter master, with orders to conform with movement of Bde Transport - keeping rail informed. A regular stream of wounded & ill chronias.	
"	23/3	6 am	We held the Chinese Army Post during the night of 22-23rd March, our only means of evacuation being our own Cars to the dressing Station at GREVILLERS from MA Car. Had two prisoners from us. We just kept ourselves clear of wounded	
"	"	10 am	We were joined by 75th F Amb who retitled from BEUGNY as the Anzacs Amb have retired; later the ambulance with them behind BAPAUME	
"	"	2 pm	As the shelling of the site began to be persistent, with HE gas & shrapnel, I shifted my ADS about 300 yds down the BAPAUME - CAMBRAI road & carried on & continued evacuating at this site of road. We attended the wounded lad until dark. The MO 1/c 121 MGC. Capt HUGHES DSO was wounded sheltering Herbeson Major RAMC 1/c 75 F Amb 4 [...]	

Army Form C. 2118.

WAR DIARY
or
INTELLIGENCE SUMMARY.
(Erase heading not required.)

Folio 14 of 77 Field Amb.

Place	Date	Hour	Summary of Events and Information	Remarks and references to Appendices
M.L.O.H. CAMP	23/IX		the afternoon & he was without any 348' BARTLETT 5 AM C D this morn We have practically ceased to be a C.W.W.D.St. but experience to us own brigade, as & also from our position on the main road, Casn from 6th & 7th R.W.K. & 11th Army come to us. We attempt to keep our old position near W.L.H. CAMP as that was the quietest spot	
"	"	7 pm	& continue in carrying stores through the night there was heavy shelling but we got no direct hit.	
			The horse 4/MAC ceased to work for us & we were entirely dependent on our 4 Lorrigan Cars & one Ford. One R.A.P. chest of the 4th Staffs was evacuated by Cw. An urgent message was sent to ADMS about asking for MAC Cars as a [illegible] the military Amb being endangered	
		8 pm	Bombed by Hostile Air Craft resulting in 2 SR killed & 4 R.w.unded 12 animals killed & one Sand Cart, one limber & two motor Cars destroyed with some equipment.	

H.Cotter Major RAMC for OC 77 Fd Amb

Army Form C. 2118.

WAR DIARY
or
INTELLIGENCE SUMMARY.
(Erase heading not required.)

Instructions regarding War Diaries and Intelligence Summaries are contained in F. S. Regs., Part II. and the Staff Manual respectively. Title pages will be prepared in manuscript.

Folio 147   77 Field Amb

Place	Date	Hour	Summary of Events and Information	Remarks and references to Appendices
In LOCH CAMP	23/3/18		Evacuation from RAPs of 7th Bde Units and in to support amb nearly continuous. Relays of bearers are established down to turn the B./G.M. Stretchers to the left side of N.H.S. on side. G. 4th S. 4th south their RAPs on the main road, are evacuated direct by car.	
"	24/3/18	9am	Certain amount of shelling during the night. AMAS visited me & ordered me to return to a previously selected place — the BRICKFIELDS about ½ a mile west of BAPAUME on the BAPAUME – CAMBRAI Road. I left a motor amb & so sitting units out near LOCH CAMP & moved back	
BRICKFIELDS		10am	Opened up ADS. Shortly afterwards ADMS informed me to prepare in the absence of the Corr statement of the LOCH CAMP BRICKFIELDS. reported that up to approximately 10 am there were on a convoy of the heavy shell fire. Our squads from the RAPs seeing that it was impossible to approach the GBt comm down to Cheshire carried our cases to A.O. see Bearers from WILTS + 10th CHESHIRES were bringing down cases. No men	

Major Bruchen M.Jr RAMC JA O.G. 77 Fld Amb

WAR DIARY or INTELLIGENCE SUMMARY

Army Form C. 2118.

(Erase heading not required.)

feb 1/18 77 Field Amb.

Place	Date	Hour	Summary of Events and Information	Remarks and references to Appendices
BRICKFIELDS	24/3		came upon 4th S Staffs who were in reserve. the 7th Bn were holding the front line some 1500 yds from the North of BAPAUME-CAMBRAI road to the west of FREMICOURT.	
"	"	12 Noon	Four M.A.C. cars appeared on duty with us for four hours. Our stretcher RAPs by the Railway Embankment were very severely shelled during the morning, many casualties were occurring in the vicinity of around 2500 so that the sending away of the RAPs to return to RAPs was frequently an impossibility, but in trying in those cases, cars were sent to fly up between the road frequent from RAPs being so buried all around, into certain hospital roads/lines made it far too hot to MDS, every shelter case that could be got away was made to do so.	
"	"	3.30 pm	W. halted RAPs reached Headquarters @ 15th CHESHIRES, where returning @ 7th Bn were ordered to retire two squads were left with M.O. of their Battalion See	

J.P Jackson
Major RAMC
¼ O.C. 77 Field Amb.

Army Form C. 2118.

WAR DIARY
or
INTELLIGENCE SUMMARY.
(Erase heading not required.)

Instructions regarding War Diaries and Intelligence Summaries are contained in F.S. Regs., Part II. and the Staff Manual respectively. Title pages will be prepared in manuscript.

folio 14.9   77 Field Ambt.

Place	Date	Hour	Summary of Events and Information	Remarks and references to Appendices
BRICK FIELDS	24/8		The bearers from the relay post were collected & all about such each regiment Emerging a stretcher case. Some wounded were brought in improvised stretchers to thickbourne & on wheelbarrows.	
"	"	4.0 pm	Enemy opened a heavy burst of H.E. shells & M.G. fire. On arrival at H.Q.S. I found orders from A.D.M.S. Kiveton Ikhnid BAPAUME. We loaded 50 cases on our own & the A.D.S. the case packing at GREVILLERS abolition & cases have to be sent to DOULLENS	
"	"	6.0 pm	marched to BIHUCOURT thro BAPAUME roll was being heavily shelled, & I pushed up transport on the way & carried them on whilst stretchers & transport. En route we were attacked by four enemy aeroplanes who flew low & machined gunned us. No casualties	
"	"		No stretcher cases were left in the A.D.S. & when we left we were leaving prepared in front of a front line system	
"	"	8.30 pm	7 th Abs Bergt arrived to this village. Orders received that both Brigade Advc topping still...	

W. Lothian
Major R.A.M.C.
for O.C. 77 F.F. Amb

Army Form C. 2118.

WAR DIARY
or
INTELLIGENCE SUMMARY.
(Erase heading not required.)

folio 150. 77 Field Amb.

Instructions regarding War Diaries and Intelligence Summaries are contained in F. S. Regs., Part II. and the Staff Manual respectively. Title pages will be prepared in manuscript.

Place	Date	Hour	Summary of Events and Information	Remarks and references to Appendices
BUCQUOY	25/3	3·0 am	Ordered to join transport lines. 70 Bde Wagons Gen Ros. Brigade is out of reinforcement in digging trenches on the high ground just west of LOG EAST WOOD from ABLAINSEVELLE to A.H.157. PETIT GRAND Brash complete south from Serre wounded both walking & stretcher cases, on little difficulty from the line & portion of Clearing Station & CCS northern division.	
"	"	8 am	In touch with A.D.M.S. Bde transport moved to a station to a point between HÉBUTERNE & SAILLY-AU-BOIS. Oc 2 Officers & 4 Motor Ambulances remained with Brigade.	
"	"	6 pm	Brigade retired during day & are reported transport.	
"	"	7 pm	Received orders that Bde H.Qrs took at BUCQUOY. One M.O. 4 men & motor ambulance opened an A.D.S. near them. Room empty with troops going east — from occupied men. transport is committed very slow & difficult as we have now only two ambulance cars & the position of CCS are not certain & are far off & every ambulance on the road so can take many hours.	

Army Form C. 2118.

WAR DIARY
or
INTELLIGENCE SUMMARY.
(Erase heading not required.)

Instructions regarding War Diaries and Intelligence Summaries are contained in F. S. Regs., Part II. and the Staff Manual respectively. Title pages will be prepared in manuscript.

Page 151

Place	Date	Hour	Summary of Events and Information	Remarks and references to Appendices
HEBERTUNE	24/3	6.0 pm	Two met Sundions & one that car left in north wounded at 4 pm on 24/3/16 again in trying they had to retreat from BAPAUME to FREVIZUS passing thro' 3 others	
	25/3/16			
	26/3	1.30 am	Bde Transport ordered to proceed to BIENVILLERS. HQuys moved with it.	
			Arrived 6.am. O visited ADS BUCQUOY, the B 7 Bde was moving to GOMMECOURT.	
		9 am	ADS withdrawn	
BIENVILLERS	"		at BIENVILLERS	
	"	1 pm	Transport ordered to proceed to ST AMAND HQuys & some sections + crew proceeded	
	"		Bde HQrs has moved to FONQUEVILLERS. the Z/S Div Amm orders to defend the GOMMECOURT Ridge. troops are striking up positions at 6.0 am	
	"	6.0 pm	Got in touch with RAPs of 7th Bde. attached hereon is each MO + exterior arr. H Leslie Hugh RAMC ½ DC 77 F Amb

2353 Wt. W3544/1454 700,000 5/15 D. D. & L. A.D.S.S./Forms/C. 2118.

Army Form C. 2118.

WAR DIARY
or
INTELLIGENCE SUMMARY.

(Erase heading not required.)

Army Form C. 2118.

7th Div 1/2 77 Field Amb

Place	Date	Hour	Summary of Events and Information	Remarks and references to Appendices
BIENVILLERS	26/3	6 AM	evacuation scheme the blows and lying down to HENNESCHAMPS were to one country ambt has been established. From they fatter patients sent be carried to an & ADS at	
			BIENVILLARS.	
		9 A.M	About wait trans at BIENVILLERS, necessary harness equipment, rations & every thing was ready to pack up.	
	27/3	12.30 am	Orders received from ADMS that Division Div artillery was to concentrate at SOUIN & brigades were to start without being relieved.	
	"	1.30 am	Orders received from Brigade that we were to march at once leaving transport moving later with Brigade Transport.	
	"	2.45 am	Started with Bearer & tent Sub div. At DS limber & water cart arriving at COIGNEUX	
		6 am		
COIGNEUX	"	9 am	Visited by ADMS. Wanted to proceed to billets in CANAPLES	

H Becher
Major RAMC 40C 77 F Amb

Army Form C. 2118.

WAR DIARY
or
INTELLIGENCE SUMMARY.
(Erase heading not required.)

No. 153 77 Field Amb.

Place	Date	Hour	Summary of Events and Information	Remarks and references to Appendices
COIGNEUX	27/3/18	12 noon	Orders received from 7th Bde that we were to march forward to Brigade at CANAPLES	
		2 pm	Earlier than been transport returned to pick up stragglers, only about 25 were brought	
		9 pm	Arrived at PUCHVILLERS - spent the remainder of the night	
PUCHVILLERS	28/3	9 am	Resumed march	
CANAPLES		12.30 pm	Arrived & now billeted at CANAPLES. Men & mules were entrained	
			Urgent indents for Army hundred & fifteen requirement. 40 men were put on	
"	29/3		Rested. All through their operation the weather has been fine though there was a total	
			absence of blankets.	
"	30/3		Received orders to entrain at DOULLENS on 31st - Expeditionary to commence 5 am	
"	31/3	midnight	Whole unit moved off to DOULLENS, arriving there at 5 am.	

H. Johnston
Major RAMC O.C. 77 Fld Amb.

Army Form C. 2118.

WAR DIARY
or
INTELLIGENCE SUMMARY.

(Erase heading not required.)

From 15th 77th Fd Amb

Place	Date	Hour	Summary of Events and Information	Remarks and references to Appendices
DOULLENS	13/3	12 noon	Entraining started at the Train	
		4 pm	Train moved off April 4 pm	
	"	12 midnight	Capts SWIFT & MACKMO R.C. U.S.A. joined for duty from No 4 General Hosp LONDON for duty	
Rest area 5A	"	12 midnight	Arrival at GOD.	
HAZEBROUCK			Received orders to proceed to Eual Amb at RAVELSBURG. This unit is to take over the evacuation of casualties from the line between DU V 15 & L/5 ready to be complete by 6 pm April 2nd.	

H. Jenkins
Major R.A.M.C.
for O.C. 77 F Amb

Army Form C. 2118.

WAR DIARY
or
INTELLIGENCE SUMMARY.
(Erase heading not required.)

Folio 155 77 Fld Amb

Place	Date	Hour	Summary of Events and Information	Remarks and references to Appendices
RAVELSBURG	31/3		Casualties suffered by the unit since 21/3/18 when active operations commenced.	
			Officers killed Capt McELREY R.G. RAMC	
			" missing Capt ARNOTT A RAMC	
			O.R. 3 killed	
			3 died of wounds	
			5 Wounded	
			1 missing	
			Horses 13 killed	
			1 G.S. wagon, 1 Mess cart-limber, & 2 water carts were destroyed or by hostile wheel gun together with some stores.	
			About 2,000 casualties passed through our hands & were evacuated since 21/3/18.	
				W Kershaw Major RAMC Lt Col 77 F Amb

April 1918

160/2902-

Volume 31

Folios 156 - 174.

CONFIDENTIAL.

WAR DIARY

MEDICAL

77th Field Ambulance.

COMMITTEE FOR THE
MEDICAL HISTORY
Date -6 JUN.1918

Army Form C. 2118.

WAR DIARY
or
INTELLIGENCE SUMMARY.
(Erase heading not required.)

Folio 15677 Field Amb.

Instructions regarding War Diaries and Intelligence Summaries are contained in F. S. Regs., Part II. and the Staff Manual respectively. Title pages will be prepared in manuscript.

Place	Date	Hour	Summary of Events and Information	Remarks and references to Appendices
RAVELSBURG CAMP Sheet 28 S.15 central	1/4/14	11 am	Field Amb, 2nd Ordered to take over ADSs & Posts from 6th Australian Division — The 20th Div is taking over the line from the Douve to the Lys river.	
"		6 pm	Relay complete — There is an ADS at UNDERHILL FM Sheet 28 T.18.d.3.3. Staff 2 officers & 14 nurses stationed with two cars equipment & 14 men. Motor cars from Ravelsberg. They have 2 institutions in the lines & one on escape. There are ADS is on the sector with the 7th Bde Posts. RAP In connection with the left AMB at about V.9.6.7.2. there are some relay posts thereby a squad of bearers at HYDE PARK CORNER V.19.3.5.9. DONNINGTON HALL, U.83.C.9.15.+ DOUVE RELAY about U.9.3.a.5.3 Evacuation from RAP down through church walk thence to MESSINES–PLOEGSTEERT Road & thence to ADS. On the right of the left sector RAP no.at about V.15.b.7.5 with a relay just at DEAD HORSE CORNER V.21.a.2.9. Evacuation by duck board push to Post 4 thence on to ADS on the right sector held by 75th Bn, the HQ is at the BREWERY Shut 36.d.5.5. The left half of the sector has an RAP at BURNT OUT FARM Sheet 20 U.28.10.2.3 with a relay post at the PILL BOX Evacuation by hand carriage down the LE GHEER W.… to relay post & thence …	

WAR DIARY
or
INTELLIGENCE SUMMARY.
(Erase heading not required.)

Army Form C. 2118.

folio 157 77 Fld Amb

Place	Date	Hour	Summary of Events and Information	Remarks and references to Appendices
RAVELSBURG CAMP Sheet 28 S15 Central	1/4/18		R.A.P. for right Sub sector is at SURRY FM, 1 Squad Bearers in Watered Shew - Cases evacuated to MOTOR CAR CORNER Sheet 36 C 8, C 7.0. & thence to M.D.S. by car. On DESPIERRE FM Sheet 36 C 2 d 6.5, where 17th EAM Heads are Mess in Corrugated Squad iron Huts. At ADS there are 2 officers post by a tent Subdivision + one Car. Evacuation from ADS by car to 76 MDS. PONT D'ACHILLES Sheet 36 B 8.5.10.	
ROMILLY CAMP Sheet 28 T 27 3 C.S.D.	5/4/18		Helph & unit moved to ROMILLY CAMP Sheet 28, T 27.3 C.S.D.	
"	"		Lt BAIN RAMC taken on our strength; strength 9 20 men joined us - Good flying men	
"			75 F Amb relieved us on left sector & took over evacuation to 7th Bde	
"			We are affiliated to 75th Inf Bde.	
"	6/4		According to 25th Div Med Defence scheme - in case of a retirement, MDS will eventually fall back on PONT D'ACHILLES with Car loading post at ROMARIN - SAHAZEBROUCK	
"	9/4		The 2nd S Lancs holds left front of 74th sector - 8th Borders left of D at sector. 11th Cheshires are in reserve.	

A.D.S.S./Forms/C.2118.

WAR DIARY
or
INTELLIGENCE SUMMARY
(Erase heading not required.)

Folio 158 77th Field Amb.

Army Form C. 2118.

Place	Date	Hour	Summary of Events and Information	Remarks and references to Appendices
ROMILLY Camp. Sheet 36 T.27.c.5.d.	9/4	3 pm	Much artillery fire on our the right of Le BIZET. Received orders to send a section as an advance party, to take over PONT d'ACHILLE M.D.S. in care 76th F.A. and ordered to proceed with 74th Inf. Bde.	
"	10/4		Heavy firing on our right & front during night & early morning. The enemy attacked & broke passed his way through on parts of our front & on our left flank.	
"	"	9.30 am	Ordered to take over site at PONT d'ACHELLES & move my headquarters there. To open an ambulance on M.D.S. Sheet 36.	
"	"	9 am	O.C. A.D.S. - the BREWERY, first C.1, d.4,5 had retired owing to the heavy shell fire & MOTOR CAR CORNER post advanced a little longer. d.8.7 The line was forced back & the infantry are retiring.	
PONT d'ACHELLES Sheet 36 B.8. v.1.5.	"	11 am	Located Battalion Hdqtrs of 7 5th Bn. at 4 near REGINA Fm Sheet 28 T.29 n Brigade Hdqts at BRUNE-GAYE B.10. 6-2.7 Sheet 36 Line held by Brigade is reported to extent from behind Le BIZET along the PLOEGSTEET road, to PLOEGSTEET. The M.O.s 6 th Border (Capt Stowell) ca missing + — of 11th CHESHIRES (Capt. OLIVER) wounded	

Army Form C: 2118.

WAR DIARY
or
INTELLIGENCE SUMMARY.
(Erase heading not required.)

4th 154. 77 Field Amb.

Instructions regarding War Diaries and Intelligence Summaries are contained in F. S. Regs., Part II. and the Staff Manual respectively. Title pages will be prepared in manuscript.

Place	Date	Hour	Summary of Events and Information	Remarks and references to Appendices
PONT d'ACHELLES	10/4	11.30 am	Capt CLARKE M.O. 1/8 2nd S Lancs is looking after all work of the brigade. The 18th S.W.Bn R.O.O & F.E.R.S RE's an application to the brigade that as urgently there MO are with them. Most of our bearers who were originally attached to MO's are somewhat or missing. ADS antiseptum consisting of Capt Boys & Lr Bart with 20 bearers + 2 nun have been established at ROMARIN, & Cases evacuated from there to the M.D.S. PONT d'ACHELLES from there to M.A.C. car	
Shut 36 B.9,6,1,5.			Take them to 76th Feld Amb OUTERSTEENE. – A Car Car to finish up to the R.A.P. Sheet 28 T29.d.8.7" Numerous Casualties are being brought in from 7,8,9,79th Bde, + from 52 nd Dvn in the two bringing to an ADS bearer Transport has been chiveted up and horse wagons ... Cooks lumber, water cart & horse ambulance, & the horse w.t of the transport from the strain	
		1.30 pm	the team with the main atm with both the unit, the latter under charge of the Divisional transp. joined the brigade transport at TROIS ROIS. MO's of Borders + RE informed of heinenhof ADS.	

Army Form C. 2118.

WAR DIARY
or
INTELLIGENCE SUMMARY.
(Erase heading not required.)

77 Field Amb & Folio 160

Place	Date	Hour	Summary of Events and Information	Remarks and references to Appendices
PONT d'ACHELLES	10/4		Casualties have been coming in all the afternoon, & we hear the use of horse ambulance	
			as MAC cars some cars are taken direct to CCSs at GODEWAERSVELDE & REMY SIDING	
			during afternoon there have been rumours of enemy in direction of STEENWERCK	
	11	4.0 pm	The firing has got nearer & bullets are coming on the road & into the camp. ADMS notified of	
			our intention to return to ROMILLY CAMP. We cleared all our patients, packed up	
	11	4.45 pm	marched out, Capt Boyce being notified to remain in Charge. On the march, orders from	
			ADMSs received by us, to open up our own MDS at WESTHOF camp, Sheet 28. T/19.b.4.4.	
			Lt Bain appointed MOi/c 11th CHESHIRES ADS	
WESTHOF Camp. Sheet 28 T19.b.4.4.	11	6.00 pm	Arrived. Bivouac notified, Vaccine line how at ROMARIN, has been received, shelters	
			Bivouac how established at CANTEEN CORNER, 4128 T 27 d 1.0 work smaller hour	
			at ROMARIN. Cars can go still to RA?	
			Bell Helps is at TROIS ROIS	

Army Form C. 2118.

WAR DIARY
or
INTELLIGENCE SUMMARY.
(Erase heading not required.)

Folio /5/ 77 Field Amb.

Instructions regarding War Diaries and Intelligence Summaries are contained in F.S. Regs., Part II. and the Staff Manual respectively. Title pages will be prepared in manuscript.

Place	Date	Hour	Summary of Events and Information	Remarks and references to Appendices
WESTHOF	10/4		R A P is still at same location, & cases can get to there.	
		9.0 pm	Received news that 5 Lancs had about 30 shell & gas & many walking & sitting cases + extra shifts became necessary using available Cars & horse drawn Amb & R A P & horse Ambulances to the Besin post.	
			No M A C Cars have turned up since about 4.0 pm A.P.M.S. helped as the movement on accumulating here	
	11/4	11.30 pm	Wounded are being cleared from line satisfactorily, but more have been re-cured.	
	"		Visited by D.A.D.M.S. 1 Am. & D.A.D.M.S. Corps 3.30 am	
	"	3.30 am	Line cleared.	

H.P. Kelly Lieut-Colonel

Army Form C. 2118.

WAR DIARY
or
INTELLIGENCE SUMMARY.
(Erase heading not required.)

Folio 162. 77 Field Amb.

Place	Date	Hour	Summary of Events and Information	Remarks and references to Appendices
WESTHOF	11/4/18	6.30 am	OC Bearer division reports that he is staying back his ADS with a Post a little forward.	T26;C;2. T26,C,2; Sheet 28.
"	"	8.30 am	Received orders to reconnoitre for an Main Dressing Stn between BERTHEN + BOESCHEPE	
"	"	"	Visited area + found that some surrounds had been brought in to Coolers Fm Sheet 28, B11; d.5, 6 front ADS west of ROMARIN. Bearers	
"	"	11 am	German attack on our front; bn has Post	
			fell back to WESTHOF, with one in conjunction with a post RAP formed by MO's	
			at KORTEPYP. KORTEPYP. T 20; d, 5,2. Sheet 28. Motor carriage to NEUVE EGLISE Rel 4 thence by motor	
			Numerous casualties coming in.	
"	"	4 pm	Received orders for main body to proceed to BERTHEN + open a MDS there.	
"	"	5.15	Started march. 36 bearers with Major Bartlett + Capt MACK MO's left behind at ADS	
			WESTHOF; with orders to evacuate casualties to 75 Fd Amb at HAEGEDOORNE	

M Kelly Lieut Colonel

Army Form C. 2118.

WAR DIARY
or
INTELLIGENCE SUMMARY.
(Erase heading not required.)

Vol.3/63. 77 Field Amb.

Place	Date	Hour	Summary of Events and Information	Remarks and references to Appendices
			until an own open MP.	
BERTHEN	11/4/18	8.30	B 75th Bde Adupt moved to WATERLOO CAMP. Sheet 28 S24 b 6.9. Arrived MDS opened up in a circus hut.	
Sheet 5A HAZEBROUCK		11 am	Cases being received from 76 F Amb. (who are evacuating OUTERSTEENE) + own own A.D.S. MAC are evacuating us to REMY Siding & PROVEN. Casualties from 25, 32, 33, 19, 49th divisions being received.	
"	12/4	10 am	Visited ADS. Only a few casualties being received - OC/ADS told to use his own discretion regarding this ADS further back.	
"	12/4/18		B OC Bearers reports heavy shelling round ADS. ADMS considers ADS too far forward.	
		6.30 pm	OC ADS ordered to withdraw from WESTHOF & establish a car loading post - go on bottom of Sheet 28 hill just west of ADS. The ADS will be established near Brigade HQrs in an esteminet S17 d 7.9. He then to retire still further back, on KEERSEBROM Sheet 28 S.11, C.6.6. or RAVELSBURG S16 C central are suitable sites. During the night ADS moved to the estaminet S17 d 7,9, which will for the time being maintained by relay posts.	

H.G. Kelly
Lieut Col. RAMC

Army Form C. 2118.

WAR DIARY
or
INTELLIGENCE SUMMARY.
(Erase heading not required.)

Feb 16th 77 Field Amb.

Place	Date	Hour	Summary of Events and Information	Remarks and references to Appendices
BERTHEN	12/4		ADS was heavily shelled during the night. Three men from direct hits on it. two OR of this unit wounded & one missing - It was moved to a farm at KEERSEBROM. S.103.d.6.5.	
"	13/4	2.15 a.m.	Situation report received from ADMS this unit held a forward collecting Station & open all shops at T.14.C.3. to S.18.d.central. OC A/93 arrived & sent to establish his 75th Fd. Amb. forward to ground round WATERLOO Rd & RAVELSBURN the brigade will shed from Caravans. ADS at KEERSEBROM or HAEGEDORNE. The car will wounded to Via Croix d. POPERINGE, & ST JEANS CAPELLE. The division is holding the line from NEUVE EGLISE - DESSURLE -	
"	10 a.m.		Visited line Inspected the ADS at the new Field amb site at KEERSEBROM, Centre being kept with line. Both Relays removed to DANOUTRE. Few wounded coming in now. The M.D.S. is kept well clear by the M.A.C.	

H.B. Kelly
Lieut-Col 77 Fd Amb

Army Form C. 2118.

WAR DIARY
or
INTELLIGENCE SUMMARY.
(Erase heading not required.)

Also 77 Field Amb. War Diary 165

Place	Date	Hour	Summary of Events and Information	Remarks and references to Appendices
BERTHEN	13/4	12.30 pm	The following situation report received from ADMS – The enemy is pressing back our troops East of NEUVE EGLISE – the troops should take up a line SHARP S5 c, 0, 1; S5 a 8, 2; S6 a, 9, 4; N3 6.0.2; N31, d, 1, 15; N31 b 5, 2. – In this event, the ADS should retire along the DRANOUTRE – LOCRE – WESTOUTRE road or along the CROIX de POPERINGHE – MOUNT NOIR road. The MDS should retire North via BOESCHEPE.	
"	"	2 pm	Visited line – fairly quiet on our front, though much firing round METEREN. Gas Conduct being kept north line, two ayrewith being kept at scrutineed RAP, & one at B relay post.	
"	14/4/18	9.0 am	Visited line & Batt. Hqts. The road to KEERSEBROM from the LOCRE–BAILLEUL road is very bad with shell holes, & it is the only one for cars, so the ADS is to go to the Fed Amb Camp Shell 86 at the Cross Roads Sq. a, 6, 7; leaving a relay post at the Old ADS site.	

H.B. Kelly Lieut-Col.

Army Form C. 2118.

WAR DIARY
or
INTELLIGENCE SUMMARY.
(Erase heading not required.)

John 116. 77 Field Amb

Place	Date	Hour	Summary of Events and Information	Remarks and references to Appendices
BERTHEN	15/4/18		Not many cases have come in the last 24 hrs. 75th F.Amb formed an advance dressing station to MDS. We are running a front line MDS.	
"		10.30 am	Orders received by A.D.M.S. to withdraw our bearers from line in conformity with 75th Bde.	
"		4.0 pm	Bearers reported here	
"	16/4	12 midnight	Orders received that to move forthwith to GODEWAERSVELDE area to about Q.18 a 6.2. Sheet 27	
			Via BOESCHEPE - LA MONTAGNE - MONTS DES CATS; to be off the road by daylight. Arrived about 5.0 am - 75th Bde is billeted this day. Our map reference is Sheet 27 R.19 a 3.3	
			In IX Corps reserve + under ½ hrs notice to move.	
R.19 a 3.3 Sheet 27	"	10 am	The 75th Bde has been formed into a Composite Battalion with our M.O. attached. 4 Squads observers to him & [crossed out] with dressings.	
	"	12 noon	Orders to received by 78th Bde to move up to hold a reserve line near LA LEVRETTE	
	"	1.0 pm	A.D.M.S. writes that if withdrawal of Fd. Amb. is necessary will be GODEWAERSVELDE km trek N. [illegible]	H.G. Kelly Lieut-Col RAMC [illegible]

2353 Wt. W2314/1454 700,000 5/15 D.D.&L. A.D.S.S./Form/C. 2118.

WAR DIARY
or
INTELLIGENCE SUMMARY

(Erase heading not required.)

Army Form C. 2118.

War Diaries 167 77 Field Amb.

Place	Date	Hour	Summary of Events and Information	Remarks and references to Appendices
Sheet 27. R.19.a.3.3.	16/4	1 pm	The remainder of the ambulances moved down to the 2nd CCS and at GODEWAERSVELDE	
			In am 75 F Amb & 78 F Amb and the latter running the MDS.	
Sheet 27. R 12 d 6.6.		3.30 pm	Found area reconnoitred for the composite battalion holds a reserve line in front of LA LEVRETTE & LES FONTAINES. O/C Amb Amb with the RAP at the latter place. Our MDS (with the 75 F Amb) is stationed at a farm house about R 23.5.7, 9, Sheet 27. with a car stand at R 17 C, 4.8, & one about R 9 d. 8.9. Evacuation from RAP in by road. Onwards to MDS & thence by Motor Ambulances to	
GODEWAERSVELDE		6.0 pm	Received orders to reconnoitre for a MDS & north of STEENVOORDE-POPERINGHE road about K 35, 6 a d on WATOU road to open up there, but for the present Casualties will be sent to 76 th F Amb.	
"		7.30	Site selected in two farm houses at K 35 a 5, 2, Sheet 27	

H.O. Kelly
Lieut Colonel

WAR DIARY
or
INTELLIGENCE SUMMARY.

(Erase heading not required.)

Army Form C. 2118.

John 16 & 77 Field Amb—

Place	Date	Hour	Summary of Events and Information	Remarks and references to Appendices
Q.12, d.6,6.	16/4	10 pm	Set out for new M D S	
		11·15 pm	Arrival at K.35, a 5,2. We are to open up but not take in Casualties till further orders	
K.35, a.5,2	17/4	10 am	Visited line. 75th Brigade has moved forward & occupied a reserve line on eastern slope of Mont Noir with R A P in Wolfenden Fm Shed 28 M 25 d 6,5.	
			The Ans on Reserve coming from. A relay post is established at about R 24 C,5,9. Evacuation is down by hand Carriage down the south western slope of MONT NOIR along the ST —— JEAN CAPELLE Road to the line at R 29 C 3,2, to relay post & thence to Relay post 4 &	
			A D S. A car in now stationed at the ADS, & another car at R.17 C 3,8,; the cars altern near BOESCHEPE is abolished.	
			There is heavy shelling in back areas & on MONT, NOIR — now known with the battalion.	
			None killed & 3 wounded — Shelling was kept up in morning & afternoon, though casualties were small	

H.G. Kelly, Lieut-Col ——

Army Form C. 2118.

Instructions regarding War Diaries and Intelligence
Summaries are contained in F. S. Regs., Part II.
and the Staff Manual respectively. Title pages
will be prepared in manuscript.

WAR DIARY
or
INTELLIGENCE SUMMARY.   Folio/5g 77 Field Amb.

(Erase heading not required.)

Place	Date	Hour	Summary of Events and Information	Remarks and references to Appendices
K35 a 52	18/4	8.0 am	Visited Lurs — 75th Bde complete Battalion had been ordered back to result new GODEWAERSVELDE. Saw Bdr Kirby's & ordered the Drevers & Cars to join the Unit at K35 a 5,2,	
"		3.0 pm	Drevers & Cars formed up here. Horses made up to establishment	
	19/4		Rested — Began to refit — ⊘ Casualties Suffered by the Unit from 10th–19 inclusive are :-	
			to other ranks Killed = 2 (17/4)	
			Died of Wounds 1 (13/4)	
			Wounded 19	
			Missing 9 (10/4) 1 (12/4) = 2	
				= 1
				= 19
				= 10
			Most of the men missing were attached to M.O. of the R.A.M.C. when the attack started	

H.O.Kelly
Lieut-Colonel

Army Form C. 2118.

WAR DIARY
or
INTELLIGENCE SUMMARY.
(Erase heading not required.)

Folio 170 77 Fld Amb

Instructions regarding War Diaries and Intelligence Summaries are contained in F. S. Regs., Part II. and the Staff Manual respectively. Title pages will be prepared in manuscript.

Place	Date	Hour	Summary of Events and Information	Remarks and references to Appendices
K35,a,3,2.	19/4		Casualties collected by this unit from April 10th – 18th sent passed through our books as	
		6 am 10/4/18	Officers 9 ORs 393	
		6 am 11/4/18		
		6 am 11/4/18 to 6 am 12/8/18	Officers 2 ORs 56	
		6 am 12/4/18 to 6 am 13/4/18	Officers 10 ORs 174	
		6 am 13/4/18 to 6 am 14/4/18	Officers 3 ORs 67	
		6 am 14/4/18 to 6 am 15/4/18	Officers 10 ORs 113	
		6 am 15/4/18 to 6 am 16/4/18	ORs 8	
			Total Officers 34 ORs 831	
			But in addition many wounded sick came through our ABS were not taken through the books of the 75th & 76th F Ambs.	

H.W. Kelly Lieut Colonel

Army Form C. 2118.

WAR DIARY
or
INTELLIGENCE SUMMARY.
(Erase heading not required.)

Files 171   77th Field Amb.

Instructions regarding War Diaries and Intelligence Summaries are contained in F. S. Regs., Part II. and the Staff Manual respectively. Title pages will be prepared in manuscript.

Place	Date	Hour	Summary of Events and Information	Remarks and references to Appendices
Sheet 27. ~~DOZINGHAM~~ W 35 a.3.2.	21st	3.30 am	Received orders to march under orders of G.O.C. 75th Inf. Bde. to POPERINGHE area.	
		9 am	Started arrived at 4 pm at DOZINGHAM Sheet 27. F.11.a.57. an old CCS site.	
Sheet 27. DOZINGHAM	22nd		Attachment to 7th Inf. Bde. + are collecting their sick.	
F.11.a.5.7	23 & 24		Rested + refitting	
"	25 &	1.0 pm	7th Bde. under orders to move in half an hour.	
"		1.30 pm	7th Bde. ordered to move to Sheet 28 G.26.a. to be in support to XXII Corps Bde. heights at HOOGRAEF Cabaret.	
"	"	4.30 pm	3 Squads to Bearers + one officer sent up to Brigade concentration area. 3 squads to be attached to MO Jends.	
"	"		4 other squads went up at — with 2 ccws. The rest 7th + 74th Bdes. with the 75th in support are ordered to counter attack at 3 am tomorrow.	

[signature]

Army Form C. 2118.

WAR DIARY
or
INTELLIGENCE SUMMARY.
(Erase heading not required.)

Folio 172 77 Fld Amb

Place	Date	Hour	Summary of Events and Information	Remarks and references to Appendices
25/4/18	25/4/18		the line KEMMEL VILLAGE, LINDENHOEK, STORE FM, M.29, a.7.5. the jumping off line is the KEMMELBEEK stream.	
DOZINGHAM				
M.6, a, 2, 9. Sheet 28	26/4	1.0 am	The bearers moved up with the Brigade & established an A.D.S. in an internment about M.6.a.2.9. & the bearers with some equipment in a car & kept by the limit front them then we have a car front about G.3.4.a.2.8. & a horse Amb. RAPs limbers & water cart, with a tent subdivision & the remainder of the bearers proceeded to VANSOHIER FM G.2.1 c.5.7. Sheet 28.	
"	"	4 am	numbers of casualties coming in. Visited RAPs & brigade - all in dugouts in the LA CLYTTE, DICKEBUSCH road. Evacuation is by hand carriers & lorries or by cars to RAPs & thence by FA Cars to Corps M Dressing Station REMY SIDING.	
"	"	11 am	7th Bde brought both in support. RAPs established behind LA CLYTTE to forward lines. seen juried. All casualties have been brought in about 200 in Brigade - mostly machine gun bullets.	
"	"	12 noon	Headquarters of unit moved to VANSOHIER FM	

A.R.Kelly
Lieut Col ?????

Army Form C. 2118.

WAR DIARY
or
INTELLIGENCE SUMMARY.
(Erase heading not required.)

John 173. 77 Fld Amb

Place	Date	Hour	Summary of Events and Information	Remarks and references to Appendices
VANSOHIER	25/4.		ADS + farm shelled during the afternoon	
F.M	26/4.		ADS shifted down to RED LODGE about M.9.a.07. on account of shelling. Shared with 76 F Amb.	
Sh 28			Staff consists of 1 M.O & Seven Squads + 1 Car. Relieved every 24 hrs. There is one dugout with dicks & duckdown	
G.21.3, C.5.7.			There is a good deal of shelling behind the line. Casualties are few from this line	
"	27/4	11:30 pm	7th Batt brought back to reserve round our ADS	
			On account of the shelling the ADS has been moved to the a dug out on the OUDERDOM –	
			RWENINGHELST Rd	
"	28/4	11.0 am	Orders received from A.D.M.S. to leave division of 77 Fld Amb to remain with 2 M.O. &	
			Clear Casualties of 7th Bde under orders of O.C. 75th F.Amb.	
			77 F Amb is to open up a MDS at DOZINGHAM for division, it be opened at 6.0 pm	
			for Sick men & Gas cases. 1h. 75 & 76th Fld Ambs are to each send one M.O. & a tent	
			subdivision.	

M.C.Cxxx Lt Major
Kxxxx Lt Major

Army Form C. 2118.

WAR DIARY
or
INTELLIGENCE SUMMARY.
(Erase heading not required.)

folio 17 77 Field Amb.

Instructions regarding War Diaries and Intelligence Summaries are contained in F. S. Regs., Part II. and the Staff Manual respectively. Title pages will be prepared in manuscript.

Place	Date	Hour	Summary of Events and Information	Remarks and references to Appendices
VANSOHIER FM. G.21.6.5.7 Sheet 28	28/4		A collecting post for walking wounded to is to be formed by OC 76 Fd Amb at VANSOHIER farm. Evacuation by light railway to the Corps walking wounded Dressing Station at BANDAGHEM.	
	29/4	6pm	Opened up. Evacuation is by MAC Cars to LCS at ARNEKE & ESQUELBECQ. Casualties admitted this am officers 9	
DOZINGHAM Sheet 27 F.14.c.5.7. Sheet 27	29/4		Also a good number of Casualties have come in due to an unsuccessful attack by the enemy. Casualties admitted from 6am 29/4 to 6am 30/4 officers 3 OR 106	
"	30/4	6 pm	Received orders to open a MDS at the site of No10 CCS REMY SIDING, as the place is now in II Corps area. To be opened by 12 noon. 1. Casualties admitted 6am 30/4 to 6am 1/5 officers 2 OR 58	

2353 Wt. W2344/1454 700,000 5/15 D. D. & L. A.D.S.S./Form/C. 2118.

Army Form C. 2118.

WAR DIARY
or
INTELLIGENCE SUMMARY.
(Erase heading not required.)

Vol 32

140/3076.

Confidential

War Diary

Medical 77th Ambulance

May, 1918.

Volume 32.

Army Form C. 2118.

WAR DIARY
or
INTELLIGENCE SUMMARY.
(Erase heading not required.)

Folio 175 77 Field Amb.

Instructions regarding War Diaries and Intelligence Summaries are contained in F. S. Regs., Part II. and the Staff Manual respectively. Title pages will be prepared in manuscript.

Place	Date	Hour	Summary of Events and Information	Remarks and references to Appendices
DOZINGHAM	31st May	7.30 am	One officer & tent subdivision & equipment moved off & took over site at REMY SIDING from 18th Field Amb — spared by horse.	
F 11, a, 5, 7. Sheet 27. S.E.			Tent-sub-div of 78th Fd Amb left us at 9.30 am for REMY. Four horses marching down the Switch Rd were	
POPERINGHE			Three shells burst & killed 11 O.R. & wounded 15. Four horses were killed.	
			Dressing Station at REMY opened at 12 noon, at which time cars from the front were even diverted. Personnel	
REMY SIDING	"	12 noon	from DOZINGHAM marched to REMY as soon as their Camps were clear.	
			Lt SEIDLER M.O.R.C. U.S.A. taken on our strength.	
SHRAPNEL Sheet			Casualties 6 am to May 1st to 5 am May 2nd at Officer 3 O.R. 82	
		5 pm	As there was a battery of 9.2 guns behind us an alternative site at WIPPENHOEK being looked at	
			& a holding party put in.	
	2 May		Lt TYDSDALE from 31st Fd Div taken on our strength	
			Casualties from 6 am May 2nd - to 6 am May 3rd Officer 4 O.R. 98.	

H.B. Kelly / Lt Col
O.C. 77 Field Amb
OC 77

Army Form C. 2118.

WAR DIARY
or
INTELLIGENCE SUMMARY.
(Erase heading not required.)

Folio 17b 77 Field Amb.

Instructions regarding War Diaries and Intelligence Summaries are contained in F. S. Regs., Part II. and the Staff Manual respectively. Title pages will be prepared in manuscript.

Place	Date	Hour	Summary of Events and Information	Remarks and references to Appendices
REMY SIDING	3 May	4 pm	The division is to be relieved night of May 3/4 by 32nd French Division. 7th Brigade is to forward to Support around the A28 at 2 am & to march to Transport lines around K.32 - about 2.8 at 5 am.	
			We are to march out with the 7th Bde.	
			Tent subdivision of 76 F.A. supposed there was to as the French Ambulance may not be up, until a note from Division morning not to to stay in & clear	
		6.30 pm		
		Midnight	The French took the French Ambulance relieves us.	
			No representation from the French lines arrived	
			Casualties from 6 am - May 3rd to 6 am May 4th: Officers 3 O.R. 50.	
	4th May	5 am	O.C. & bearers of A68 return by French by 8.0 am	
			As no French Ambulance cars arrived, ours stayed in W-Chain & cleared French casualties.	
			Until 2 am. One car got a direct hit, but no one was injured. The cars suffered considerable returned Amb at 11.30 am	
		11 am	Tent Subdivision of 75th F Amb. reported their unit	

H.Q. 77 Field Amb

Army Form C. 2118.

WAR DIARY
or
INTELLIGENCE SUMMARY.
(Erase heading not required.)

John 177 77th Field Amb.

Place	Date	Hour	Summary of Events and Information	Remarks and references to Appendices
REMY SIDING.	4th May	2.30 pm	At this hour all our cases had been evacuated — We marched out & formed near Steenvoort & camped for the night at K32 – Sheet 27. Casualties admitted since 6 am D.R. 26.	
K32 (Sheet 27)	5th May	2.30 am	Received orders from G.O.C. 7th Inf Bde to march at tomorrow to ESQUELBECQ upon Steenvoorde Church at 10.20 am. Billeting officers were sent ahead & met one to meet us at terminus billings. Arrived at ESQUELBECQ 4 km & marched on to BISSEZEELE (Sh HAZEBROUCK Sheet). Arrived at 5.30 pm to billets as Canyon Wood filled. As it was too wet no trousers cd be kept. Proxy a bulk of accumulation. Capt WITTE M.C. arrived from 39th Div & so as taken in our strength.	

H.Q. [signature]

Army Form C. 2118.

WAR DIARY
or
INTELLIGENCE SUMMARY

(Erase heading not required.)

Volu 17.6 77 Field Amb.

Place	Date	Hour	Summary of Events and Information	Remarks and references to Appendices
BISSEZEELE	May 6th	4 pm	Rest.	
"	May 7th	4 pm	Lieut FINDLAY from 34th Div taken on our strength. Casualties suffered by this unit from 25/4/18 to 4/4/18. O.R. killed 2, Wounded 9 (5 men own shell fire). John our billets vacated by French. Sent an officer to reconnoitre entraining station. Drew two extra deep return. Capt NASON RAMC & Lieut SEIDLER MORC USA were sent from this unit to relieve Capt WELLS MD I/C DAC & Capt MACK MOI/C 2nd S.Amo respectively. Received orders to entrain to join the 9th Corps. 1st French Army. This unit will entrain at REXPOEDE at 2.30 a.m. 9th inst.	
"	9/4/18	2.30	Major BARTLETT 2 Officers, 2 dunkeons M.T. Ambulances & 1 Ford & one cycle left by road for new area for duty at detraining centre & at filtering pt. One ambulance M.T. ambulance detained at entraining station for sick.	

H.O. Aby Fortell
R.A.M.C.
O.C. 77th Field Ambulance

Army Form C. 2118.

WAR DIARY
or
INTELLIGENCE SUMMARY.

(Erase heading not required.)

Instructions regarding War Diaries and Intelligence Summaries are contained in F. S. Regs., Part II. and the Staff Manual respectively. Title pages will be prepared in manuscript.

Place	Date	Hour	Summary of Events and Information	Remarks and references to Appendices
Hut 22 Sois 4/15	11/7/18	4:40	Arrived and marked the lie on in spot with the whole Brigade Group engaged. Front Subject. The Division will rest at town. We are looking to front.	
ARCH 18-45 WITHINE			Lechi. Stationed is of 37. C.C.S.	
"	14/7/18	9 am	The Brigade Group implanted a review by the G.I.C.	
"	15/7/18	5 pm	moved forward	
"	15/7/18	5 pm	Capt. HITER, M.O.R.C. USA. left for duty with American Army	
"	16/7/18	6:20am	Major F. A. LEUCHER of this unit proceeded on special leave to England	
Amatruy	21/5/18		the 4th Brigade meals moved to ordinary area	
			7/7 Amb. occupy site of the French Hospital. H.O.C 15	
	26/5/18		25th Divisional Orders May 25 1918 H.O.20 Honours & Awards	
			T. Capt. (A Maj.) B. F. Carlile M.C. Conf. Military Cross	
			No. 3921/5 S.t. C.H.B.S.K L. Hannon M.M. awarded D.C.M.	

2353 Wt. W2344/1454 700,000 5/15 D. D. & L. A.D.S.S./Forms/C. 2118.

WAR DIARY
or
INTELLIGENCE SUMMARY.
(Erase heading not required.)

Army Form C. 2118.

Place	Date	Hour	Summary of Events and Information	Remarks and references to Appendices
Acheux	26.9.16	1/pm	Orders received to move up to Crown Sector. Enemy about to attack. Main Body under Major O'Donnell fell in at 9.30. & march off to Guyencourt to form an A.D.S. 100 Bearers with Capt Wilson & Lt Sunburn Amb. Casgy O.B.E. mostly linking with ever. moving of B Guyencourt via Dernancourt — Becourt established an A.D.S. on the edge of road in a sunken part outside Guyencourt	
Guyencourt	27.9.16		Got in touch with Comrade H.Q. in early hours of morning. C.R.M.S. with R.C. Findlay came up to reconnoitre line. About 1 am Bearers went down many hundreds of yds slates sent over during early hours of morning. 14th Infy Brigade in advance — Push to the S.W. of Guyencourt about midday. the 4 Comrade took up a position in the wood W. of Guyencourt in about the same latitude as the village of Beaupreaux. Walls on our extreme left then H.B. Staff & 10 Division with 6 S.W. on extreme right & holding Bank on far Down to Hamenville. 1 squad of Bearers at 1 stretcher squads up with each Battn then through the wood was a very difficult carry, so sent up a team to the Coln. — Staff. — 1 to Brecherin. During afternoon Col Wellim Major Crabbit went up to the Walls and got wounded was attended in a small Sunken, Man near Croft H.Q. commenced attack machine gun fire. R. Findlay got in touch with Division Staff. About 4 pm enemy then including Aerocraft aimed a Counter attacks & Cartridge main hand aided after a tount Batch Cardross from Beaupreaux. OC 1/1st C Amb.	

WAR DIARY
or
INTELLIGENCE SUMMARY.
(Erase heading not required.)

Army Form C. 2118.

Place	Date	Hour	Summary of Events and Information	Remarks and references to Appendices
Beauvincourt	27.5.18	6am	Opened A.D.S. at Beauvincourt on the site of Beauvincourt Civil Station occupied by 3 Bearers sharing the Dug-Outs with 25's 26's & ambes, this area was being heavily shelled. Means Shuttling motor ambulance was waiting for evacuation. Cat. Bn. Col. Kelly sent down Major Boultill who had been O/C H.Q. Transport Stores at Montescourt & in touch with 2 LS. my Col. H.O. Fuller D.D.O. Major Reichwald & Lieut-Couch m.O. LOC'B (ambers) evacuated with x Fuel Sub Bearers & about 30 Crowns. On arrival at Montagne Major Boultill found about 100 wounded awaiting evacuation, made all wounded cases walk towards Savecourt, in it was evacuating the CCS whilst M.T.A. cars were working our cars & ten ambulances of not motor Bearers, Major Corball C.O. of 3rd Can. re-inf'd A.D.m.S. got in touch of German armies 4thH at Savecourt. Could not is manage S.S.A. Coffeulle ahead at Sauchigne in men and a Sheffield order would not yet through to Grenancourt. We therefore this and in an ambulance and some traffic leaving the Grenancourt road 2 miles to of Grenancourt picked up A.D.m.S. of Grenancourt in Major Boultill immediately sent off all transport under Capt. Dyson to previous camp South of 25+S Division. Capt. Webb was in charge of Major Stephen Station at Montescourt Running	

WAR DIARY
or
INTELLIGENCE SUMMARY.
(Erase heading not required.)

Army Form C. 2118.

Place	Date	Hour	Summary of Events and Information	Remarks and references to Appendices

	27.5.18		Casualties to date. Room C
			Sgt. W.J. Addicott
			Sgt. S.F. Bradley
			Sgt. A.E. Simpson
			Cpl. M. Crouchland
			Pte. N.W. Brown
			    H. Keiller (Wounded)
			    A.S. Ridge
			    A.S.C. HT
			Dvr. J. Bell A.S.C. M.T.
			Pte. A.H. Abbott (non Quincement)	

Anazarcy	28.5.18		Camp being shelled all night about 4.30am bombs being nearly shells" several of wooden huts on fire. Machine gun (enemy) on hill at camp puttin through the huts. Arabs had to evacuate camp had to leave about 40 skeleton cars behind. The CCS left a rear.... Sent off under Capt. Willis rest of personnel Sgt Major about 10 brancas staying behind under order Col Craddock until the last wounded & rear of an Ambulance returned wounded about 30 men were then evacuated about 30 other bus cars. Lieut Evans & Fawley Cpl. Robb killed on the road. Enemy aircraft very active on Sinai Guminary road. Marched down to Arien & killed all remains of the MT & Cars	C. Craddock - Col comdg TT ola TT

2353 Wt. W2544/1434 700,000 5/15 D. D. & L. A.D.S.S./Forms/C. 2118.

Army Form C. 2118.

WAR DIARY
or
INTELLIGENCE SUMMARY.
(Erase heading not required.)

Instructions regarding War Diaries and Intelligence Summaries are contained in F. S. Regs., Part II. and the Staff Manual respectively. Title pages will be prepared in manuscript.

Place	Date	Hour	Summary of Events and Information	Remarks and references to Appendices
On wire Ground			Roll Call the following Officers & men present	
			Lt. Col: H.O Mellin DSO	
			Maj. H.A Boeher CMG	
			Capt C Bolter MC	
			Lieut A.S Hendley	
			Sgt Wallis A	Q.M Longworth T
			Sgt Thom	" Floyd W.E
			L/Sgt Ward AL	Anselm A.S
			L/Sgt Bain TL	Marler L.G
			Pte Ackland F.W.	Sundon G.H
			" Coates W	Glenn E.F
			" Gould H	Sart H.G
			" Crosley F	
			" Egan T	4 Officers
			" Goode W.H	24 O.R
			" Hannan T	
			" Holvuk F.A	
			" Ingham S	
			" Jenman H	
			" Lain N.D	
			" Lain W	
			" Neely Q	

WAR DIARY
or
INTELLIGENCE SUMMARY.
(Erase heading not required.)

Army Form C. 2118.

Instructions regarding War Diaries and Intelligence Summaries are contained in F. S. Regs., Part II. and the Staff Manual respectively. Title pages will be prepared in manuscript.

Place	Date	Hour	Summary of Events and Information	Remarks and references to Appendices
Vezilly	28.5.18		Marched on to Dezillis attack connection to A.D.M.S. 25 Division stayed in that area until 2.30 — then marched to 1 Kilometre south of Villers Agron camped in a field for the night. Major O. Caullet was put in Command of M.A. Comdie of few wounded arrived on the road, being shortly seen through machine gunning, picked up about 10 walking wounded	
Dormant	29.5.18		About 10 am advanced on Dormans Wounded in a lorry encountered by road side in small wood about 2 Kilometre N. of that town picked up A.D.M.S about 10 p.m — Set up a small post in the S. of the Dormans. Lieut Nodali applied for duty. Coll Waite & Major O. la Chapelle shared the mean. About midnight On the Dormans road until early hours of morning — no casualties about 6am moved up to La Chapelle. Lt Nodali asked to form up a Collecting post near Dormans	
La Chapelle	30.5.18		About 9am moved to Le Nodali after an attack at Cot Thievry & Smith Composite Odettes at Dormans unsuccessful in affair but is Middle half grand Moved Ordette & La Perrielle Servet & that Col Comber Croft — had moved back to Chomeron & Lt Nodali, 4 bearers + 1 ambulance car remained with Cot Thievry Small Village shelled retired on to small gallery of chaper near La Chalpelle late evening	O. Caullet O.C. ? ? commd To Cang? ? C.O. T.V.

2353 Wt. W2511/1454 700,000 5/15 D. D. & L. A.D.S.S./Forms/C. 2118.

WAR DIARY or INTELLIGENCE SUMMARY

Army Form C. 2118.

Place	Date	Hour	Summary of Events and Information	Remarks and references to Appendices
En Chapelle	30.5.15		55th then adopted nursery system	
	31.5.15		Col General Guffin slightly wounded in buttock wound passed at S.F.W. evacuated to H.O.C. Elverner	
			111.F. Amb. attached to Col Thuncard Smith Cadet at 6am marched up Oden St Menin-en-Ronne camped for the night Carried 12 men in Horse Ambul: with 1 CT Yeo	

Army Form C. 2118.

WAR DIARY
or
INTELLIGENCE SUMMARY.
(Erase heading not required.)

Vol 3 140/3076

War Diary
- Medical -
77th Field Ambulance, R.A.M.C.

COMMITTEE FOR THE
MEDICAL HISTORY OF THE WAR
Date 7 AUG 1918

4

Instructions regarding War Diaries and Intelligence Summaries are contained in F. S. Regs., Part II. and the Staff Manual respectively. Title pages will be prepared in manuscript.

Place	Date	Hour	Summary of Events and Information	Remarks and references to Appendices
	June 1918			

WAR DIARY
or
INTELLIGENCE SUMMARY.

(Erase heading not required.)

Army Form C. 2118.

Place	Date	Hour	Summary of Events and Information	Remarks and references to Appendices
La Chapelle	30.5.18		3rd Field ambulance morning reported. B39 General Guilfer reported wounded in Buttock wound dressed at S.G..m wounded to H.O.E at Estaires	
	31.5.18		77th FA and attached to Col. Thuncaid Smith Battn at 6am marched under his order to amannid-en-cour carried on their work	
Amanid-en-Cour	1.6.18		Capt. T. Colman & 8 bearers returned to Col. Thuncaid Smith. So Buty with Inn and Mills gone. 12 men chosen from A.S.D. m.S. reported to Stramen 7th Inf. Brigade H.Q. & prepare to take on Brigade Bror and given available kooden & tent & erected in a field.	
	2.6.18		Weather very hot 6 Buty men cart. Watts & 1 ent subalturn to H.C..r. Estaires S. Buty 1st Beds men, 0 and 2 later van Chatham St. Lee Granville from 7th Inf. Brigade	
Chatham-St.Lee Granville	4.6.18		9 non-n.c. hospital to collect sick from 7th Inf Brigade 4th Inf Brigade D.T.H.Q. 112 RFA & Co of A.S.E. (m.g.) Battn occup. accompanied in leg. Gaam Ja Wart. H.T. Saulshaw can & carlage for another 20 cases in Capt Given reported for duty	
	5.6.18		Capt Wilson Ditcham joined So Buty with ambulance 20 cases in hospital. Sent Cdr Scotts wounded to 1/5 Siteland T.A. at Buitin	
	7.6.18		M. Tisdale wounded at Scramm Y.C.S. So Buty coday	

Army Form C. 2118.

WAR DIARY
or
INTELLIGENCE SUMMARY.
(Erase heading not required.)

Instructions regarding War Diaries and Intelligence Summaries are contained in F.S. Regs., Part II. and the Staff Manual respectively. Title pages will be prepared in manuscript.

Place	Date	Hour	Summary of Events and Information	Remarks and references to Appendices
Chocques or La Creuse	10/6/19	AM	March off under 7th Inf. Brigade Orders at 10.30am to Pernes. West 8 miles arrived Pernes 3.25. Awaiting requisites to proceed. Good accommodation for hospital & personnel in camp.	
Pernes	10.6.19		7th Field Ambulance to collect sick from 7th Inf. Brigade details 7th Inf. Brigade. No field ambulance with A.S.C. 7th Inf. Brigade S.H.Q. Several cases of P.U.O. in 7.A.C.	
"	12.6.19		115 C.C.S. Sevenne Sa serious cases. Slight cases to Chichy. 24 men cases from D.A.C., P.O.O. admitted from J.A.C. 52. C.C.S. open at Sevenne. 63 cases now in hospital.	
"	13.5.19		Another 13 cases of P.U.O from D.A.C. Temperatures very high.	
"	14.6.19		Lt. Tisdale returns this unit from 12 C.C.S Sevenne.	
"	15.6.19		Lieut. Col. H.H. Cannon onc. name to take over command of 7th Fd. Ambulance.	

2353 Wt. W2344/1454 700,000 5/15 D.D.&L. A.D.S.S./Forms/C. 2118.

WAR DIARY
or
INTELLIGENCE SUMMARY.

Army Form C. 2118.

(Erase heading not required.)

Place	Date	Hour	Summary of Events and Information	Remarks and references to Appendices
	16/6/16	P.M.	Lieut Colonel HM LEESON McMunn arrived and assumed command of 17th Field Ambulance vice Lieut Colonel KELLY D.S.O. been taken prisoner of war. Weather fine.	
GOURGANÇON	17/6/16	A.M.	Morning spent in packing up & preparing to move to fresh address from REEVES	
		4.30pm	Unit marched from REEVES to new area an ambulance with mess Cooks from 74th Brigade billets went together. The payment by ? ? march in hot weather and arriving at GOURGANÇON at 9pm. The men billeted in the town	
GOURGANÇON	18/6/16	A.M.	Morning spent in settling in new Billets & opening a Small Rest Station of 50 beds	
		P.M.	Officer Brother John Weather fine	
GOURGANÇON	19/6/16	A.M.	Train cars of Stretchers received from 25 Div Ambulance. Had trouble in a hole ambulance went round houses in 3 villages trying all out without a medical officer collected to train court and brought ? some back to Rest Station. Afternoon	
			Weather cloudy.	
GOURGANÇON	20/6/16	A.M.	Hospital Train ? ? from ? they in very ? order. Captain MADDEN	
		P.M.	Rev appointed duty from 9th Royal North Lancashire Regt ready to return on the Strength of Unit our 2nd Lt T2/24721 Driver BATCHELOR arrived from 21st Coy A.S.C. and was taken on the strength accordingly of the Unit.	
GOURGANÇON	21/6/16	A.M.	Work on Rest Station & ? buggy ?	
		P.M.	? returning from A.P.M.S. 25 Division that and will move to a new area ? others from 7th Brigade!	
GOURGANÇON	22/6/16	A.M.	Returns put ready to move.	

Army Form C. 2118.

WAR DIARY
or
INTELLIGENCE SUMMARY.
(Erase heading not required.)

Instructions regarding War Diaries and Intelligence Summaries are contained in F. S. Regs., Part II. and the Staff Manual respectively. Title pages will be prepared in manuscript.

Place	Date	Hour	Summary of Events and Information	Remarks and references to Appendices
GOUY-EN-ARTOIS	22/8/16	P.M.	Unit marched under orders of 17th Inf. Brigade from GOUY-EN-ARTOIS to CONNANTRAY, arriving there at 6 p.m. Billeted in the town, weather fine	
CONNANTRAY	23/8/16	A.M.	Morning spent in getting weighing bills and provision. Small unit station for 12 patients. Orders to move to new area received from 145 Brigade at 9 p.m.	
		P.M.		
CONNANTRAY	24/8/16	A.M.	Unit marched from CONNANTRAY & SOMMESOUS at 10.40 a.m. in advance with 74th Brigade transport (6th) arriving there at 2.30 p.m. was billeted in the Gare. Orders received late from A.D.M.S. 75 Division (attd to 1st Army) to Railway-transport stations proceed by train to 1st Army area from SOMMESOUS and HAILLY-LE-CAMP stations. Half train can proceed each station, 1 commencing at 7.30 p.m. Next day.	
SOMMESOUS	25/8/16	A.M. P.M.	Reading in billets. General Routine work. Weather cloudy	
SOMMESOUS	26/8/16	A.M.	Unit entrained for 1st Army area. Nos. 1 & 2 a.m. on armoured under 25 km. Nos. 3 & 4 - 22/8/15 at the station, was found to not very well & sent up	
			station punctually & have weather fine	
In the train	27/8/16	A.M. P.M.	Proceeding by train to new area. Nothing unusual occurred.	
PREHEDOE	28/8/16	A.M.	Unit arrived at HESDIN Station at 9 a.m. and proceeded to château	

WAR DIARY
or
INTELLIGENCE SUMMARY.

(Erase heading not required.)

Army Form C. 2118.

Place	Date	Hour	Summary of Events and Information	Remarks and references to Appendices
PRAE MESRE	24/11/17	AM	Battery fired 14th HE Rounds of Gas Shells on enemy Battery if PRE MESRE 10 rounds fire later. Hostile Battery stating fired ranged our station at 12 noon and around the south of our concrete hut. The work was dismissed at 1 pm & the weather	
PRAE MESRE	25/11/17	AM	Weather fine & warm of.	
		PM	Unit very quiet. Enemy firing a little work. 6:50 hostile Battery fired 3 shells over front in a field on east of gully. From the Battery. Billets & Bivouacs as their were all still there. Weather fine.	
PRAE MESRE	26/11/17	AM	Confirmation about station. Major BARNETT ames Sergeant Major IVINS, 2 Sergeant to mover. Major BARNETT Amer Sergeant Major IVINS, 2 Sergeant & 20 other ranks returned to proceed to 39th Division for dismounted Staff for 15th Australian Divisional Artillery. OR S & RC Army 25/11/17 Weather warm.	

J.H.H. Keown
Lieut Colonel Anned
Commanding 77th Tin Field Artillery

War Diary

Medical

July 1918.

Army Form C. 2118.

WAR DIARY
or
INTELLIGENCE SUMMARY.
(Erase heading not required.)

Instructions regarding War Diaries and Intelligence Summaries are contained in F. S. Regs., Part II. and the Staff Manual respectively. Title pages will be prepared in manuscript.

Place	Date	Hour	Summary of Events and Information	Remarks and references to Appendices
PRÉHEDAE	1/7/18	A.M.	Office and Routine work in hospital. Major Bartlett Reid reported Major from a 10 O.R. proceeded to ADMS 39th Division for temporary duty. Weather fine.	
Do.	2/7/18	A.M. P.M.	Routine work. Inspected cases of foot and mouth disease amongst cattle in field where sent in quarantine. Reported to O.C. 37 Mobile Veterinary Section. Weather fine.	
PRÉHEDAE	3/7/18	A.M.	Orders received to move to LEBIEZ owing to risk of infection from those cattle from O.C. 26th Division details.	
		P.M.	Unit marched from PRÉHEDAE to LEBIEZ at 3.50 pm and arrived at the area at 5 pm where they unit bivouacked in a field for the night. Weather fine.	
LEBIEZ	4/7/18	A.M.	C.O. interviewed local commandant and obtained a good site for the ambulance in a farm with field adjoining.	
		P.M.	Unit moved to this site and found a thoroughly fit reception of local sick. Weather fine.	
LEBIEZ	5/7/18	P.M. P.M.	Formation of Hospital and provision of equipment. Office & Routine work. Weather fine. Visit of Bookman Latumes & Francois.	
LEBIEZ	6/7/18		Visit of area commandant to see if necessary sanitary appliances had been provided for use. Promised to supply 1, 4 seater & 1 two seater latrine as soon as possible.	

WAR DIARY
or
INTELLIGENCE SUMMARY.

(Erase heading not required.)

Army Form C. 2118.

Place	Date	Hour	Summary of Events and Information	Remarks and references to Appendices
LE BIZET	6/7/16	PM	Inspection of Regiment of stretcher bearers and new found to the in good order. 17 O.R. so reinforcements arrived from Reinforcement Camp ROUEN and were taken on the strength of the unit. Weather fine.	
" "	7/7/16	AM	Office work. Weather fine.	
" "	8/7/16	AM	5 O.R. from Reinforcement Camp ROUEN arrived and were taken on the strength.	
		PM	Heavy Thunderstorm tow had to evacuate their bivouacs & take shelter in a barn.	
" "	9/7/16		Routine work. Weather wet.	
" "	10/7/16		Capt Ryan Rant proceeded to 112 Brigade A.T.A. for temporary duty. Weather wet & stormy.	
" "	11/7/16		Staff Sergeant Powell proceeded to Office of A.D.M.S. 26th Division division for duty. Weather stormy.	
" "	12/7/16		Weather very stormy. Thisled out Bivouacs + good tents.	
" "	13/7/16	AM	Annual return of A.D.M.S. 25th Division desires vice Lieut Colonel TYRRELL Rant proceeded to England for duty. Weather fine & hot.	

WAR DIARY or INTELLIGENCE SUMMARY

Army Form C. 2118.

Place	Date	Hour	Summary of Events and Information	Remarks and references to Appendices
LE BIEZ	14/7/16		Weather Showery. Routine work all day.	
" "	15/7/16		Routine work. Heavy thunderstorm at night with much lightning.	
" "	16/7/16	A.M.	At about 3 a.m. severe peal of lightning struck a tree and killed Dvr Theobald A.S.C. who was somewhere under it & injured slightly Driver Granger & Bird.	
		P.M.	Routine work. Arrangement for the funeral of Driver Theobald.	
" "	17/7/16	A.M.	Funeral of Driver Theobald A.S.C. at HESDIN. Routine work. Weather showery.	
" "	18/7/16	A.M.	No. 38034 Pte Barron transferred to Corps (?) to be acting Sergeant. Pte Thomas to be acting Sergeant. Pte Palmer from duty hospital to be Acting Sergeant. Pte Bellinger from acting L/Cpl	Authority D.G.M.S. D.3/84/143/1/11/16
		P.M.	Routine work. Weather showery.	
" "	19/7/16		Routine work. Weather showery.	
" "	20/7/16	A.M.	Driving (Winterbottom?) & Woodruff A.S.C. reported for duty from 2nd London G.S.C.	
		P.M.	Routine work. Weather heavy & cool.	
" "	21/7/16		Routine work. 6 O.R. went to Paris on leave. Weather cool.	

Army Form C. 2118.

WAR DIARY
or
INTELLIGENCE SUMMARY.
(Erase heading not required.)

Instructions regarding War Diaries and Intelligence Summaries are contained in F. S. Regs., Part II. and the Staff Manual respectively. Title pages will be prepared in manuscript.

Place	Date	Hour	Summary of Events and Information	Remarks and references to Appendices
LEBIEZ	22/7/18	AM	Visited D.D.M.S. XVII Corps who informed me that this unit is to hold itself in readiness. The school for temporary duties Officers being strong 75 of Field Ambulance in the Division when we proceed and that weather fine.	
" "	23/7/18		Another heat wave. Weather wet and stormy.	
" "	24/7/18		Routine work. Weather showery.	
" "	25/7/18		Dr Watson A.S.C. reported for duty from 201 Co. A.S.C. Weather showery	
" "	26/7/18	AM	Captain Matthews R.A.M.C attended Court Martial on Corporal Kelly A.S.C. as member of Court. Instructions went in Sergeant Major Miller A.S.C. received and forwarded to 75th Field Ambulance. Weather very wet.	
" "	27/7/18		B.O.R. Reinforcements arrived from Reinforcement Camp ROUEN and were taken on the strength. Captain Ryan R.A.M.C. returned from temporary duty with 112. Brigade R.F.A. Weather showery	
" "	28/7/18		Handed over duties of A.D.M.S. 25th Division to Lieut. Colonel Davidson R.A.M.C. O.C. 75th Field Ambulance. Weather showery.	
" "	29/7/18		Captain Ryan R.A.M.C proceeded to C.R.E. 25th Divisional Details for duty. Weather fine.	

Army Form C. 2118.

WAR DIARY
or
INTELLIGENCE SUMMARY.

(Erase heading not required.)

Instructions regarding War Diaries and Intelligence Summaries are contained in F. S. Regs., Part II. and the Staff Manual respectively. Title pages will be prepared in manuscript.

Place	Date	Hour	Summary of Events and Information	Remarks and references to Appendices
KEBIEZ	29/7/16	am	Routine work.	
		pm	Received orders to move to ENQUIN sur BAILLON estab. to form morning and report for duty to 47th Infantry Brigade, 16th Division. Weather fine & warm	
KEBIEZ	30/7/16	am	Marched at 5 am from KEBIEZ to ENQUIN sur BAILLON arriving there at 10 am. Interviewed Area Commandant who allotted the unit a very good site in a farm with excellent accommodation for Patients Personnel and Transport.	
ENQUIN sur BAILLON	31/7/16	am	Routine work in office. Unit preparing the hospital for the reception of 50 patients trailing cookhouse & ablution benches.	
		pm	Visited ADMS 16th Division at SAMER and reported arrival of the Ambulance and its situation. Weather fine and hot.	

N. McLeod
1/8/16

J. H. Leeson
Lieut Colonel R.am.C
Commanding 77th Field Ambulance

Army Form C. 2118.

WAR DIARY
or
INTELLIGENCE SUMMARY.
(Erase heading not required.)

WM 35

War Diary
Medical
77th Field Ambulance

Date Aug. 1918

COMMITTEE FOR THE
MEDICAL HISTORY OF THE WAR
Date 5 OCT. 1918

Army Form C. 2118.

WAR DIARY
or
INTELLIGENCE SUMMARY.
(Erase heading not required.)

Instructions regarding War Diaries and Intelligence Summaries are contained in F. S. Regs., Part II. and the Staff Manual respectively. Title pages will be prepared in manuscript.

Place	Date	Hour	Summary of Events and Information	Remarks and references to Appendices
ENGUIN	1/8/18	A.M.	Arranged for collection of sick of 47th Infantry Brigade. Interviewed Brigadier and discussed medical arrangements.	
"		P.M.	A.D.M.S. 16th Division inspected camp & surroundings. Sanitary arrangements for the Brigade of our command satisfactory. Weather fine and hot.	
"	2/8/18	A.M.	Formed Recreation Room in a Barn close to Hospital lines. Sergeant Major J. Moore Ass returned from PARIS leave.	
"		P.M.	One J.M. Henry Dragst. Moore embarked dysmpanitis. Veterinary Officer sent for.	
"	3/8/18	A.M.	A.D.V.S. inspected Horses and found them in good condition.	
"		P.M.	Routine work. Weather very hot.	
"	4/8/18		Routine work.	
"	5/8/18	A.M.	Routine work.	
"		P.M.	Brigadier 47th Inf. Brigade inspected camp & arrangements for holding sick. Everything found satisfactory. Weather hot.	
"	6/8/18	A.M.	Very heavy rain. Visited Oau Commandant to get our billets for men who went in Bivouacs. Attended a large repast sheet from him with open sides, which would accommodate 30.	
"		P.M.	Routine work. Weather dull all day.	
"	7/8/18		Office & Orderly work all day. Weather fine.	

Army Form C. 2118.

WAR DIARY
or
INTELLIGENCE SUMMARY.
(Erase heading not required.)

Instructions regarding War Diaries and Intelligence Summaries are contained in F.S. Regs., Part II. and the Staff Manual respectively. Title pages will be prepared in manuscript.

Place	Date	Hour	Summary of Events and Information	Remarks and references to Appendices
ENQUIN	8/9/18		Office & Routine work. Weather fine	
"	9/9/18	AM	Inspection by C.O. & of 16th Division who had hospital arrangements and transport who were satisfied with everything. Officers Aitken & Brown arrived for duty from the Base. New Staff Captain 47th Infantry Brigade and arranged for a medical Inspection Room for surrendering details to be found at Brigade H.Q.	
"	10/9/18		Routine & Office work. Weather fine	
"	11/9/18		Routine work. Very hot and sultry.	
"	12/9/18		Routine & Office work. A draft of eight reinforcements arrived from Base. Weather fine & hot.	
"	13/9/18	AM	Detachment which was away with 78th American Division returned.	
"	14/9/18	AM	Route Lille, Bebey, Benan, more U.S.A. arrived for duty from Base. Interviewed D.A.D.M.S. re disinfection of Indian clothing who made such arrangements for it to be done.	
"	15/9/18		Revised accommodation for scabies patients to 36 owing to large numbers coming in for treatment of Biviouacs in the outside the Hospital fence. Weather fine.	

Army Form C. 2118.

WAR DIARY
or
INTELLIGENCE SUMMARY.
(Erase heading not required.)

Instructions regarding War Diaries and Intelligence Summaries are contained in F. S. Regs., Part II. and the Staff Manual respectively. Title pages will be prepared in manuscript.

Place	Date	Hour	Summary of Events and Information	Remarks and references to Appendices
ENGUIN	16/8/16	P.M.	Routine work. Weather fine & hot. Warning order received from 47th Infantry Brigade to be prepared to move.	
"	17/8/16	A.M.	Routine work. Arrangements for move received from ADMS 16th Division	
"	18/9/16		Much time table received from 47th Brigade. Transport move at 5.20 p.m.	
"	19/8/16	6 P.M.	Unit moved to new area by Busses and lorries and took over the old occupied by No 1 Field Ambulance at BARLIN. Sheet 44, B, K 33.	
BARLIN	20/8/16	A.M.	Settling down in new area. Visit of ADMS and D.A.D.M.S. 16th Division. Arranged with them about collection of local sick. Transport arrived 6 p.m. 1st William Road arrived from base and taken in charge.	
"	21/8/16	A.M.	Office & routine work. Made arrangements with Town Major for treatment of civilians in air raids on the town. Major Bartlett Rowe proceeded on leave to U.K. Very hot and sultry.	
"	22/8/16	P.M.	Detachment 19 O.R. to 22 C.C.S. for temporary duty. E.A. activities over us last night but no bombs dropped. Weather fine.	

Army Form C. 2118.

WAR DIARY
or
INTELLIGENCE SUMMARY.
(Erase heading not required.)

Instructions regarding War Diaries and Intelligence Summaries are contained in F. S. Regs., Part II. and the Staff Manual respectively. Title pages will be prepared in manuscript.

Place	Date	Hour	Summary of Events and Information	Remarks and references to Appendices
BARLIN	23/8/15	A.M.	Routine Work.	
		P.M.	Went to 22 C.C.S. to see Detachment and Mg Chm. Lieut Brown M.O.R.C to 18 G. Scottish Rifles for temporary duty. Brother pris but slowly	
"	24/8/15	A.M.	Completed arrangements for evacuating civilians during air raids. Office routine	
"	25/8/15		Office & Routine work. Weather fine	
"	26/8/15		Office & Routine work. Weather cool	
"	27/8/15		Protective work against bombing at first line. frequency with Routine work	
"	28/8/15	A.M.	Arranged accommodation for incoming reinforcement at Hersgarbis and three hours who is to take over from me.	
		P.M.	O.C. 111 Field Ambulance arrived & discussed taking over at time etc.	
"	29/8/15	A.M.	Explained scheme of work to O.C. 111 F. Ambulance & showed him around.	
"	30/8/15	A.M.	Handed over to O.C. 111 F. Ambulance & moved with unit to Three huns	
RUITZ	31/8/15	P.M.	Office work. Awaiting orders to move. Instructions received through A.D.M.S. 16th Division to join 25th Division details; proceeding by road. Marched out at [illegible] bivouacked for the night. [illegible]

To D.A.G. **17**   SECRET.
   G.H.Q., 3rd Echelon.
   ---------------------   -------

        Herewith copy of my War Diary for the month
of September.   It is much regretted that during the many _and_
moves this Ambulance has had during the last fortnight this _military_
matter was overlooked, and War Diary not sent on the First _operations_
of the month in accordance with regulations.

                                    [signature]
                                    Lt. Col. R.A.M.C.
14/10/18.   Commndg. 77 Field Ambulance.
---------   -------------------------------

Army Form C. 2118.

WAR DIARY
or
INTELLIGENCE SUMMARY.

(Erase heading not required.)

CONFIDENTIAL

September, 1918

140/3324

WAR DIARY
MEDICAL

77th Field Ambulance

Army Form C. 2118.

WAR DIARY
or
INTELLIGENCE SUMMARY.
(Erase heading not required.)

Place	Date	Hour	Summary of Events and Information	Remarks and references to Appendices
PERNES	1/9/18	13.4	Unit marched by road at 13 hours from PERNES to CREPY. Hqrs Reference arriving there at 18 hours. Good billets and accommodation were obtained from the Area Commandant. 3 pm full out on the march and one carried to the destination.	PERNES 11 1Z.10.S.N. 1C 57 Aujoucourt
CREPY	2/9/18	10.00 hr.	Unit marched off at 10.00 hr by road to LEBIEZ. On the way one Ford lorry broke down and had to be sent to 25th Division M.T. (company) workshops at FRUGES. Hqrs Reference HAZEBROUCK 5A G.B. G.2. Arrived at 15 hours, no billets available but good accommodation was a Hop field. Ends hours field at Shelty. Hqrs Reference DIEPPE 16 4 I 3.8 of the unit received orders to proceed to HAUDRICOURT by rail convoy from G.H.Q.	3/9/18
LEBIEZ	3/9/18	10.00	Unit marched by road from LEBIEZ to LE BOISLE a halt being made for lunch outside HESDIN. The march was completed by 7 p.m. good billets for men & horses in the town, weather fine. Under instructions from G.H.Q.	Mg... LEBIEZ BOISLE MISEVILLE 3.4 8.3
LEBOISLE	4/9/18	10.00	Unit marched from LE BOISLE to PLESSIEL, 5 k S.B. arrived at 3 pm. Billets for 3 days procured from Detail Issue S/d at ABBEVILLE. Weather fine.	N/ota...
PLESSIEL	5/9/18	10.00	Marched by Road from PLESSIEL to MOUFLIERES. Kopje I Z 8.2 Horses were found to be fresh in the town and the march was through pleasant country. a FOUCAUCOURT kopje I 3.4 I 7.2 advance accommodation was found in a Chateau.	

Army Form C. 2118.

WAR DIARY
or
INTELLIGENCE SUMMARY.
(Erase heading not required.)

Instructions regarding War Diaries and Intelligence Summaries are contained in F. S. Regs., Part II. and the Staff Manual respectively. Title pages will be prepared in manuscript.

Place	Date	Hour	Summary of Events and Information	Remarks and references to Appendices
FOUCAUCOURT VIA NESLE	6/9/18	10 AM	Unit moved from FOUCAUCOURT to HAUDAICOURT. Buses 16 A.I. 3.8 arriving at 3pm. Bivouacked for the night in a field at VILLERS. Buses 4.I.8.8 on their standing hospital of 150 beds is to be formed. O.C. interviewed Camp Commandant	
			HAUDAICOURT area and secured marquees where necessary stores to be drawn for formation of hospital	
VILLERS	7/9/18	AM	Commenced formation of Hospital. Saw ADMS (Command) and ADMS CG Division re army medical arrangements of transport & equipment & delivery of stores	
VILLERS	8/9/18	pm	Went of to M.S. L of 8.8 re the units of hospital & proposed plan viewed & approved.	
" "	9/9/18	AM	Went of 101 DALRYMPLES of sane the advice on Malaria who gave us trucks about the treatment of Malaria cases existent in hospital when open & form.	
" "	10/9/18	AM	Interviewed C.R.E. of the area about necessary R.E. work to be undertaken - internal formation of hospital.	
" "	11/9/18	AM	Interviewed Brigadier 199 I.B. who promised to send us the engineers of detachment of Units to commenced hospital roadway for entrance & exit & also	
" "	12/9/18		Erection of Armstrong Sheds & Washroom Officer Quarters	

Army Form C. 2118.

WAR DIARY
or
INTELLIGENCE SUMMARY.
(Erase heading not required.)

Instructions regarding War Diaries and Intelligence Summaries are contained in F. S. Regs., Part II. and the Staff Manual respectively. Title pages will be prepared in manuscript.

Place	Date	Hour	Summary of Events and Information	Remarks and references to Appendices
VILLERS	13/9/18	AM	Office Routine. Return of Hospital contents. S.M.O ABANCOURT interviewed re Medical Officers for Motored Batteries when contact was exploited to them.	
" "	14/9/18	AM	Returned sent to ABANCOURT to take over Hospital there from 55th Division. Orders are given by the End, 1 MMSR WELLS R.A.M.C & 32 Other Ranks with one Motor Ambulance received from M.D.M.S. 66th Division.	
		P.M.	Returned out to SEA.RUEX. Supp 16 5 6 6 4. to take over Hospital from 55th Division. Captain HADDOW M.C. R.A.M.C. & 20 Other Ranks sent in Motor transport under orders of D.D.M.S. 66th Division.	
" "	15/9/18	AM	Office Routine. Return of hospital contents.	
" "	16/9/18	AM PM	Office Routine. Arrival of Rations Maps & Plots for Hospital.	
" "	17/9/18	PM	Commandant ABANCOURT area inspected work of section of Hospital & saw plan of Division on this return to FRANCE and Hope 66th Division on the enemy who wanted one of unpending move of 66th Division from this area.	
" "	18/9/18	AM	Informed A.D.M.S. 25th Division on the return to FRANCE and Hope 66th Division on the enemy who wanted me of unpending move of 66th Division from this area.	

Army Form C. 2118.

WAR DIARY
or
INTELLIGENCE SUMMARY.
(Erase heading not required.)

Instructions regarding War Diaries and Intelligence Summaries are contained in F. S. Regs., Part II. and the Staff Manual respectively. Title pages will be prepared in manuscript.

Place	Date	Hour	Summary of Events and Information	Remarks and references to Appendices
VILLERS	19/9/18	AM PM	Officer Posted. Lieutenant SERQUEX reported to Headquarters during day & left same day and was to Corps Demobilisation Centre and hence for A.D.M.S. 66 Divn	
	20/9/18	AM	Medical Board held. "State of Health" of Pte LONG 5th Leicestershire Rangers Present Lt Col HADLESON, M.C. and Members Major POWELL R.A.M.C. (T.F.) Captain HUDSON M.B. R.A.M.C. (T.F.) Pte LONG recommended to No. 8 General Hospital ROUEN	
			Report sent to A.D.M.S. 66 Division	
	21/9/18	AM	Received telephone from D.M.O. ADANCOURT that rail was opened for evacuation within next 48 hours to new area. Division of Hospital concerned	
	22/9/18	AM	Major WEIR placed to XIII Corps H.Q. to attend a conference to give exchange Major BARTLETT proceeded to ADANCOURT to witness Army Hospital	
		PM	Preparations at ADANCOURT closed and fresh transport for H.Q. which were then ready completed. Intermediate equipment Requisitioned	
	23/9/18	PM	Received warning order from 197 Inf. Brigade that unit will move to-morrow in work to join Headquarters of the Division at ST RIQUIER.	
	24/9/18	AM	Unit marched off at 9 AM having loaded own kit/stores and all done received as a Detachment and up by O.O.M. ROVEN to take own form no. and proceeded to G. FOUCAUCOURT km VESLE when the right [...] of to [...]	

2353 Wt. W2541/1454 700,000 5/15 D.D.&L. A.D.S.S./Forms/C. 2118.

Army Form C. 2118.

WAR DIARY
or
INTELLIGENCE SUMMARY.
(Erase heading not required.)

Place	Date	Hour	Summary of Events and Information	Remarks and references to Appendices
ROUVROY EN SANTERRE NESLE	24/1/16	AM	Was about to start on short trip journey to ST AIGNIER when a Wire was received by Registrar RASC to divert route to MOLLIENS VIDAME. Annexe 17, 2, 4, 37. Started off at 12:30 & arrived about 6 pm. Billets had been arranged.	
MOLLIENS VIDAME	26/1/16	AM	Started off at 10.000 hrs for MILLY sur SOMME. Arrived about 3 pm. Interviewed A.S.O. about rations for 3 days on arrival with instructions. P.S.O. kept but how about an arrival but succeeded in getting them upon consultation with S.S.O. 25th Division who had arrived first.	
MILLY sur SOMME	27/1/16	pm	Marched to QUERRIEU by road at 10 am. Arrived about 3 pm. 25th Division at 6.30 pm but also in regions unknown.	
QUERRIEU	28/1/16	am	Left at 6 am & marched to FRICOURT-VILLERS. Obtained billets from town commandant and found hospital (& infantry with 29 R.A.M.C. unit) of G.O.C. who inspected hospital and accepted. Received orders also to have M. or 3 pm. Inspected future of future evacuated to C.C.S.	
FRICOURT	2/2/16	am	Went when arrived at 2am marched off at FAM for BERNAFAY WOOD & LENSM ED at arrived there 3 pm. Billets in dug outs. Hospital in wooden shed.	

2353 Wt. W3514/1454 700,000 5/15 D.D.&L. A.D.S.S./Forms/C. 2118.

Army Form C. 2118.

WAR DIARY
or
INTELLIGENCE SUMMARY.
(Erase heading not required.)

Instructions regarding War Diaries and Intelligence Summaries are contained in F.S. Regs., Part II. and the Staff Manual respectively. Title pages will be prepared in manuscript.

Place	Date	Hour	Summary of Events and Information	Remarks and references to Appendices
BEAN+FAY WOOD	39/9/40	AM	Office Routine. Whilst out for a walk. Inspected billets and surroundings. Saw A.D.M.S 26th Division in evening to discuss framing question and efforts in front situation of ambulance weather cold & windy.	
" "	3		H.H.Kenny Lieut Colonel R.amc comm 77 F Ambulance	

2353 Wt. W2544/1454 700,000 5/15 D. D. & L. A.D.S.S./Forms/C. 2118.

Confidential

Vol 37
WL 37
40/3401

War diary of
77 Field Ambulance
From 1st – 31st of October
1918

Army Form C. 2118.

WAR DIARY
or
INTELLIGENCE SUMMARY.
(Erase heading not required.)

Instructions regarding War Diaries and Intelligence Summaries are contained in F.S. Regs., Part II. and the Staff Manual respectively. Title pages will be prepared in manuscript.

Place	Date	Hour	Summary of Events and Information	Remarks and references to Appendices
BERNAFAY WOOD	1/1/18	0900	Marched road from the Nord to Bois de L'Eppinette. Arrived there at 11.30. Small Field Oppt met on the side of the road for 10 periods & detailed until more room in forming. Nothing unusual to report. Weather fine.	Sketch 920 D.14.c.2.2.
BOIS DE L'EPPINETTE	2/1/18	11h am	Routine work.	
		15.30	Received marching orders from the 1st Infantry Brigade to move to St Emilie. Marched off 17.15. arriving at ST. EMILIE at 21.30 hrs. The Unit bivouacked without in a most faulty. Some shelling round about with ??? & heavy shells. ??? horses enough rooms to remember. Weather fine.	Sketch 6x2 B.24.T.2.3.
ST. EMILIE	3/1/18	09h	Summoned to Conference 10 ock of 1st Infantry Brigade concerning plans operations to be undertaken the following day. Proceeded to A.D.M.S. at 1.37. Australian Division to ascertain more ??? arrangements in the same area. Going treatment subsequently interviewed A.D.M.S. 25th Division. Supplied him with this information.	Sketch 622 B.24. T. 2. 3.
			Proceeded to Conference & relaxed site for Main Dressing Station next to Bellevue farm. On returning called at the 1st Infantry Brigade Gover's & was informed that the Unit marched off at 13.30. The Brigade ??? ??? 1.50. Brigade ??? left one ??? & Brigade at their Headqr. ???. 5. 3. ??? ??? ??? hours subsequently marched ??? to field in the Bellevue Road. T. 2. c.65. where they bivouacked for the night.	

Army Form C. 2118.

WAR DIARY
or
INTELLIGENCE SUMMARY.
(Erase heading not required.)

Instructions regarding War Diaries and Intelligence Summaries are contained in F. S. Regs., Part II. and the Staff Manual respectively. Title pages will be prepared in manuscript.

Place	Date	Hour	Summary of Events and Information	Remarks and references to Appendices
BELLICOURT ROAD	4/11/18	0640	Received warning order from the 7th Infantry Brigade that Battalions were going in north and were to Aragon at 0800. The Battalion Broong arrived at 8 in. A. & D. pm. Dressing Station at G.2.26.10.2. Most Wounded men turned forward a stripped with personnel ready to receive wounded who moved to arrive about 0730 hr. Owing to the Spin Broong Status their having left forward with Battalion it was necessary at night. This was moved in the afternoon to S.11. d. 6.4.	Markham G.2, 4, & 5
HARGICOURT	5/11/18	am	O.O. inspected the Advanced Dressing Station & forward posts at B.11.a.16.10.4 & B.45.a.10.2. Advanced Dressing Stations forward of forward. Casualties of recent fighting few, at heavy ones and almost mostly of light machine gun wounds.	Markham G.3.a.4.72
		pm	Nothing much.	
HARGICOURT	6/11/18	am	K.O.C. + to the A.D.M.S. 25th Division round the R.A.P's of the 7th Brigade & forward Ambulances marched a R.B.S.M.D.S. when Ks system of evacuation was explained. Everything working smoothly.	Markham G.3.4.72
		19.30	The A.D.M.S. 25th Division addressed the Field Ambulance Commander to Conference at Ks Headquarters of the 74 Field Ambulance to discuss Medical arrangement to forthcoming operations. The Conference lasted 1½ hours.	

WAR DIARY
or
INTELLIGENCE SUMMARY.
(Erase heading not required.)

Army Form C. 2118.

Place	Date	Hour	Summary of Events and Information	Remarks and references to Appendices
HARGICOURT	7/10/18	09.00	An advanced party consisting of One N.C.O. and Other Ranks were sent up this Relay Post at Mont Espee & convert Mont place into an Advanced Dressing Station in preparation for the receiving operation. This was prepared & ready to receive casualties by 14.00 hours.	
		14.00	The Advanced Dressing Station on the BELLICOURT — GRAND MONT road marched as a complete unit to a Main Dressing Station. The former M.D.S. at Cérisicourt being about the same hour. The personnel, equipment and organization of the Ambulance moving from there to the new M.D.S. on arrival the staff of the original Advanced Dressing Station on the Bellicourt — Grandcourt Road was sent forward to reinforce the Advanced Party at the new A.D.S. at Mont Espee. All moves were completed by 17.00 hours. A conference was held of the O.C. 77th Field Ambulance & various arrangements made for operations to take place the next day & O/C All concerned.	
BELLICOURT GRANDCOURT ROAD	8/10/18		Night operations undertaken by the THIRD and FOURTH ARMIES at 05.17.M. Medical situation zero — Relay Post, Quadroon Quarry, Advanced Dressing Station Mont Espee, M.D.S. entered Mont Farm. Excellent programs was made by the attacking troops & at 15.00 hours the A.D.S. had been formed on the main Bellicourt – Le Catelet road at the entrance to Gonaire, the original A.D.S. being about 3/4	
		16.00		
		18.50	Mont Farm to Gomans. Owing to the large number of cases arriving information	

Army Form C. 2118.

WAR DIARY
or
INTELLIGENCE SUMMARY.
(Erase heading not required.)

Instructions regarding War Diaries and Intelligence Summaries are contained in F.S. Regs., Part II. and the Staff Manual respectively. Title pages will be prepared in manuscript.

Place	Date	Hour	Summary of Events and Information	Remarks and references to Appendices
Continued	8/10/18		a rear party had to be left behind at the former A.D.S. in order to evacuate all cases. By M.A.C. Cars. Leys goes to the main party at 0200 hours	
		19.00	On the 9/10/18. At 1900 hours the A.D.S. was subject to a heavy attack from hostile aircraft during which Capt. M.K. Niles R.A.M.C. & 7 O.R.'s that rank be were wounded and two other ranks killed. One ambulance tent being put out of action.	
Estrees	9/10/18	15.00	The attacking infantry having made good progress the A.D.S. at GENEVE was closed at 1500 hours and reopened at the mill at MARETZ. There was about a small advanced party no before having rear cart forward to progress since had been during and evacuating cases at C.C. remaining at ESTREES. Orders received during the afternoon from A.D.M.S. 25th Division that the ambulance is to take over the M.D.S. for the Division on relief of the own Brigade note.	P. 22. C.
	10/10/18	08.00	Our advance having again progressed satisfactorily on advanced party was again sent forward to form the new A.D.S. at P.22.C. The old A.D.S. moving up	
		11.30	There at 1130 hours & the M.D.S. from Estrees moving up & being overtaken at the former A.D.S. at the mill MARETZ. Owing to the rapidity of the advance during the day it was found necessary to again move the M.D.S. during the afternoon of this appointment to BUSIGNY where it was opened at 1800 hours. A relay post being formed at Noelly at the A.D.S. at 2.19.d. and R.A.P.s being at Q.25. Central. The note that throughout this day was fine.	Q.19.d. Q.25.Central.

2353 Wt. W254/1454 700,000 5/15 D. D. & L. A.D.S.S./Forms/C. 2118.

Army Form C. 2118.

WAR DIARY
or
INTELLIGENCE SUMMARY.
(Erase heading not required.)

Instructions regarding War Diaries and Intelligence Summaries are contained in F. S. Regs., Part II. and the Staff Manual respectively. Title pages will be prepared in manuscript.

Place	Date	Hour	Summary of Events and Information	Remarks and references to Appendices
BUSIGNY	11/10/18	06.00	So as to facilitate the treatment and evacuation of wounded the M.D.S. was divided into two parts; Apportion was on the site for receiving cases & good place for forming up Walking Wounded Dressing Station formed immediately opposite in an old German Rest Camp. This was cleaned out & ready for their reception by 0800 A.M. At the same time the O.C., M.D.S. moved his Dressing Station from its previous position to a more suitable place close to the Church at CONNECHY, which is nearer the routes of evacuation.	
		14.30	Instructional A.D.M.S. was informed that the O.C. 76 Field Ambulance has been relieved to find the O.C. M.D.S. at once & 3 men for M.D.S. sub medical charge of the 75th Infantry Brigade. Relays to be completed by 2000 A.M. this evening. Stretcher Squads to work three runners were accordingly distributed for this duty and proceeded to O.C. A.D.S. at HONNECHY, who had them	
		16.00	placed in position & reported the relays complete.	
		20.00		
		20.00	Received warning order that the Division would be relieved on the line commencing the 12 inst.	
BUSIGNY	14/10/18	10.00	The A.D.M.S. 50th Division, the O.C. 1/1st, O.C. 2/2nd Northumbrian Field Ambulances here to the taking over of my M.D.S., Walking Wounded Dressing Station. It was decided that I should only hand over my established Market Stump & O.C. 2/2nd Northumbrian Field Ambulance as they had formerly made their arrangements for the treatment and — wounded. The 1/1 M.A.C. Cars & 4 lorries attached to me to transit	

Army Form C. 2118.

WAR DIARY
or
INTELLIGENCE SUMMARY.
(Erase heading not required.)

Instructions regarding War Diaries and Intelligence Summaries are contained in F.S. Regs., Part II. and the Staff Manual respectively. Title pages will be prepared in manuscript.

Place	Date	Hour	Summary of Events and Information	Remarks and references to Appendices
Continued				
AUSIGNY	12/9/18		over to O.C. 1/1st Northumbrian Field Ambulance. There were only two beds left at the Unit moved out to ELINCOURT, which is the village allotted to the 7th Infantry Brigade group.	
		13.45		
		12.50	Order sent to O.C. A.D.S. to close his Dressing Station as soon as the 7th & 75th Brigades were clear of the forward area & to open my new Headquarters at ELINCOURT as soon as possible. O.C. went ahead with N.A.C. Barrage This Unit is selected in order for the Ambulance in a farm on the Estourmel – Malincourt Road just outside the village of Elincourt.	
		16.00	The Unit arrived & moved into billets. Found a small Rest Station of 30 beds in a field adjoining the farm in which we were billeted.	
		17.30	The A.D.S. party rejoined.	
ELINCOURT	13/9/18 a.m.		Office Routine. The rest of the day spent in Medical inspection & taking personnel.	
ELINCOURT	14/9/18 a.m.		Office Routine.	
		14.30	Conference at A.D.M.S. Office re forthcoming operations. It was decided in future that one Ambulance should be responsible for clearing the line and one A.D.S. party for the purpose the Bearers and cars of that Unit should act in Divisional Rest Station & the Motor Ambulances in reserve pending developments.	

WAR DIARY
or
INTELLIGENCE SUMMARY.
(Erase heading not required.)

Army Form C. 2118.

Instructions regarding War Diaries and Intelligence Summaries are contained in F.S. Regs., Part II. and the Staff Manual respectively. Title pages will be prepared in manuscript.

Place	Date	Hour	Summary of Events and Information	Remarks and references to Appendices
ELINCOURT	17/9/18	a.m.	Office routine.	
		14.30	Conference at A.D.M.S. Office. Heard further the means of plans for the next operation. Decided that so our Brigade is to go into the line first that we shall move up with them and be responsible for clearing the forward area.	
ELINCOURT	18/9/18	06.30	Worked with O.C. of A.D.M.S. & Walking Wounded Collecting Post at 1/3rd Northumbrian Field Ambulance, chose site for out transport when moving up.	
		14.00	The Unit moved from ELINCOURT to a small field in the village of Banteux road just before going in to the village of Banteux.	
		16.30	Arrived there. The Unit bivouacs for the night in tents & transport in the field immediately behind. O.C. proceeded to Headquarters of 1/3rd Northumbrian Ambulance and subsequently A.D.M.S. 50th Division, conferred with O.C. 1/3rd Northumbrian Field Ambulance about the work in co-operation with 1/3rd Northumbrian Field Ambulance for commencement of operations. Transport lines were formed at R.26.d.9.2. only A.D.S. Limber, Water Cart proceeded with Headquarters and Water Cart proceeded with Headquarters, Cook's Limber, Quartermaster Limber, & Water Cart parking at this place.	R.35.a.10.9. R.26.d.9.2

Army Form C. 2118.

WAR DIARY
or
INTELLIGENCE SUMMARY.
(Erase heading not required.)

Instructions regarding War Diaries and Intelligence Summaries are contained in F.S. Regs., Part II. and the Staff Manual respectively. Title pages will be prepared in manuscript.

Place	Date	Hour	Summary of Events and Information	Remarks and references to Appendices
HONNECHY	17/10/18	05.20	Attack on enemy's position made by 50th Division, with the 75th Brigade in reserve. Arrangements with O.C. 1/3rd Northumbrian Field Ambulance that if our Brigade was called on that 2 mounted forms an A.D.S. and the Bearer Sections starting post in conjunction with form on the Bapaume - LE CATEAU road, just south Honnechy. Meanwhile the Ambulance was called up on mounted standard, which remained the same throughout the day.	
HONNECHY	18/10/18	03.10	Having orders received that the 75th Brigade were to attack at 08.25 hours after preliminary operation of 50th Division.	P.30.a.3.2.
		05.30.	The Unit marched off & formed the A.D.S. and Walking Wounded Collecting Post. This was ready to receive patients by 0800 hours. During the formation of the Dressing Station we were subjected to heavy shelling, partly by high velocity guns & secondly by shrapnel & air amunition.	
		10.00	O.C. proceeded forward & ascertained the A.D.S. to far back for wheeled transport, & came up to ST SOUPLET, & before an advanced party going forward, & ambulances arrived.	Q.33.a.9.2.
		12.00	A.D.S. then moved to this point, arriving up by 12.00 hrs & while holding forty beds left behind to evacuate the two places all the previous cases. This leaving two establishments, a forward Collecting Post and Cart Stand unaltered. Evacuation being performed by hand carriage from R.A.P's to Cart Post, by Ford Cars on Cart Post to A.D.S. and by Sunbeam Cars from A.D.S. at Les Pâtures, the outskirts of SERAIN. Walking Wounded Ambulance from the A.D.S. to the Walking Wounded Collecting Post & by M. Corps Ambulance from W.W. Collecting Post by the 1/3rd Northumbrian Field Ambulance from By 10 P.M. all the C.M.D.S.	Q.28.c.3.4. P.30.a.3.2.

Army Form C. 2118.

WAR DIARY
or
INTELLIGENCE SUMMARY.
(Erase heading not required.)

Instructions regarding War Diaries and Intelligence Summaries are contained in F. S. Regs., Part II. and the Staff Manual respectively. Title pages will be prepared in manuscript.

Place	Date	Hour	Summary of Events and Information	Remarks and references to Appendices
ST. SOUPLET.	19/10/18		O.C. with advanced party proceeded in Ambulance Car to the outskirts of ST. BENIN and there to ascertain if and where to push forward the A.D.S. in accordance with the existing situation. This being not practible No ST. BENIN was not occupied by the enemy. Returning & stalling with Good Hill.	P.22.c.2.2.6.
		11.00.	The V.A.D.S. was parked here, the wounded being cleared the same time. Ammts. holding party being left there to the evacuation of the area, their earliest treatment. O.C. reconnoitred forward area and established post in road at crossroads to get to find Ears in four minutes. The A.D.M.S. visited the Ambulance during the afternoon & gave warning order that we were to be relieved in the line on the 20th inst. by the 76th Field Ambulance, when we shall go back into rest.	Q.19.c.6.6.
ST. BENIN.	20/10/18	07.00.	The 7th & 75th Brigades attack enemy's position.	
			Major E.B. Galdos N.C. R.A.M.C. Effected a change of demies with 7 subordinates A.D.S. as before, three squads. Three runners were attached to Battalions of the 7th Brigade, three squads & one runners & new runners attached to Battalions of the 75th Brigade. Ford Cars running between Coll. Post and A.D.S.	Q.19.c.6.6.
		12.00.	O.C. 76th Field Ambulance arrived and took over duties of clearing the line from me at that time.	Q.19.c.6.6.
		14.00.	We packed up, marched out to our transport lines, having being relieved by O.C. 76th Field Ambulance, Major G.B. Galdos, N.C., R.A.M.C., all ranks, Horses Ambulances, 2 Ford Cars.	
		16.00.	Arrived at the transport lines. Canvas was pitched for accommodation of unit as the field weather was not...	

A.D.S.S./Form/C. 2118.

Army Form C. 2118.

WAR DIARY
or
INTELLIGENCE SUMMARY.
(Erase heading not required.)

Instructions regarding War Diaries and Intelligence Summaries are contained in F. S. Regs., Part II. and the Staff Manual respectively. Title pages will be prepared in manuscript.

Place	Date	Hour	Summary of Events and Information	Remarks and references to Appendices
	21/9/18.		Lieut. Little M.O.R.C., U.S.A., detached for temporary duty attd. 61 M.D.S. Owing to bad weather the percentage is not so healthy and the Unit moved with our intercourse, who sent 6 cooks limber down farm where excellent accommodation was obtained.	P.26.d.8.2.
		14.00.		V.4.d.5.2.
Farm	22/9/18.	15.00 a.m.	Arrived there. The remainder of the transport remained in formation for the night. Transport moved down to our Headquarters. Visited A.D.M.S., who thought that in view of forthcoming operations we were not to pack up O.C. accordingly proceeded forward and above next with further up men horses with further arrangement for transport. In accordance instructions from A.D.M.S., two armfuls Cars, two Motor Ambulances, two Wheeled Stretchers, and two grades of Bearers were despatched to O.C. 76th Field Ambulance, St. BENIN for temporary duty.	V.4.d.5.2. 7.30.e.6.6.
		16.00	2nd Unit marched off and arrived at 17.00 hours at new situation where accommodation for the night was provided.	
	23/9/18.	07.00.	Visited O.C. 76th Field Ambulance at his Headquarters St. BENIN. Operations progressing well. Returned to Headquarters; reconnoitred a situation for Unit to move to by end sector equipment is the left in our present site in change of O/C Green R.A.M.C. when Unit movement to new Area.	Q.9.c.8.7.
		14.00	Unit & transport moved to new site, arriving at 15.00 hours. Personnel accommodated in a house, transport in a field behind.	Q.9.c.8.4.

2353 Wt. W2544/1454 700,000 5/15 D.D.&L. A.D.S.S./Forms/C. 2118.

Army Form C. 2118.

WAR DIARY
or
INTELLIGENCE SUMMARY.
(Erase heading not required.)

Instructions regarding War Diaries and Intelligence Summaries are contained in F. S. Regs., Part II. and the Staff Manual respectively. Title pages will be prepared in manuscript.

Place	Date	Hour	Summary of Events and Information	Remarks and references to Appendices
	24/10/18	07.00	Visited Brigadier of Infantry Brigade, who reported enemy shell fire great. Infantry were in front of BOIS-l'EVEQUE. On the way took O.C. Motor Ambulance with me over a large portion of the corner of the LE CATEAU – BAZUEL and LE CATEAU – POMMEREUIL roads.	Q.9, 2, 3, 4.
		10.15.	The Unit moved and arrived at 11.15 hours. Some slight shelling round about by High Velocity Guns.	Q.5, 2, 3, 9.
Cross Roads	25/10/18 a.m.		Officer i/c unit Major Bartlett M.C., R.A.M.C., proceeded to ESCAUFORT to attend to some French Civilians who were suffering from gas poisoning. All three were evacuated to C.C.S. at POIX L'AMPLE, twice sent by D.A.D.M.S. was treated and found to be suffering from Metallic poisoning.	Q.5, 2, 3, 9.
	26/10/18 a.m.		Officer Routine. Lieut. Benson M.O.R.C, U.S.A. relieved Major E. H. Cuddon, M.C., R.A.M.C., as Officer in charge of Bearers in the line. Bearers from personnel of Major Bartlett ATMS [?] wounded on the 25 inst. to that day completed 9 weeks personnel.	Q.5, 2, 3, 9.
	27/10/18 a.m.		Some gas shelling at 02.30 hours. Office routine. A fine day spent in training	Q.5, 2, 3, 9.
	28/10/18	10.00	Acting A.D.M.S. called to discuss formation of Divisional Rest Station by this Ambulance, as the Rail Station now of the 154 Field Ambulance was badly shelled during the night. It was decided to find at each either on HONNECHY or ESCAUFORT. Four staff Ranks admitted to hospital with Influenza	Q.5, 2, 3, 9.

WAR DIARY
or
INTELLIGENCE SUMMARY.
(Erase heading not required.)

Army Form C. 2118.

Place	Date	Hour	Summary of Events and Information	Remarks and references to Appendices
	29/10/18	08.30	Proceeded to BOONNERY to find a/49 further Personnel had arrived. Interviewed the Quartermaster about 2 together found no more available places in HONNECHY CHATEAU, where there was good accommodation for 100 beds. Advanced party of one N.C.O. and four men sent down to prepare the place. Interviewed D.D.M.S. XIII Corps and A.D.M.S. about the site and they approved of us being taken over to-morrow.	Q.5. F.3.9.
		17.00	Orders given to transport to move at once as possible. The buildings were unlit, no accommodation available and by 19.30 most were receiving patients.	
		19.00 to 20.30	Considerable numbers of sick were sent in during evening owing to enemy's bombing.	
HONNECHY	30/10/18 am		Continued treatment of sick and wounded. 30 cases of Influenza admitted accommodation to near. Decided to form an Corps Rest Room to a hut, minimum of about 150 beds being the necessary Influenza patients.	
		18.00	20 Bearers were sent to Field on the task.	
HONNECHY	31/10/18	09.30	Summoned to a conference with Lieut. A.D.M.S. at Busigny. It being impossible in my mind. Decided that situation continues to turn the Personnel of Rest Station present must move up with the attacking Divisions. 20 more men nominated. Throughout the day with Influenza — Throughout the activity under review the unit at Honnechy suffered from Influenza...	

M. M. Keown Lieut (actual) Gort. Comm. 77 Far. Ambulance
2/11/18

Volume

Confidential

Nov 1918

WAR DIARY

MEDICAL SERVICES

77th Field Ambulance

NOVEMBER 1918

COMMITTEE FOR THE
MEDICAL HISTORY OF THE WAR
6 MAR 1919

149/34/51

WO 38

WAR DIARY
or
INTELLIGENCE SUMMARY

Army Form C. 2118.

Place	Date	Hour	Summary of Events and Information	Remarks and references to Appendices
HONNECHY	1/11/18	A.M.	Office Routine. Major Haddow M.C. Rank in bed with Influenza. Found annexe to hospital in tents for 20 patients, also new out-patient department in old stable at entrance to hospital. In very many sick & also to be used as general receiving room. Lot of sick in hospital. Weather wet & cold.	
"	2/11/18	A.M.	A.D.M.S. 25th Division here to discuss [Influenza] Epidemic. Decided that I should remain here & have Officers RYAN & NASON allotted for Influenza duty. For R.E. & M.A.C. regiments. Sanitary officer FOSTER to take charge of our trains. Capt BENSON and I/C to go to C/Sgt Main ammony station. Capt FOSTER left & Capts RYAN & NASON reported by 1900 hrs. Weather wet & damp. 14 patients discharged to duty.	
"	"	P.M.	Major HADDOW still in bed.	
"	3/11/18	A.M.	Office Routine	
"	"	16.00 hrs	Visit of his A.D.M.S. 25th Div. Col HAMERTON C.M.G. D.S.O. who inspected hospital & thought all patients recently very comfortable.	
"	"	18.00	One sick our Division sent to C.M.D.S. for temporary duty.	

HWR

Army Form C. 2118.

WAR DIARY
or
INTELLIGENCE SUMMARY.
(Erase heading not required.)

Instructions regarding War Diaries and Intelligence Summaries are contained in F. S. Regs., Part II. and the Staff Manual respectively. Title pages will be prepared in manuscript.

Place	Date	Hour	Summary of Events and Information	Remarks and references to Appendices
HONNECHY	4/x/18	8 am	Attack by 25th Division on enemy's position west of LANDRECIES until 1000 of January. Spent of day in front in when our turn in advanced had come with Divisional First Station.	
		14.00	Visited ADMS 25th Division to discuss the situation, decided to remain at HONNECHY. Was informed that Captains BURWELL M.C. & HOWSON had been failed to be on duty, called for their car a hangar from road to Busigny.	
		18.00	Two Bombs dropped in vicinity of MARETZ-LE CATEAU road junction with HONNECHY road.	
"	5/x/18	am	Office Routine	
		14 h.	Wire from ADMS 25th Division asking for O.C. to come to Divisional Headquarters to discuss site & new situation of D.R.S. Proceeded to LANDRECIES and found suitable site. Called at ADMS Office on return when it was decided at arrival of wounded to our vehicle at Division who wished to be relieved in due course to form D.R.S. at LE CATEAU in its stead by 75th Field Ambulance. Decided to move to reserve with patients.	
"	6/x/18	12.15	Moved D.R.S. and 50 patients complete with Staff of M.A.C. cars to new site at LE CATEAU. On arrival being moved complete with staff & equipment at a time the Dressing & Reception Room, Store & Stores also being moved complete horse most satisfactory & the Patients ten second at new site by 17.00 hrs.	

Army Form C. 2118.

WAR DIARY
or
INTELLIGENCE SUMMARY.
(Erase heading not required.)

Instructions regarding War Diaries and Intelligence Summaries are contained in F. S. Regs., Part II. and the Staff Manual respectively. Title pages will be prepared in manuscript.

Place	Date	Hour	Summary of Events and Information	Remarks and references to Appendices
LE CATEAU	7/11/18	0900	Conference at A.D.M.S. Office to decide on suitable situation for D.R.S. in Orion was carried out to the West about LANDRECIES. Decided to inspect BUSSIES on the North and South flanks. A first site was actually chosen but on return some improvements of hut had been elected to form D.R.S. in the Barracks at LANDRECIES.	
LE CATEAU	8/11/18	0900	O.C. 77th Field Ambulance & ADMS 25th Division went to inspect 2 Barracks at LANDRECIES found D.A.D.M.S 46th Division there. D.A.D.M.S 25th Division O.S. 77 Field Ambulance & ADMS 25th Division there selected one GERMAN HOSPITAL in which was a small building for 5.7. East Lancs Field Ambulance as they were not of their own (viz) 66th Division they were ordered to move and it was agreed to form a D.R.S.	
	1400	Advance of 5.7. 1.F.A.&.C & 4 CoR proceeded to new site to commence clearing out floor coats of everything & what huts F. ambulance still there a.a. - a.m.g. 25th Division about them to prepare to move out at once.	
LE CATEAU	9/11/18	0900	Moved to LANDRECIES with whole unit and 56 patients arrived at 12.00 hrs 2/5 East Lancashire Field Ambulance still in occupation. Placed patients in an empty room & proceeded to a.a. - a.m.g. for instructions who ordered to take over site & that O.C. 9/2 East Lancs Field Ambulance was to separate at once being only his own. As the invalids it was arranged to show rooms by accommodation there Remainder of the day spent in clearing up preparatory to taking over from them as Divisional Rest Station.	

WAR DIARY
or
INTELLIGENCE SUMMARY.
(Erase heading not required.)

Army Form C. 2118.

Place	Date	Hour	Summary of Events and Information	Remarks and references to Appendices
LANDRECIES	10/XI/18	09.00	Received information from A.D.M.S. 25th Division that the matter of movement of our front line had been referred to Corps "Q" and that they had ruled that 3/2 East Lancs Field Ambulance might remain where they were & we were to share with them.	
		10.00	Proceeded with ADMS 25th Division and D.A.Q.M.G. to find a new site for the Rest Station at BOUSIES & found an excellent one in an old Château, L'EPINETTE with accommodation for 200 patients. This was empty and was accordingly taken over.	
		12.30	Advance party of 1 H.C.O. & 12 men went on ahead to take over & clean up new site.	
		13.45	Ambulance with patients moved to new site, all patients being comfortably housed & the Rest Station complete by 18.30 hrs. Later have complete by 16.30 hrs.	
BOUSIES.	11/XI/18	A.M.	Formation of Hospital continued; accommodation provided for 100 patients.	
		11.00 14.30 hrs	Visits of ADMS & A.A. & Q.M.G. 25th Division to see work in progress. Notified from H.Q. 25th Division that hostilities would cease as from 11.00 hrs & to suspend further outward movement of personnel. O.C. 25th Division Train in early instalment of arrival. O.C. 77th Field Ambulance was asked to spend on this subject arranged to start early treatment rooms with all Battalion Medical Officers from 19.00 hrs until the hour of 19.00 hrs and 07.00 hrs on days on which he wished Medical & ways to be supplied in behalf by Officers. Ambulances. VV	

WAR DIARY or INTELLIGENCE SUMMARY

Army Form C. 2118.

Place	Date	Hour	Summary of Events and Information	Remarks and references to Appendices
BOUSIES	12/10/18 AM	11.00	Office Routine. Received A.D.M.S. 25th Division who informs that unit will be moving to-morrow probably to H.Q. of old XIII Corps Main Dressing Station at LECHTEAU. Owing to our present shortage of cars managed for the loan of 2 ambulances from 76 & 76 Field Ambulances for the move. This was agreed to. 130 patients to be transported with D.A.S. to new area.	
BOUSIES	13/10/18	03.00	Orders have cancelled and have received orders to proceed to POMMEREUIL and clear the Divisional Aid Station; all cars being evacuated; received from MDS 25th Division O.C. 75 & 76 Field Ambulances to provide 2 cars each & 16 MAC & vans. Move to commence at 07.30 hours. M.A.C. commenced at 07.30 hours. Patients kept up being cleared at 07.00 hrs. all cars evacuated and D.A.S. cleared by 09.30 hrs. Ambulances worked by Road under Divisional arrangements at 11.00 hrs to POMMEREUIL Bullets being retained from the Army (mounted troops) settled in by 13.30 hrs Divn. arrived at 14.00 hrs. Interviewed ADMS 25th Division re disposal of dressing stations and blankets when it was decided to fit ambulances from Corps re their disposal.	
POMMEREUIL	14/10/18 AM		Office Routine. Visited 37 C.C.S. re the disposal of Red Cross Stores before we move to our new area when the Division hopes.	RW

WAR DIARY or INTELLIGENCE SUMMARY

Army Form C. 2118.

Place	Date	Hour	Summary of Events and Information	Remarks and references to Appendices
POMMEREUIL	13/11/18	A.M.	Office Routine. Attended band given by G.O.C. 25th Division to all Officers of the Division in a section of Pho Lable.	
POMMEREUIL	16/11/18	A.M.	Office Routine. 141 Reinforcements arrived. Was inspected and posted to stations.	
		11.00	Saw A.D.M.S. 25th Division who asked me to arrange duties of Officers having his sons on leave to the United Kingdom. It was agreed that O.C. 77 F. Ambulance should remain at Cour Ste Marabin. Conference to A.D.M.S. Office to be held from 9.10.a.m. to 12.00 hr. daily.	
POMMEREUIL	17/11/18	10.00	Proceeded to ADMS Office 25th Division and arranged duties of Sons. Office Routine until 17h00	
POMMEREUIL	18/11/18	a.m.	Office Routine. Circular re Railwaymen & Coalminers attached.	
POMMEREUIL	19/11/18	a.m.	Office Routine. Circular re Education Scheme received.	
POMMEREUIL	20/11/18		Further circular re Education Scheme & Coal Miners returns received. O.C. to Office, A.D.M.S. all day.	
POMMEREUIL	21/11/18	a.m.	Office Routine. Extra of work - general cleanliness. Route march. Headquarters.	
Do.	22/11/18		Office Routine. Attended Sports meeting at D.H.Q. Head-Quarters June.	
Do.	23/11/18		Office Routine. Educational Forms "B" completed, rendered to A.D.M.S. Weather fine.	

Army Form C. 2118.

WAR DIARY
or
INTELLIGENCE SUMMARY.
(Erase heading not required.)

Place	Date	Hour	Summary of Events and Information	Remarks and references to Appendices
POMMEREUIL	24/11/18		Office Routine. Weather fine.	
		11.00	Attended Sports Sub-Committee at Yr Brigade Hdqrs.	
			Conferred Mr D.H.Q. in afternoon when further details of Demobilisation scheme were submitted & discussed.	
POMMEREUIL	25/11/18	10.00	Meeting of Educational Officers at D.H.Q to discuss further development of Educational Scheme. O/C Educational Officer present to answer & arrange.	
		15.00	Meeting of Ambulance Commanders at the office of A.D.M.S. to represent A.F.B.179A.	
			The G.O.C. 25th Division to inspect Ambulance on the 28th inst. Weather fine.	
POMMEREUIL	26/11/18		Office Routine. A.F.B.179A. completed & forwarded for use of personnel who are married. Weather fair but cold.	
POMMEREUIL	27/11/18		Office Routine. During the afternoon a preliminary inspection for use of G.O.C.'s inspection. Weather fair but dull.	
POMMEREUIL	28/11/18	09.00	Inspection by G.O.C. 25th Division. Unit complimented highly on excellent turnout.	
		18.45	Received orders to move tomorrow with 7th Infantry Bde to QUIEVY	
QUIEVY	29/11/18	10.10	Moved to QUIEVY by march route.	
		14.30	Passed starting point. Arrived QUIEVY. Weather fine.	
			Preliminary meeting & new appointments by incoming meeting.	

VALENCIENNES
Sheet 12
4. F.2.0.

Army Form C. 2118.

WAR DIARY
or
INTELLIGENCE SUMMARY.
(Erase heading not required.)

Instructions regarding War Diaries and Intelligence Summaries are contained in F. S. Regs., Part II. and the Staff Manual respectively. Title pages will be prepared in manuscript.

Place	Date	Hour	Summary of Events and Information	Remarks and references to Appendices
QUIEVY	30/11/18	8 am	Officer Commanding Hospital opened for 12 cases, not requiring more than 5 days treatment. Village very dirty - men employed in cleaning up. Weather fine.	

149/3481

Confidential

9/Field F.A 39

Volume 39

Dec 1918 War Diary of O.C. 77 Field
Ambulance

for the month of

DECEMBER 1918

Army Form C. 2118.

WAR DIARY
or
INTELLIGENCE SUMMARY.
(Erase heading not required.)

Instructions regarding War Diaries and Intelligence Summaries are contained in F. S. Regs., Part II. and the Staff Manual respectively. Title pages will be prepared in manuscript.

Place	Date	Hour	Summary of Events and Information	Remarks and references to Appendices
QUIEVY	1/xi/15	p.m.	Office Routine. Weather fine	MW
"	2/xi/15	"	Office Routine. Visit of DDMS 2nd Division to inspect arrangements from sub/unts.	MW
"	3/xi/15	a.m.	Office Routine.	
		p.m.	His Majesty the King inspected 7th Brigade in afternoon within thing's of the village.	MW
"	5/xi/15	a.m.	Office Routine. Lecture at 11.00 hrs. By Captain Donaldson on Reinstatement First School. LEESON returned to command ambulance at 21.00 hrs on return of ADMS 25th Division from leave to England.	MW
"	6/xi/15	a.m.	Office Routine.	
		a.m.	Pte Lawton Rawd left to proceed to O.C. Transportation at CORMIS on a course with nurse from D.A.y 3rd Echelon.	MW
"	7/xi/15	a.m.	Visit of ADMS 25th Division who inspected puncture a transport ADMS School for an Early Treatment room to be started use the inspection Room. Office Routine rest of day.	MW
"	8/xi/15	a.m.	Office Routine. Weather fine	MW

WAR DIARY
or
INTELLIGENCE SUMMARY.

Army Form C. 2118.

Place	Date	Hour	Summary of Events and Information	Remarks and references to Appendices
QUERY	8/xii/18	P.M.	Офр Rankin. A.D.M.S. 25th Division asked O.C. 11 Field Ambulance to ascertain cause of first outbreak of Influenza amongst men of 113 Brigade R.F.A. W.A.	
	9/xii/18		Офр Rankin visited unit and showing W.A.	
	3/xii/18		O.C. 11 Field Ambulance furnished a case to the United Kingdom Major MOODY M.O. Rank arrived convalescent and was absent without leave W.A.	
	9/xii/18	A.M.	Офр Rankin.	
		14.30 t	Officers of MOMS Office on the use of "Influenza Vaccine" 75 samples on experiment were handed in. All ordered officers in Division attended. W.A.	
	13/xii/18	09.00	LIEUT LITTLE. M.C. R.P. U.S.A. reported to O.C. 3rd Division Reception Centre for Enquiry only.	
		15.00	Divisional Sanitary Officer at Marymiller of Division W.A. meeting of Captain & J. MELVIN R.A.M.C. T.F. reported for duty.	
	14/xii/18	11.45	A.D.M.S. 25th Division visited unit and interviewed O.C. 25th Division List and affairs of the adoption of experimental measures which cannot by having a in the Division, the two recently then meeting was in hand.	G.M.S.

Army Form C. 2118.

WAR DIARY
or
INTELLIGENCE SUMMARY.
(Erase heading not required.)

Instructions regarding War Diaries and Intelligence Summaries are contained in F. S. Regs., Part II. and the Staff Manual respectively. Title pages will be prepared in manuscript.

Place	Date	Hour	Summary of Events and Information	Remarks and references to Appendices
QUIEVY	15/XII/18	A.M.	T.O.R. Reinforcements arrived from Base Depot and were taken on the strength	
" "		P.M.	Office Routine weather fine	
" "	16/xii/18		Office Routine. Very wet	
" "	17/xii/18		Serjeant BESTEN Reme reported for duty from the Base Depot and as there is no vacancy by 4 and posted to "6" Section as I could not struck off strength in accordance to 3rd Army R.O.W. 1068 with Seventeen Ambulance Car A/7105	
" "	18/xii/18		Five O.R. Candidates reported to look morning returning evening section CAMBRAI for demobilisation Weather very wet	
" "	19/xii/18	A.M.	Captain G.S. McKean R.A.M.C. (TF) proceeded to Belart 46 C.C.S. R.H. for [unclear] as a Postal Officer	
		P.M.	Warrant g.n. STONE R.A.M.C. (SA) reported as employed and to join 6 as strength	
			as a clerk	
" "	21/xii/18	15:00	Education officer attended meeting of Divisional Education Officer at the Quarters held at ST. HAMA. R.A.M.C. (SA) deputed for Company who he hope to to 2nd in Monocle Rd	
			Weather had a cold	

Army Form C. 2118.

WAR DIARY
or
INTELLIGENCE SUMMARY.
(Erase heading not required.)

Instructions regarding War Diaries and Intelligence Summaries are contained in F.S. Regs., Part II. and the Staff Manual respectively. Title pages will be prepared in manuscript.

Place	Date	Hour	Summary of Events and Information	Remarks and references to Appendices
QUIEVY	21/10/18		Office Routine. Weather fine cool	
"	20/10/18		Office Routine. Weather fine cool	
"	23/10/18		All moves running with and exp. as hoped to have appeared to last morning	
"			Collecting centre CAMBRAI for demobilisation	
"			Major Nell and two furnals Aut. Inst. reported their arrival for duty and were shown into their UK	
"	24/10/18		Office Routine. Weather fine	
"	25/10/18		Christmas Day. General Holiday and our 20th Divisional Concert Party at chez Soeurs. First visit was followed by a (concert & dance) in the evening at YCA	
"	26/10/18		Office Routine. The Buckless Range was to to CSMS XII Corps no church note	
"	27/10/18		Office Routine. Weather wet and wild	
"	28/10/18		Office Routine on sent. A.J.Z.S. ——— (S.Adm.) + Officer engineers (Imma) to attend 25th Division	

Army Form C. 2118.

WAR DIARY
or
INTELLIGENCE SUMMARY.
(Erase heading not required.)

Instructions regarding War Diaries and Intelligence Summaries are contained in F. S. Regs., Part II. and the Staff Manual respectively. Title pages will be prepared in manuscript.

Place	Date	Hour	Summary of Events and Information	Remarks and references to Appendices
RUSY	29/10/18	11/10	Recd Wire DESA Rear. Showed from here & received orders from Major Y. G. FOSTER refunded to A.D.M.S. 25th Division for carrying out an A.D.M.S. duty as when of M.O.R. DVN A.D.M.S. proceed on time to time on Leigh.	
"	30/10/18	AM	Office & Routine work	
"	"	PM	Interview with ADMS 25th Division when front situation, ambulance arrange, & arrang, in various a were explained. WL	
"	31/10/18	1900	Received a report on riding of POIX TERRASON & VENDEGIES into Staff by War G Infantry Brigade prior to be Brigade moving this to the 3rd of Common stored pack of ammunition to an VENDEGIES had salvage to be stored & sanitary work to be done similar form.	
			31/10/16	

McKwa Lieut. Foster Recent Camp 44 2nd Ambulance

25 DIV. Box 1999
No. 40

140/254

4
War Diary & Intelligence

Summary / O.C. 77
Field Ambulance for the
month of JANUARY
1919

Jan 1919

Army Form C. 2118.

WAR DIARY
or
INTELLIGENCE SUMMARY.
(Erase heading not required.)

Instructions regarding War Diaries and Intelligence Summaries are contained in F. S. Regs., Part II. and the Staff Manual respectively. Title pages will be prepared in manuscript.

Place	Date	Hour	Summary of Events and Information	Remarks and references to Appendices
QUIEVY	1/1/19	AM	O.C. visited 20th 25th Division & learnt we had anycases in next morning forward. It was decided that the 2nd were previously asked to 25 F.A. Field Ambulance for medical & sanitary work should be recalled as there has been flu.	
		PM	Orders for move of the Brigade to VENDEGIES-aux-BOIS & thro' AUF VALENCIENNES H.Q. received from Brigade Major.	
"	2/1/19		Office routine. Packing up ready for move.	
"	3/1/19	AM	Tent needed by road at 10.20 hrs to VENDEGIES au BOIS arriving there at 13.00 hrs when dinner was served immediately in an area good flag of room for billetting of men and provision of hospital H for 12 cases. 1 room attached; Questin's Educational Room, winter ???.	
VENDEGIES	4/1/19	AM	Office + Routine work. Two went round rural collecting sick from 7th Brigade at POIX and also 7th Brigade at SOLESMES; two cars went under own medical administration; a small reception room consisting of a bedroom and two rooms with medical equipment was established in the village of SOLESMES, and a medical officer from the unit was detailed daily to attend to sick & all until such time the unit all until such.	

WAR DIARY
or
INTELLIGENCE SUMMARY

Army Form C. 2118.

Place	Date	Hour	Summary of Events and Information	Remarks and references to Appendices
VENDEGIES	5/1/19	A.M.	Office & Routine work. T/48182 Driver Baker A. 201 Company R.A.S.C admitted at 11.30 hrs suffering from injuries to aunt [arm?] & [hand?] poisoning. Bomb [unknown] O.C. proceeded to interview O.C. of Base & obtained from him the [bottle] from which the dose was taken and also the spare unit. Major SHADDON MC R.A.M.C assumed medical charge of the case but in spite of every effort he died at 16.45 hours hospitalisation sent to H.Q. 3rd Echelon and O.C. 201 Company R.A.S.C. MWL	
VENDEGIES	6/1/19	A.M.	Body of the late T/42182 Driver Baker sent to O.C. No 3 C.C.S at CAUDRY for a post mortem examination to be made. A sample of the powder also sent for analysis. Statement sent to A.D.M.S. 25th Division. S.M. JUKES Regt. & Private CHAPIN Regt. proceeded on leave from H.Q. Ypres Bgde Conf CAMBRAI en route for Demobilisation as men from H.Q. [Ypres] Bgde Conf considered non-permanent. MWL	
"	7/1/19	A.M.	Office & Routine work. General clearing up of village previously unattempted, weather unsuitable & cold to-day. MWL	
"	8/1/19	A.M.	Office & Routine work. Visit of A.D.M.S 25th Division. O.C. 77th Field Ambulance & O.C. 75th Field Ambulance visited Headquarters. 75th Infantry Brigade to enquire about movements ([return?]) [from] their disposition of clothing of Brigade. Weather fine. MWL	

WAR DIARY
or
INTELLIGENCE SUMMARY

Army Form C. 2118.

Place	Date	Hour	Summary of Events and Information	Remarks and references to Appendices
VENDEGIES	9/11/18	AM	Office & Routine work. Proceeded to Brigade. Lecture held to no[?] put on at Brigade and visited Companies as to the possibility of bringing it into line for the Brigade scheme[?] to 65 & get the Divisional Percussion Lamp. It is ok & made it[?] go there.	WW
"	10/11/18	AM	Representative from O.C. to Sandle Italian arrived with intent to put up a South Observation[?] nets with a Cheveral[?] Stove & Blankets, on experiment to see whether it would be efficient. This will be given a thorough trial at Div. Officers warm-remainder of day.	WW
"	11/11/13	AM	Visited the village of APRIGNIES[?], BERLAIMONT, a LOUVIGNIES to see villagers-civils & find out if they need receiving industrial attention, all unite great interests. Ascertained that on M.O. Can Should be posted at BERLAIMONT to attend each from Servoirs[?] which will & then draw on the Camp to be at our disposal if & when[?] the 9th 16 & 19th Kashmir[?] Regiment[?].	WW
"	12/1/18		Office & Routine work, Weather fine & wet	
"	13/1/18		Inspection of around 25th Division went on parade. Everything satisfactory. Office & Routine work on afternoon.	WW
"	14/1/18	AM	Office & Routine Work. Saw about 25th Division a Court of Enquiry to be held on the Body of the late No BAKER 2nd Co. A & L Pushball[?] Battle[?] from which he[?] died[?].	WW

Army Form C. 2118.

WAR DIARY
or
INTELLIGENCE SUMMARY.
(Erase heading not required.)

Instructions regarding War Diaries and Intelligence Summaries are contained in F.S. Regs., Part II. and the Staff Manual respectively. Title pages will be prepared in manuscript.

Place	Date	Hour	Summary of Events and Information	Remarks and references to Appendices
VENDEGIES	15/1/18	a.m.	Office & Routine work. Visit of Asst. D.A.D.M.S XIII Corps to inspect new Type of Chloride absorption. Visit ended & no Con. Weather hint of cold snow. WM	
"	16/1/18	a.m.	Office & Routine work. Weather fine WM	
"	17/1/18	09.15	O.C. & II full Cavalrymen, Major HADDON R.A.M.C. Sergeant LOUNGE R.A.M.C. proceeded to Headquarters of 25 Divisional Train to give evidence at Court of Enquiry on Pte Baker D.C.L.I. A.S.C. As to the circumstances under which he met his death. Lasted all day. Returned to these HQ at 16.15 hours WM	
"	18/1/18	a.m.	Office & Routine work. Weather fair. Forwarded further recommendations for "Pearl Gazette" to A.D.M.S 25th Division WM	
"	19/1/18	a.m.	Parade service Church of England 9.45 a.m. Rest of day a holiday. WM	
"	20/1/18	a.m.	Office & Routine work. O.C. & Major HADDON went to give evidence in case Baker D.C.L.I. A.S.C. at H.Q. 4 Co R.A.M.C. Searches & enquiry WM	
"	21/1/18	10.00	O.C. Major HADDON RAMC & Sergeant LOUNGE R.A.M.C proceeded to H.Q. 4 Co R.A.M.C. to give evidence in the case of Driver BAKER R.A.S.C. Returned at 13.00 hrs. Visit of A.D.M.S 25th Division to discuss the case & interview his dispenser, a private, whom it seems is history fully explained. Both Soldiers exonerated. WM	

D. D. & L., London, E.C.
(A8001) Wt. W17771/M2931 750,000 5/17 Sch. 52 Forms C2118/14

Army Form C. 2118.

WAR DIARY
or
INTELLIGENCE SUMMARY.
(Erase heading not required.)

Instructions regarding War Diaries and Intelligence Summaries are contained in F. S. Regs., Part II. and the Staff Manual respectively. Title pages will be prepared in manuscript.

Place	Date	Hour	Summary of Events and Information	Remarks and references to Appendices
VENDEGIES	22/1/19	pm.	Office & Routine work. Rev. C.H. THOMPSON, C.F. evacuated to C.C.S. with "Influenza". Weather fine.	
" "	23/1/19	am.	Morning spent in reviewing Equipment for a Field Ambulance on the scale of 2 instead of 3 Stations.	
" "	24/1/19	am. pm.	Office & Routine work. Visit to NWDHQ 25th Division to enquire if troops were comptable. Every they reported satisfactory.	
" "	25/1/19	am.	Office Routine. Major JACKSON visited outlying villages of ROCQUIGNY, BEAURIMONT & AULNOYE to inspect billet troops units & found all satisfactory. Weather very cold	
" "	26/1/19	pm.	Fall of Snow for the 1st time this year. Office + Routine work	
" "	27/1/19	pm.	Completed Divisional transfer & forwarded to NWDHQ 25th Division. Also completed Cadre establishment of this unit consisting of 3 Officers & 58 other ranks & forwarded to NWDHQ 25th Division for transmission to higher authority.	
" "	28/1/19	am.	Return of troops available for demobilisation rendered to NWDHQ 25th Division.	
" "	29/1/19	am.	Office + Routine work. 1 Demobilisation allotment received for R.A.S.C. (MT) personnel "return on Demobilisation" by O.R. 16 at 18.30 hrs at not taken forward.	

Army Form C. 2118.

WAR DIARY
or
INTELLIGENCE SUMMARY.
(Erase heading not required.)

Instructions regarding War Diaries and Intelligence Summaries are contained in F. S. Regs., Part II. and the Staff Manual respectively. Title pages will be prepared in manuscript.

Place	Date	Hour	Summary of Events and Information	Remarks and references to Appendices
VENDEGIES	3/11/18	AM	O/Pc & Routine work. Visit of CUSMS 25th Division when demobilisation problem was discussed. On G.S. Waggon 1 hundred waggon despatched to CAMBRAI to obtain three 3/11/18 for demobilisation + N.C.O. & 2 men spent the night at 76 Field Ambulance.	
" "	3/11/18		O/Pc & Routine work. Divn Centre RASC (HT) despatched to CAMBRAI for demobilisation. Weather very cold & inclined to snow all day.	H.M.Kevan Lieut. Kings Island Regt Lieut Ambulance Commander 77

VOLUME 41

5/4

War diary of the Officer Commanding 77 Field Ambulance
in the month of February 1919.

WAR DIARY
or
INTELLIGENCE SUMMARY.

(Erase heading not required.)

Army Form C. 2118

Instructions regarding War Diaries and Intelligence Summaries are contained in F. S. Regs., Part II. and the Staff Manual respectively. Title pages will be prepared in manuscript.

Place	Date	Hour	Summary of Events and Information	Remarks and references to Appendices
VENDEGIES AU BOIS	1/2/19	AM	Office + Routine work. Snowing. AM	
"	2/2/19	AM	Office + Routine work. Morning spent in preparing lecture on "Armies of Occupation."	
		18:00	O.C 77 Field Ambulance delivered a lecture to all troops in the village on the advantages of volunteering for the new Armies of Occupation & the attractive terms offered. A large attendance was present. AM	
"	3/2/19	AM	Office a Routine work. 4 horses sent to Staging camp BEAUVOIS entg Y.F. demobilisation. (Mjr Newby RASC accompanied them)	
"	4/2/19		Office a Routine work. Capt Kelly RASC proceeded to O.C Divisional Train to arrange for a further party of 2 grooms proceeding to this attraction.	
"	5/2/19	AM	Office a Routine work. Received intimation from corps that no 30/= Bount Coys to be demobilised, & various willed to this unit Troops had been cancelled. Transp Sisters D.R. Wagoner to be sent to Inf Rgts to await rejoining wagt into coming despatches AM	
"	6/2/19		Office a Routine work.	
"	7/2/19		Office a Routine work. Ptes Miller + Wilson proceeded to Inf Concentration camp prior to demobilisation AM	

Army Form C. 2118

WAR DIARY
or
INTELLIGENCE SUMMARY.
(Erase heading not required.)

Instructions regarding War Diaries and Intelligence Summaries are contained in F. S. Regs., Part II. and the Staff Manual respectively. Title pages will be prepared in manuscript.

Place	Date	Hour	Summary of Events and Information	Remarks and references to Appendices
VENDEGIES	8/7/19	AM.	Office work. Divine Service in Recreation Room.	
"	9/7/19		Office & Routine work. Pte Jones T. Pte Gee proceeded to Corps Inoculation Camp for demobilisation.	
"	10/7/19		Office & Routine work. Major Baldwin Rene assumed duties O.C. O/c vice Major Ridley. Hon. Sergeant BEATON & Pte LEGG proceeded for duty with 3rd Army Remount depot	
"	11/7/19		Office & Routine work.	
"	12/7/19	AM.	Office & Routine work. (Major RIDLEY proceeded to OSTM 18th Division for duty. Q.M.S. King proceeded to O.C 76 Fd Ambulance for temporary duty	
"	12/7/19	PM.	Reverend A.E. BANKS C.F. reported his arrival for duty & was taken on strength.	
"	15/7/19	AM.	Office & Routine work. Hospital completed nominal roll of "bodies" of Ones unit to ADMS 25th Div to obtain approval of HQrs III Army	

Army Form C. 2118

WAR DIARY
or
INTELLIGENCE SUMMARY.
(Erase heading not required.)

Place	Date	Hour	Summary of Events and Information	Remarks and references to Appendices
VENDEGIES	14/2/19	AM	Officer & Routine work. Capt. Evans, Pte. Paul and Cpl. preceded to (W/P Concentration Camp for demobilisation.	
"	15/2/19	AM	Office & Routine work. Warning order received for the Ambulance to move to IWUY at an early date. Lieut. Williams Paine reference QM & King Paine for temporary duty with 76 Field Ambulance.	
"	16/2/19	AM	Office & Routine work. Weather dull & cloudy.	
"	17/2/19	AM	Interviewed Staff Captain 74th Infy. Brigade, about billets in new area, was shewn list of Barns allotted to us & 6. to 77. Field Ambulance proceeded to IWUY to report. Ambulance was found sufficient accommodation. Returned to H.Q. at 14.30 p.m.	
"	18/2/19	AM	Advance Party consisting of Major Foster Band and 7 ORs with 1 Car and 2 G.S. Wagons (loaded) proceeded to IWUY at 10.00 am. to prepare billets, &c. Sunbeam Car with orderly sent to HAUSSY to spend night & in readiness to rejoin by his o c/2 Tunis of 74th Brigade on the march to IWUY who were staying the night there.	
"	19/2/19		Office & Routine work. One Sunbeam Ambulance Car parked at ST PYTHON and HAUSSY during the night 19-20 for use of medical officers 76 & 74 Fd Amb in respect of urgent cases.	

Army Form C. 2118

WAR DIARY
or
INTELLIGENCE SUMMARY.
(Erase heading not required.)

Instructions regarding War Diaries and Intelligence Summaries are contained in F. S. Regs., Part II. and the Staff Manual respectively. Title pages will be prepared in manuscript.

Place	Date	Hour	Summary of Events and Information	Remarks and references to Appendices
VENDEGIES	20/2/19	am	Unit marched to new area at IWUY by road at 09.30 hrs leaving IWUY at 14.30 hrs. Advance party arrived willed in an unoccupied house. Baths stove etc in adjoining yard. Hospital consists of reception Room and one ward for 10 patients (fixed in a barn). Small wire gates and STR in large barn in the IWUY CAMBRAI main road. Transport in uniform from ...	
IWUY	21/2/19	AM	Office & Routine work. Day spent in cleaning up and settling down in new area	
"	22/2/19	"	Office & Routine work. S.O.R. provided time for demobilisation	
"	23/2/19	"	Unit meeting. Divine Service held at HQ.	
"	24/2/19	"	Office a Routine work. 2. O. R. provided to (HP Imbrication camp) for demobilisation	
"	25/2/19	"	Office & Routine work. Windows fine 3. O. R. volunteered for a gun for heavies of occupation.	
"	26/2/19	"	Office & Routine work. Weather showery.	
"	27/2/19	"	Office & Routine work.	
"	28/2/19	"	Office & Routine work. 3. O. R. proceeded to (HP Concentration camp for demobilisation. Fifteen Potland Pennard remainder 17 Fresh Yorkshire	

www.ingramcontent.com/pod-product-compliance
Lightning Source LLC
Chambersburg PA
CBHW080925230426
43668CB00014B/2195